YANKEE MAGAZINE.'s

Panty Hose, Hot Peppers, Tea Bags, and more— for the Garden

1,001 INGENIOUS WAYS
to Use Common Household Items
to Control Weeds, Beat Pests,
Cook Compost, Solve Problems,
Make Tricky Jobs Easy,
and Save Time

YANKEE BOOKS.

Yankee Publishing Staff

PRESIDENT: Jamie Trowbridge
BOOK EDITOR: Veronica Lorson Fowler
CONTRIBUTING WRITERS: Marianne Binetti, Monica Moran Brandies,
Rebecca Chesin, Sally Jean Cunningham, Kate Carter Frederick, Annette Hentz,
Arden Moore, Nan Sterman/Plant Soup, Inc., Cathy Wilkensen-Barash
TECHNICAL REVIEWER: Erin Hynes
BOOK DESIGNER: Jill Shaffer
INTERIOR ILLUSTRATOR: Michael Gellatly
COPY EDITOR: Barbara Jatkola
INDEXER: Ellen Sherron
PROOFREADERS: Jenny Donelan, Brenda Witherspoon

Rodale Inc. Editorial Staff

EDITOR: Christine Bucks
SENIOR PROJECT EDITOR: Marilyn Hauptly
COVER DESIGNER: Tara Long

The information in this book has been carefully researched,
and all efforts have been made to ensure accuracy. Rodale Inc. and Yankee Publishing Inc.
assume no responsibility for any injuries suffered or damages or losses incurred during
or as a result of following this information. All information should be carefully studied and
clearly understood before taking any action based on the information or advice in this book.

When using any commercial product, *always* read and follow label directions.
Mention of specific companies, organizations, or authorities in this book does not imply endorsement
by the publisher, nor does mention of specific companies, organizations,
or authorities imply that they endorse this book.

Internet addresses and telephone numbers given in this book were accurate
at the time it went to press.

Printed in the United States of America on acid-free ∞, recycled paper ♻.

Library of Congress Cataloging-in-Publication Data

Yankee magazine's panty hose, hot peppers, tea bags, and more—for the garden : 1,001 ingenious ways
to use common household items to control weeds, beat pests, cook compost, solve problems, make tricky jobs
easy, and save time.
     p.   cm.
Includes bibliographical references and index.
ISBN-13 978–0–89909–394–9 hardcover
ISBN-10 0–89909–394–9 hardcover
   1. Gardening—Miscellanea.   2. Organic gardening—Miscellanea.   3. Home economics—Miscellanea.
I. Title: Panty hose, hot peppers, tea bags, and more—for the garden. II. Yankee (Dublin, N.H.)
SB453.Y295   2005
635'.0484—dc22   2005008126

12   14   16   18   20   19   17   15   13   11   hardcover

RODALE
LIVE YOUR WHOLE LIFE™

We inspire and enable people to improve their lives and the world around them
For more of our products visit rodalestore.com or call 1-800-848-4735

Contents

Recycling That Helps the Planet and Helps You

Where better to recycle than in the garden, where innovation and frugality have long been honored traditions? Many people, after all, have gotten into gardening because they love the idea of taking a few pennies' worth of seeds and seeing them produce armloads of vegetables, fruit, and flowers far more varied and delicious than anything they could find in stores.

The concept of using—and reusing—common household items outdoors is nothing new to gardeners. Yet gardeners, resourceful though they may be, are always looking for more ways to save money, time, and trouble in the garden.

That's where *Panty Hose, Hot Peppers, Tea Bags, and More—For the Garden* comes in. In this book, you will find hundreds of ideas for using in new and unusual ways common household items or items you'd otherwise toss into the garbage can. Why make a special trip to the garden center when the solution might be lurking right in your garage, your closet, or your pantry?

You'll find hundreds of earth-friendly tips that put everything from laundry baskets to dental floss, margarine tubs to newspapers, to work in the garden. For example, is powdery mildew a problem? Dig through your cabinets and come up with an effective spray made of baking soda, water, and liquid soap. Has that pretty wicker basket's bottom sprung out? Sink it into the ground, fill it with soil, and plant it with flowers for a clever garden accent. Frustrated with the waste of all that foam packaging that electronics and other goods are sold in? Use it in the bottom of large planters and pots. It creates excellent drainage, minimizes weight so you can move containers easier, and reduces the amount of expensive potting soil needed to fill the pot.

Turn a plastic milk jug into a clever bird feeder. Or dust off that old golf caddy and use it to store and wheel garden supplies to wherever you need them. The ideas you'll find in this book are practically endless and will get you looking around your home with an eye to recycling in ways you'd never have thought possible.

Chapter 1 takes us, well, from the ground up with tips for improving your soil and mulching wisely. Chapter 2 is written for those who aspire to raise more and better plants from seed, with great tips on seed-starting containers, indoor lighting for seedlings, and more. Chapter 3 is full of cool tools you can make or create with scraps from around the house. Chapter 4 focuses on one of the most popular forms of gardening, container gardening, and the many creative containers and innovative growing techniques you can try for little or no money.

To help you spend less time searching for stuff and more time with your hands in the soil, we've devoted Chapter 5 to getting organized, with great ideas for tool and supply storage (an old chandelier is perfect for keeping all those hanging baskets neat and at hand), labeling plants, and keeping plant and garden records. Chapter 6 is all about planting and caring for trees and shrubs with materials you have lying around.

Flower gardening is extremely popular these days, so we have lots of tips in Chapter 7 for annuals, perennials, flowering vines, bulbs, and weed control, as well as tips for drying and cutting flowers. If you like to grow your own fruits and vegetables, turn to Chapter 8, where you'll find innovative tips for planting, growing, and harvesting.

Even lawns are included, in Chapter 9. There you'll find lots of ways to get maximum results with minimum efforts and no chemicals. Gardening without chemicals, after all, is important in attracting birds, butterflies, and other beneficials, such as toads and pest-devouring wasps, which we tackle in Chapter 10.

Gardeners in cold-winter regions will appreciate Chapter 11, where old materials are recycled into clever gadgets for extending the growing season in both the spring and fall. Explore fun and creative ways to build cold frames and create cloches, row covers, and other frost protectors.

Pests and disease are a problem in any garden and we present a number of ways to take items from your kitchen and use them to fight pests in the garden. Find out in Chapter 12 how aluminum foil, pinwheels, and nutshells can keep your garden healthy.

Chapter 13 reveals tips for keeping houseplants in top form, using everything from chopsticks, plastic lids, leftover tea, and more. Chapter 14 is a potpourri of tips, including better ways to bring cut flowers indoors and how to create a healthier water garden.

Also keep an eye out for recurring boxes.

"One Man's Trash" features information on how and what to "mine" for great stuff for your garden from resources such as dumps, salvage stores, and the curb, for excellent garden materials that can be used as is or "repurposed" for something new.

"Pass It On" is filled with ideas on how to share good stuff with those who could use it, whether it's donating perennials to a day-care center or giving your old mower to the local battered women's shelter.

"Save the Planet" contains tips with an emphasis on the environment. These are tips that better help you use up products and items you may have around the house, preventing them from being hauled off to a landfill, an increasing problem in a world where almost everything is considered disposable. At the end of the book, we list more resources for frugal gardeners to use in recycling, reusing, and repurposing items around their homes in the garden.

The tips found in this book are sure to make you rethink the way you garden and help you to do your part in healing our fragile and fractured environment, or at least your little corner of that environment. *Panty Hose, Hot Peppers, and Tea Bags, and More—for the Garden* is sure to become a well-worn favorite in your garden library—a sensible and useful resource for creating a garden that is as earth-friendly as it is beautiful and productive.

Use the Right Thing

A wise gardener once observed that, when recycling materials in your garden, "if you wouldn't put it in your mouth or let it touch your skin, you probably shouldn't put it in your garden."

That's because, as every experienced gardener knows, gardens are living, changing, evolving things. The tangle of plastic twine that got wrapped around the buried graft of the rose bush may well eventually strangle the poor thing as its grows and thickens. Soap sprays and soapy water applied to the garden may seem like a good idea at the time, but they can pollute your soil in much the same way nonbiodegradable detergents pollute our water. While cow and chicken and sheep manures may provide top-notch nutrients for our compost piles and soils, getting rid of cat and dog waste in the garden has the potential to spread harmful pathogens shared by all meat-eating creatures.

In this book, you'll find lots of specific tips on planet- (and people!) friendly ways to minimize waste in your home by using gentle materials in your garden. On the next few pages, we discuss overall guidelines and cautions in the hope that they free you to get creative and think up new uses for everyday items in your garden, but to do it in a way that benefits both you and the environment around us.

Wood Ash

▶ Ashes from logs burned in your fireplace are a fine addition to alter soil that is mildly to strongly acidic. (A soil test, performed with an inexpensive kit obtained from your local garden center, can tell you exactly how acidic or alkaline your soil is.) Ash adds readily available calcium, magnesium, potassium, and trace minerals to the garden, lawn, or compost pile. And, because it is alkaline, it quickly raises the soil pH.

However, don't add ash in these situations:

• If the soil pH is 6.5 or higher. Otherwise, you risk making the soil too alkaline, which makes soil nutrients less available to plants.

• Near plants that prefer acidic soil, such as azaleas, blueberries, and some hydrangeas.

• In the potato patch, because alkaline soil encourages potato scab.

One guideline is to apply no more than one 5-gallon bucket of ash per 1,000 square feet of soil per year—that's not a lot. Because soil types vary in how drastically ash affects the pH, it's wise to test your soil every few years if you use ash.

Engine Oil

▶ Environmental regulations for disposing of motor oil from your car, mower, or other power tools raise questions about the oft-recommended practice of dipping metal tools into a bucket of sand moistened with used motor oil to clean the tools and protect them from rust. Eventually you have to dispose of the oily sand—but where? You can't throw it in the compost or trash. Automotive service stations won't accept it. Perhaps your local hazardous-waste site might accept it; ask first. Or better yet, skip the risk and use other methods to clean and protect tools.

Household Wastewater

▌ It's tempting to recycle the water used in your home and, in some arid areas, entire systems have been created to reuse household water, such as that from a washing machine, in the landscape. Watering the garden with soapy water left from washing dishes and clothing—also called gray water— is more controversial than you might expect. Some communities ban using gray water in the garden, for fear of contaminating homegrown vegetables with harmful microorganisms. Also, dumping the suds from soap containing phosphorus might put you at odds with ordinances banning phosphorus fertilizers.

If using gray water is legal in your area, keep these points in mind before dumping the baby's bath on the baby's breath:

- Do use soap that's especially recommended for use in gray water systems.
- Don't use greasy water or water that has been in contact with raw meat or human waste (that includes diapers and soiled baby bottoms).
- Use the water within 24 hours so bacteria don't have time to grow.
- Irrigate only nonfood plants.
- Add the water to the soil; spraying leaves might damage them.

Cat Litter

▌ Tossing used cat litter into the compost instead of the landfill is tempting, but the practice isn't recommended. Cat waste can contain

Beware of Leftovers?

Recycling household items in the garden is a wonderful practice, but take care that the recycled item doesn't create more work than it saves. Be especially careful when using materials that don't biodegrade, such as metals and plastics. Mulch with that pine garland leftover from Christmas? You'll have a tangle of wire and sticks once the pine needles fall off. Truss up a vine with twine? Fine if it's a natural material such as jute, but think twice if it's not. If in doubt, start small—it's easier to remove a packing peanut mess from one flower pot than 10.

Much Ado about Newspaper Mulch

Newspaper is a cheap, abundant, and useful mulch. And it's safe. You can ignore outdated cautions about newsprint containing lead—it's been decades since newspapers got the lead out. And the amount of hydrocarbons in colored inks is insignificant.

As a mulch layer under a decorative material such as bark chips or stones, newspaper smothers weeds and sod more effectively than the decorative material alone. And unlike some landscape fabrics and weed barriers, newspaper breaks down completely, so you don't have to extricate it in five years, when it's shredded and roots are tangled in it.

How quickly a layer of newspaper mulch breaks down varies greatly, depending on several factors. The rate is faster if the soil is rich in microorganisms, if your region is damp or you water often, or if temperatures are warm but not hot. Experiment to find what works best in your garden. As a starting point, if you live in a warm, damp climate, make your layer about five sheets thick. If your climate is dry or cold, use two sheets. Make the layer thicker if you want it to last more than a season or if you're trying to smother an aggressive plant, such as a lawn of bermudagrass or St. Augustine.

When using newspaper mulch, keep these pointers in mind:

• Slick inserts are safe, but their size and slickness makes them harder to work with than regular newsprint.

• Cover the newspaper completely with a decorative mulch. Exposed newspaper turns brittle quickly, especially if it gets damp and then dries. Then it's prone to breaking up and blowing around.

• Don't cover seeds with newspaper—they can't push through it.

• On a slope, the covering of decorative mulch is more likely to slip downhill with newspaper under it, so cover newspaper with a thicker layer of decorative mulch that you would on flat ground.

• Because newspaper is high in carbon, it could set off the chain of events among soil microbes that temporarily reduces the amount of nitrogen in the soil immediately below the mulch. The deficit should not affect established plants, but might make young, small plants turn a bit yellow. If so, treat them to a spritz of an organic foliar fertilizer.

the parasite that causes toxoplasmosis, a dangerous disease for pregnant women, those with compromised immune systems, and children. EPA standards for composting waste from cats and other meat-eaters are far beyond the scope of a backyard compost pile.

Clean cat litter is safer, but even then, read the label carefully. Depending on what brand and formulation you buy, the litter may or may not be made of biodegradable materials and may contain various chemicals you don't want in your garden, especially a vegetable or herb garden, or around other edible plantings. When in doubt, leave it out.

Paper in the Compost Pile

▶ You can compost paper, including magazines and newspaper. Composting is a great way to dispose of the unsolicited credit card applications you run through the paper shredder. These suggestions will make paper composting successful:

• If possible, shred the paper first; smaller pieces break down faster. If nothing else at least tear it into strips. If possible, make the strips no wider than 1 inch.

• Mix the paper into the pile to make it break down faster and, if the pile is open, to keep it from blowing away. Wet paper that isn't mixed in can form a tough papier mâché-like shell that sheds water once the paper dries.

• To offset the high carbon content in paper, add kitchen scraps, grass clippings, and green leafy material to keep the pile cooking.

Pressure-Treated Lumber

▶ Raised beds are a great solution if the native soil is infertile, shallow, or drains poorly. But is it safe to use pressure-treated lumber left over from a building project? Absolutely not. Pressure-treated lumber is soaked in chromated copper arsenate to prevent rot and the copper, chromium, and arsenic will leach into the soil, especially the soil closest to the lumber—creating a toxic mess.

However, when building a raised bed, there are a number of alternatives to pressure-treated wood.

Check into naturally rot-resistant woods, such as redwood and cedar. They last just as long and there are no concerns about chemical contamination.

Stone is also an excellent alternative to pressure-treated wood when building raised beds. Simply stack flat or cut stone around the edge of the bed and fill with topsoil. (Salvaged fieldstone from fields and ditches is fine; just be sure to get permission first.) Depending on how securely the stone rests upon the lower stone, you can build a bed anywhere from a few inches to roughly a foot high.

There are also a variety of solid concrete wall-building blocks on the market today in a number of natural-looking colors. Some of the blocks simply stack together while others interlock, creating a fairly strong wall. Like natural stone walls, these concrete building blocks are suitable for raised beds up to about a foot or so high.

If your raised bed is in a vegetable garden where appearance is less of an issue, old-fashioned plain concrete block can be used. It's easy to stack and best of all, if you place the holes facing upward, they make great planting nooks for herbs that like excellent drainage, such as thyme, oregano, and rosemary. They're also a great planting spot for succulents, such as chicks and hens and small sedums. Raised beds made of traditional concrete block can be built two to three blocks (about 18 inches) high.

Don't forget brick, either. Salvaged brick can often be had for the hauling from a dump or landfill (again, be sure to ask first) and is often quite beautiful. Bury the bricks, side by side and upright, to make a raised bed just a few inches high. Or, if you're feeling handy, go ahead and mix up some mortar and lay a low brick wall six to eight bricks high (about 18 inches).

Soap Sprays

▶ A solution made from dish detergent and plenty of water has long been a popular control for killing soft-bodied insects on contact. But before you reach for the spray bottle, heed these cautions:

- Ingredients in some detergents can burn plant tissue. And because environmental conditions—such as sun intensity and temperature—change how susceptible plants are to damage, you can't assume that a spray that was safe last week will be safe tomorrow. Always try a spray on a few leaves first and check the leaves a few days later for damage.
- Plants that are susceptible to soap damage include some tomato varieties, portulaca, plums, and cherries. To get an idea of which plants soap might harm, check the label of a commercially available insecticidal soap, bearing in mind that a homemade mix might be more dangerous to plants.
- The solution must be extremely weak. Only about 2 percent should be soap.
- Dishwasher and laundry detergents are not safe for plants.
- Small insects are susceptible to soap sprays, but large ones usually are not. Exceptions are box-elder bugs and Japanese beetles.
- Identify the insect before you spray it, to make sure it's a pest. Some mite species, for example, help control spider mites. Killing them could actually make a spider mite infestation worse.

Carpet Remnants

▶ Carpet remnants (those made of natural fibers and without an kind of treatment or backing) are an effective, dense mulch, although not a particularly attractive one. Consider using them for pathways in the vegetable garden or to smother an especially tough patch of lawn or weeds. But plan to remove them at the end of the season, and don't use them as a permanent mulch under trees and shrubs. As a long-term mulch, they easily become a mess. Depending on how the carpet is made, it can unravel and tangle in plants or, worse, the mower or weed trimmer. Tough weeds can grow into the backing, making removal difficult.

CHAPTER ONE

Soil-Improving Secrets

Don't treat your soil like dirt! Good soil is the foundation of the garden, and taking some time and care with your soil before you plant—rather than after—can be the difference between a garden that sulks and a garden that thrives. In this chapter, you'll learn how to make the best compost ever, as well as many other soil-improving tips that will help you build the richest, blackest soil possible. Your plants will thank you for it.

COMPOSTING SECRETS

Making a Racket

▶ No matter how well you compost, there will still be some large particles left after the pile is "cooked." Get rid of those clumps by sieving the finished compost through an old tennis racket. The webbing will catch large particles (throw them back in the compost pile with a strong forearm), while the finer compost will go right through into your bucket or wheelbarrow.

A Big Fan

▶ When a box fan meets its maker, unscrew one of the grids and use it as a compost sifter. Because it's plastic and weatherproof, you can store it neatly right by your compost bin.

Junk That Mail

Tired of all that junk mail piling up? Get it off your desk and into the garden, where it will feed your plants for months.

First, put it through a shredder, removing staples as needed. Then place a 6-inch layer of shredded paper around your plants. Water well; the paper will settle down to about 1½ inches deep. Top with a thin layer of organic mulch or topsoil. After a couple of seasons, the paper will break down completely, enriching the soil.

Blowing More Than Hot Air

▶ Hang on to that old metal vent you tore out during a home improvement project. It makes a super compost sifter. Depending on its size, just lay it across a wheelbarrow or large bucket. Use a spade to pile the compost on top of the vent. Then use your hand or the flat portion of the spade to push the compost through. You'll have a beautiful, fine compost perfect for filling containers or mixing with amendments such as perlite, vermiculite, or sphagnum peat moss for your own custom potting soil.

Box Yourself In

▶ Create a mini–compost bin with an old cardboard box. Fold the top and bottom flaps inward and set on the soil behind shrubs, in your vegetable garden, or in any out-of-the-way

Turn an empty cardboard box into a convenient mini–compost bin.

spot. Bury the bottom inch or two in the soil to prevent the box from blowing away. If wind is really a problem, anchor the box by driving a stake through one corner.

Add layers of yard refuse to the box, and allow them to break down over a year or two. Remove the compost when desired and then tear up and bury the remainder of the box, which by that time will be soft and broken down.

This technique works well with small boxes, but you can use large appliance boxes, too, for larger compost bins.

Bag It

▶ While you're going around your garden weeding, deadheading, and just generally cleaning up, toss yard waste into a small paper bag recycled from a fast-food restaurant or other shop. When the bag is full, dig a hole in your garden large enough to contain it (among perennials or shrubs is ideal), and tuck it into the soil to turn into compost right on the spot.

Drumroll, Please

▌ Drum-type composters are terrific time- and energy-savers, but with a price tag of hundreds of dollars, they sure hurt the wallet. The good news is, you can make your own in a snap with a spare garbage can.

Start with a very large (55-gallon or so) plastic cylindrical trash can with a tight-fitting lid. Using a paring knife heated over a candle, punch $1/2$- to 1-inch aeration holes in the top, bottom, and sides of the container. Space the holes 6 to 8 inches apart.

Fill the trash can with carbon- and nitrogen-rich materials, such as grass clippings and autumn leaves, and give them a thorough soaking. Pop on the lid. Every week or so, tip the container on its side, roll it around a few times, check to make sure the contents are still moist, and stand it back up. You'll have compost within several weeks.

16 Weird Compost Materials

We all know you can add orange peels to the compost heap. But what about wine corks? Here are a number of items that you might not have considered as potential fodder for the compost pile.

1 Cotton balls
2 Used matches
3 Tissues
4 Paper towels
5 Paperback books (remove the covers)
6 Cardboard ice cream containers
7 Seashells
8 Wine corks
9 Chewing gum
10 Nutshells
11 Pizza boxes
12 Tea bags
13 Contents of vacuum cleaner bags
14 Olive pits
15 Water from an aquarium or fishbowl
16 Hair from hairbrushes and haircuts

Trash Trick

▌If you have an old wastebasket that's getting ratty or that you don't need anymore, put it to good use next to your compost bin. When working with your compost, you'll find materials popping up that won't decompose—everything from plant labels and plastic twine to cracked Legos. A wastebasket near the compost heap will give you a convenient place to toss these items.

If the wastebasket is lightweight, weight its bottom with a stone or

Drink Up

Coffee grounds have long been a favorite addition to compost piles. But did you know that they are also an excellent amendment to potting soil? They're light-weight, porous, high in organic matter, and attractively dark. Plus, if your soil is alkaline, their natural acidity helps balance the pH. A good source of used grounds is your local coffee shop, where they're usually happy to give them away. You'll be surprised at all the other uses you can find for them.

• Grounds make a dark, attractive mulch around acid-loving plants, such as azaleas, hydrangeas, hollies, and blueberries.

• Slugs don't like caffeine, so a mulch of coffee grounds, which retain much of the chemical, will help keep the slugs away from your hostas and other vulnerable plants. Just be sure to spread the coffee grounds no more than 1 inch deep around the plants. In cool, moist weather, an unsightly but harmless mold can form on the mulch.

• Keep grounds on hand for mixing into potting soil. Spread them out on newspaper for a day or so to dry, then store them in a plastic bag.

• If you have grounds from only a pot or two of coffee, add a spoonful or two to houseplants and a cup or two to larger con-tainer plantings. Work the grounds lightly into the soil.

• Put a paper filter full of coffee grounds in the bottom of a plant container or planting hole to nourish new plants.

brick. If it's watertight, use a heated nail to punch some drainage holes in the bottom so it won't collect rainwater.

Warm Toes, Frosty Compost

▶ In the winter, you often don't feel like trekking through the cold to the compost bin just for a few eggshells and orange rinds. Instead, place a flexible plastic container, such as an ice cream container, in an inconspicuous spot right outside your back door. When the container is full, simply pop the frozen compost into your bin.

We All Scream for Compost

▶ During warmer weather, a plastic container makes a handy indoor compost collector. Place it under or beside the kitchen sink to collect vegetable peelings, eggshells, coffee grounds (filter and all), dead flowers, and more. (Do not add grease, soap, or meat scraps.)

Once every day or so, empty the container onto your compost pile. Or make compost on the spot by dumping the contents under a bush or between vegetable rows. Cover it lightly with grass clippings, leaves, or soil, if you wish.

Our Pet Ideas

▶ Dig through Fido's and Fluffy's supplies to help speed up your compost pile. A bowlful or two of dry dog food is a good catalyst. It's high in nitrogen, which feeds the soil

Ways to Stir Compost

A compost pile decomposes faster when air is circulated into the pile. To achieve this, some gardeners insert bamboo sticks or other rods into their compost heaps, either horizontally or vertically, then wiggle the sticks to mix the compost slightly. Here are some other super mixing sticks.

1 Golf clubs. Put the base at the bottom of the pile to help lift the compost slightly.

2 Tall, heavy-duty, cardboard packing tubes, such as the kind used to send large posters or tall, slender objects.

3 Old curtain rods, especially those that are L-shaped (they'll catch the compost as you lift it).

4 Old table or barstool legs.

5 An old floor lamp—minus the shade, of course—with the electrical cord cut off. When building the compost heap, do so around the floor lamp. Simply lift it to mix the pile.

6 Old snow or water skis.

microbes, encouraging them to give off more heat and facilitating the composting process. Sprinkle a thin coating over every several layers of compost.

Unused cat litter containing alfalfa meal (check the ingredients on the package) is also an excellent activator because it's fairly rich in nitrogen. Even better are horse alfalfa pellets, which are extremely high in nitrogen.

A Taste for Tea

▌ Get crazy at your next tea party in the garden. Toss used loose tea or tea bags into the compost pile or even around shrubs and perennials. The tea will decompose on the spot, releasing much-appreciated nitrogen in the process.

Breakfast Brew

▌ Whirl together your breakfast scraps for a nourishing brew that your compost pile will love. In a heavy-duty blender or food processor, pulverize coffee grounds, fruit peels, and eggshells. All will feed the soil nicely.

Ash Bash

▌ Wood ashes are great to add to the compost heap, but a little tricky to handle—there's always the chance that a seemingly dead ember will reignite. In the winter, when you don't want to haul those ashes out through the cold and damp to the compost heap, store them in one of those large metal tins that popcorn and other holiday goodies come in.

Note: Adding ashes to compost piles and soils with a low pH, such as those found in many areas of the West, is not recommended because they won't break down. If in doubt, leave them out.

Party On

▌ The next time you have a backyard bash, collect all those bottles or cans with a little wine or beer in them and empty them onto your compost pile. The alcohol will not only moisten the pile but also will activate the compost by providing sugars for the microbes.

Indoor Compost

▶ Turn large plastic garbage bags into treasure sacks of black gold—compost, that is. Fill the bags with fallen leaves each fall. Top off each bag with at least one shovelful of soil or compost and one-third shovelful of grass clippings or alfalfa pellets. Water well, tie up, and poke airholes in the bags. Store them in a spot where they won't freeze over the winter, such as a heated garage or basement. In the spring, you'll have bags of leaf mold—a dark, crumbly soil conditioner that is a magnet for earthworms and a humus-rich soil amendment.

A Rind Is a Terrible Thing to Waste

It's easy to save all that kitchen waste for your compost heap in the summer when the weather is pleasant. But tromping through the cold and dark out to the compost pile in the winter is another story.

For wintertime composting, consider doing it indoors in a black plastic garbage bag. Add 1 to 3 gallons of garden soil and/or finished compost to a bag or two in the fall to promote enzyme action. Tie each bag closed, and keep it in the basement or garage or on the back porch. Add kitchen waste every day or so, shaking the bag a bit to mix the old with the new.

The materials will actually break down more quickly than if you had pitched them onto the frozen compost heap. Plus, they'll be nicely primed for adding to your compost bin or soil when spring comes.

Afterlife for Faded Bouquets

▶ When that fresh spring bouquet or potted Easter lily fades and dies, don't throw it away. Instead, let it continue to "bloom" by adding it to your compost pile. Pour the water from the vase onto the pile, too. All that slimy green stuff (and the additional moisture) is good for the heap.

Note: Don't add the green floral foam to the pile. Crumbly as it is, it won't break down.

Worms in Your Drawers

▶ Before you send that old dresser to the dump, save the drawers to make worm compost bins. Clean out one or more drawers and drill a line of 1/8-inch holes about 6 inches apart in the bottom of each. Line it with several layers of dampened newspaper and add worms sold specifically for composting, such as red wigglers (available through mail-order sources). Keep moist.

If you really want a lot of worms, keep the dresser and use all the drawers. Or use the lower drawers for worm composting and reserve those on top for garden tools.

8 Soil Don'ts

Sometimes it's as useful to know what you *shouldn't* put in your soil and compost heap as it is to know what you should. Here's a list of no-nos. Some may seem silly, but you'd be amazed what people might consider.

1 Anything you'd use for a household painting or refinishing project, including paint, paint thinner, paint remover, turpentine, varnish, and varnish stripper. Would you drink these? If not, don't put them in your garden.

2 Household chemicals, such as cleaners and drain uncloggers.

3 Meats or animal fats. They attract rodents, dogs, cats, and other pests.

4 Table or pavement salt. Salt bursts plants' cells, making the plants look burned. In high-enough concentrations, it can even kill them. (Many weed killers—

both synthetic and organic—are salts.)

5 Dog doo-doo, used cat litter, or, heaven forbid, solid human waste. The droppings of any meat-eating mammal can carry harmful pathogens.

6 Drywall. It has become popular in recent years to soak drywall in water, then add it to soil to help break up clay. Not only is drywall's effectiveness as a soil amendment dubious, but it also can contain compounds you don't want your plants (especially edibles) to be taking up.

7 Pressure-treated wood, which contains arsenic, a toxic heavy metal.

8 Black walnut leaves, bark, or chips. Black walnut contains juglone, a chemical that inhibits the growth of many plants, especially tomatoes.

Rather than pitch that old dresser drawer, turn it into a compost sifter to make the richest, crumbliest soil amendment around.

Sifting Through Drawers

▶ An old drawer with the bottom knocked out can make a nifty compost sifter. Just staple or nail scrap or salvaged screening to the bottom.

Diaper Pail Duty

▶ Have an old diaper pail collecting dust in your attic? Put it to a new and inventive use collecting food scraps for your compost heap. The tight, odor-proof lid will keep smells in and flies out. Tuck a brown paper grocery bag into the pail, and put it in your pantry or near your kitchen sink. Throw all your compostables into the bag. When it's full, toss the waste onto the compost heap—bag and all, if you want.

Compost Where You Like It

▶ That old garbage can on wheels can make a handy portable pre–compost bin for longer twigs and sticks. Let them soften and break down a bit before snapping them in two and adding them to your compost heap. This technique is especially good for rose prunings, which are problematic when tucked directly into the compost heap. They take a long time to decompose and seem to rake your skin every time you turn the pile or remove finished compost.

If the garbage can doesn't already have lots of holes in the bottom from wear and tear, poke some into it so that rainwater will drain away. Tuck it into an out-of-the-way corner and roll it out as needed.

Wall-to-Wall Disguise

▶ Use old, neutral-colored indoor-outdoor carpeting to make your compost pile blend seamlessly into the background.

For a 5-foot-high barrier, use 6-foot 2-by-4s as posts, spaced 2 feet apart. Dig a 12-inch hole for each post. Place the posts in the holes and backfill with soil or concrete. Staple the carpeting (green or brown seems to work best) to the posts. Make a straight fence or create a three-sided privacy screen. For a finished look, wrap the carpeting completely around the end posts.

The carpet will limit your access into the pile, but as long as the pile is low enough for you to get to the compost comfortably, the carpet should not interfere.

Alternatively, use a carpet screen to hide tools, wheelbarrows, or an unsightly work area of the garden.

MIRACULOUS MULCHES

Shag Mulch?

▶ Scrap or salvaged carpeting, turned upside down, makes an excellent mulch in many situations.

Use it as a non-permanent mulch for several months to make paths in a vegetable garden, as a mulch between rows of plants in a vegetable or cutting garden, or to smother a tough patch of weeds, removing the carpet at the end of the season. If looks matter, top with an inch or two of wood chips, gravel, pine needles, or other attractive mulch.

Roll out the red (or shag or Berber) carpet for your plants! Old carpeting makes a nearly weed-proof mulch to put around trees, shrubs, and other plantings.

You can also use old carpeting as permanent mulch in areas where you won't need to mow or whack weeds with a string trimmer. Some carpets will come unraveled over time and can become tangled in power equipment, so use it only in areas where this won't be an issue.

Lazy-Bed Gardening

Creating a flowerbed does not have to mean back-breaking work and tedious grass removal. Instead, use cardboard as an uber-mulch to turn lawn into planting beds.

In early spring or early fall, break down some cardboard boxes and tear the cardboard into 12-inch-wide strips. Wet them thoroughly, then completely cover the future garden area with a layer or two of strips. If desired, cover the cardboard with a mulch that can be worked into the soil (chopped leaves, straw, or shredded bark). Water as necessary to keep the cardboard moist, which will hasten its deterioration.

In about 6 months, the grass will be dead and most of the cardboard will have broken down into beneficial organic matter. Using a spade, turn the mulch into the soil, pulling out any large pieces of cardboard. You're ready to plant.

For-Real Landscape Fabric

▶Those old blue jeans make fantastic landscape fabric. They're durable; they're a dark, earthy color; and they'll let in air and water while blocking weeds. Cut off any metal parts and slit the sides to create a single thickness. (You could also just lay 'em on the ground as is, if you wish.) Top with mulch, straw, or grass clippings.

Tuck In Your Flowerbeds

▶Old blankets and sheets make terrific mulch. Just be sure to use those that are 100 percent natural fibers, such as cotton or wool.

Alternatively, synthetic bedding can be used as a landscape fabric. Cut each item into long, wide strips and use as an underlayer for straw, mulch, or gravel paths. You could even position the strips under brick or gravel patios.

Magnificent Mulch

▶Have a bunch of chipped or cracked, unglazed terra-cotta pots lying around? Break them into 1- to 1½-inch pieces, and use the shards as mulch around plants that like somewhat dry conditions—including prickly pear cactus, sedum, and Mediterranean herbs such as rosemary, lavender, oregano, and thyme. The shards will keep the crowns drier and create the baked conditions these natives of arid regions love.

RAISED-BED KNOW-HOW

Salvage for a Raised Bed

▶ If you redo a sidewalk or driveway, it can be inconvenient—and costly— to dispose of the broken concrete. Fortunately, chunks of concrete make perfect building blocks for a surprisingly natural-looking raised bed or low terrace.

Stack the pieces, fitting the irregular shapes together as best you can. Keep the height at no more than 12 to 18 inches so the wall is stable. Fill or backfill with soil, and add planting material. Place trailing plants such as ivies, petunias, and ground-cover roses along the edge to camouflage and soften the appearance of the concrete.

Make a Splash with a Raised Bed

▶ Don't toss out that rigid kiddie pool once the kids have outgrown it or merely because it's sprung a leak. Instead, turn it into an attractive raised bed—an outstanding solution for problem planting areas, such as clay, hardpan, rocky, or root-laden soils.

Use a utility knife to slash holes in the bottom to provide drainage. Position the pool where you want it, then fill it with a blend of topsoil and

7 Mini–Raised Beds

A number of vegetables do best when planted in "hills"— mounds of soil just a few inches high and a foot or so across. Beans, squash, pumpkins, and other plants that germinate only in adequately warmed soil all do well in hills. Plants that like to start out in soil that is cool but not too wet also benefit from hills or raised beds. Check out this list of items you can use to create hills and mini–raised beds for your favorite edibles.

1 A pie plate with the bottom cut out
2 The rim of an old spring-form pan
3 A shoe box with the bottom cut out
4 A garbage can cut into circular "slices"
5 A plastic ice cream container with the bottom cut out
6 A milk jug with the top and bottom sliced off
7 An old drawer with the bottom knocked out

An old wading pool creates the ideal environment for moisture-loving plants that are difficult to keep adequately watered.

compost. Mound more soil around the pool to hide it (or stack stones around it), finishing with stones that slightly overlap the edge to hide it completely.

Bogged Down

▶ A kiddie pool is just the thing to create a bog garden. Dig an appropriate-size hole for either a rigid or inflatable pool. Position the pool (without air, if it's inflatable) in the hole. Using a sharp knife, slash a number of drainage holes in the bottom, depending on what plants you'll be adding and how much moisture they like. Fill with good-quality soil, and add your plants. Some moisture-loving plants to try include astilbes, leopard's-bane, rushes, and water cannas.

New Life for an Old Litter Pan

▶ When that cat litter pan gets too disgusting and needs to be replaced, give it a decent (not to mention useful) burial in the flowerbed, right underneath a plant or two that love moisture. When planting astilbes, ligularias, hydrangeas, or other perennials and small shrubs that like it wet, position the top of the litter pan about 10 inches beneath the soil surface. It will keep moisture right where the plants like it—at their roots.

Read Up on This

▶ When a bookcase has gotten old and wobbly, don't pitch it. Instead, turn it into a raised bed. Just knock or cut out the back, lay the bookcase on the ground, and bury at least

Beds of Wine and Rose Patterns

The things you'd normally find on your dinner table can also be turned into funky and whimsical edgings for raised garden beds.

Chipped, cracked, or otherwise disposable plates can be set on edge and used to make a garden border. Bury the bottom half of each plate in the soil and use the top half to create an edge. Use a collection of saucers to edge a tiny bed or dinner plates to make a taller border. Chip-proof enamelware or other crack-resistant pottery is best for gardens where power mowers or other garden machinery could damage the plates.

Innovative gardeners may even want to recycle an entire set of matching china by using plates and saucers to edge a bed, hanging teacups from cup hooks on a fence, and using teapots or tureens as planters set into the garden.

If you really want to keep the fine-dining theme going, use old forks to label plants. Insert the handles into the soil. Cut plastic tags from a clean bleach bottle, write the plant names on the tags with a permanent marker, and tuck the labels into the tines.

And what would an elegant table be without wine? Recycle wine bottles as funky but functional walls for your raised beds. Stick the narrow neck of each bottle into the soil and backfill the bottle with soil. (*Note:* This is not recommended for gardens where children might be playing, as the bottles will crack and break if hit with balls and bikes.)

Finally, if you want to carry the culinary theme even further, plant these beds with herbs, salad greens, and edible annual flowers such as nasturtiums.

the bottom couple of inches. Fill with topsoil or compost and plant.

Fill 'Er Up!

▌ The next time you're making raised beds or have a hole in the landscape that needs to be filled, search your home for biodegradable materials to fill the raised beds' bottoms. Good candidates include newspapers, cardboard, flattened cardboard boxes, phone books, and trashed paperbacks.

MAKING GREAT SOIL

Go Bananas

▌ After digging a planting hole, make it a rule of thumb to check your fridge or fruit bowl for overripe bananas, badly bruised apples, shriveled grapes, bagged lettuce that has gone slimy, or other inedible fruits or vegetables. Toss them all into the hole and say good riddance—and good luck!

Treat from the Sea

▌ The next time you steam some clams for dinner or boil up a pot of shrimp, put those shells to good use. Seashells make an excellent fertilizer that is rich in calcium and other nutrients. Use the shells immediately by tossing them into a planting hole. Or let them dry outside for a day or two, then put them in a heavy paper bag and crush them with a hammer. Sprinkle the crushed shells on the soil, and then work them in lightly with a hoe.

Tuck in Tea

▌ Many shade-loving perennials such as hostas, bleeding heart, and lamiums love a rich, acid soil. Make them happy by saving tea bags and working the bags into the soil when you're planting or mulching around these plants.

Just toss wet tea bags into a paper bag, where they'll dry out. Keep them on hand to put in planting holes. The tea will add organic matter while also slightly acidifying the soil.

Hold the Silt

▌ A simple mayonnaise or similar jar is the perfect tool to use for a quick soil analysis.

Dig into your bed about 6 inches to reach the soil that comes into contact with your plants' roots. Fill the jar about halfway with soil. Add water until the jar is full, and then screw the top on tightly. Shake the jar for a minute, then let it sit for 24 hours.

Without disturbing the jar, check for any layers that have formed and mark their divisions with a crayon. (Heavy clay soil might not break up at all and instead remain solid.) The lowest, heaviest layer is sand. The next layer is silt. The top, finest layer is clay. Organic matter will usually float to the top. Ideal soil, or loam, is 40 percent sand, 40 percent silt, and 20 percent clay.

Pasta-bilities

▌ The next time you boil some pasta or potatoes, let the water cool and then use it to feed your favorite plants. It contains small amounts of starch, organic matter, and other nutrients that plants like.

Shake It, Baby

▌ Instead of throwing away an empty oatmeal container, turn it into a potting-soil mixer. If you need to mix a small amount of potting soil, put the ingredients—compost, vermiculite, dry fertilizer, sphagnum peat moss, and so on—in the container. Snap on the lid and shake thoroughly to mix. You won't even get your hands dirty. Best of all, you can store any leftover soil right in the box until you need it for your next planting project.

A Sunny Disposition

▌ Use dry-cleaning bags or a clear plastic drop cloth or shower curtain to harness the power of the sun to kill harmful organisms in your soil. Through a process called solarization, you can trap the sun's heat in the soil, killing nematodes, weed seeds, and harmful soilborne fungi.

Nearly any kind of clear plastic can be turned into an instant soil-sterilizing device, killing harmful disease pathogens in your soil. Anchor the edges with bricks.

Solarization can also kill beneficial organisms, so use it only if you know you have a soilborne problem. It works best in western or southern regions that have hot temperatures and bright sunlight and is most effective early in the growing season as the sun is ascending.

To solarize the soil, rake the surface of an established bed smooth and water thoroughly so the soil is moist 2 feet down. Cover the area with plastic, sealing the edges well with soil, rocks, or pieces of firewood. Make it as airtight as possible to encourage heat buildup.

Keep the plastic in place for 4 to 6 weeks, longer if a cool spell comes along. After removing the plastic, allow the soil to dry out to a workable texture before planting.

Break It Up

▶ Find yourself with some leftover clean cat litter? It's ideal to work into the garden. It breaks up clay soils beautifully and enriches sandy soils. Simply spread on the soil surface and work lightly into at least the top couple inches of soil.

Clean cat litter is excellent for pouring into the bottom of container gardens, where it drains freely, and eventually breaks down—usually releasing some nitrogen along the way. (Never use soiled litter, because the fecal matter of meat-eating animals of all sorts can spread disease. And check the ingredients on the package label to make sure the litter is made of all-natural and biodegradable materials.)

No Use Crying Over Broken China

▌ If yours is one of those households that seems to break a ceramic plate, coffee mug, or clay flower pot far more often than you'd like, put those bits and pieces to good use promoting drainage in the garden.

First find a container to store the pieces. A plastic, 1-gallon ice cream container or plastic bucket with lid—like the kind detergent and cat litter come in—is excellent.

Each time you break a plate or cup or pot, further break the piece into about 1-inch shards by putting it into a heavy paper bag and smashing lightly with a hammer. (Don't use glass pieces, though—they're too sharp.). Then toss the broken pieces into the container for future use.

Then next time you plant flowers or shrubs that like excellent drainage, such as roses, lavender, or bulbs, toss the shards into the bottom of the planting holes.

CHAPTER TWO

Smart Seed-Starting

Perhaps mighty oaks from little acorns grow, but let's not forget that lush perennials, gorgeous annuals, and delicious vegetables start from small seeds, too. Seed-starting is fun, allows you to get exactly the plants you want, and saves you a lot of money. Here's how to start seeds with minimum output and maximum success.

IMPROVING GERMINATION

Snug Seeds

❱ Newly planted seeds do best indoors when the soil is covered with a water-proof top to seal in warmth and moisture. There are lots of fancy contraptions on the market to do this, but why spend money when a solution is lurking in your closets and drawers?

Slip smaller pots and flats into clear plastic produce or grocery bags. Plastic bags that you can't see through will work, but it's easier to spot newly emerging seedlings with clear bags. For larger flats, use dry-cleaning bags.

Warm Thoughts

❱ Seeds sprout sooner when they receive gentle bottom heat. Professional growers use heating cables in the bottom of flats, but home gardeners can duplicate the idea without spending money on specialized equipment.

Try using an old electric blanket or heating pad beneath pots and flats in which you've started seeds. Be sure to set a metal cookie sheet on top of the blanket or pad to protect the heating elements from moisture. Also, the metal will conduct heat from the blanket and transfer it to the roots of the plants.

Read All about It!

❱ When planting seeds outdoors, it's always a challenge to keep them moist enough to germinate. Help the process along with a removable mulch made from newspaper.

Just spread the newspaper over the seedbed, or tear the paper into strips and use the strips to cover only the rows. Spray the paper with a hose, anchor it with soil or a handy brick or stone, and continue to water as needed to keep it moist. (You'll have to do this less than usual, since the newspaper will prevent evaporation.) Check the soil daily for signs of germination. As soon as the seedlings start to poke through the soil, remove the newspaper.

(Use this technique, of course, only with those seeds that don't require light to germinate. Check the seed packet to make sure it's okay to cover the seeds with soil and therefore paper.)

Are Those Seeds Any Good?

▶ Use a variety of items from your kitchen to figure out whether your seeds from last year—or the year before—are still viable. Dampen a few layers of paper towels, paper napkins, newspaper, or even coffee filters, and lay them on a plate. Sprinkle a few seeds on the paper and top with another layer or two of damp paper. Moisten the paper daily as needed to keep the seeds evenly damp.

If at least half the seeds germinate, your seeds are good enough to plant. Depending on the seeds (different seeds take different amounts of time to germinate), they may sprout in a few days or a week or two.

Zap Fungus

▶ As a rule, if seeds develop the gray cast of a fungus, you should pitch them. It's usually not worth the hassle of planting them for iffy results.

But if they're unusual or have sentimental value—or you're just plain hypercheap—give them a soak in hydrogen peroxide for a few minutes. It will kill the fungus and improve their chances of germination.

Check the Temperature

▶ You don't need a specialized soil thermometer to check the soil temperature to see if it's warm enough or cool enough to plant seeds. (Seeds such as marigolds, beans, zinnias, and morning glories, for example, need

---

3 Ways to Water Seedlings

Newly planted seeds can withstand only the gentlest of watering; otherwise, they'll wash out. Rummage around in the kitchen for containers you can turn into gentle watering devices.

1 A dribble cup. Use a slender nail to punch a few holes in the bottom of a clean tin can, yogurt container, or paper cup. Pour a little water into the container and let it dribble gently over the seedlings.

2 A seed mister. When a spray bottle of window or all-purpose household cleaner is empty, wash it well, then fill it with water. Use the bottle to deliver a fine mist to those tiny seeds.

3 A squirt bottle. Use an empty dishwashing liquid bottle filled with water to drip moisture onto delicate seedlings.

soil that is at least 65°F. Other seeds, such as larkspurs and lettuce, won't germinate if the soil is over 55°F.) Use whatever vertical thermometer you have—pool, outdoor, oral, or other—that registers 30° to 90°F.

Walls of Water

▶ Have the first tomatoes on the block by getting them off to an early start with homemade "walls of water."

Four to 6 weeks before your region's last expected frost, fill a few plastic milk jugs with water, and attach the tops. Place the jugs in a 12-inch or so circle around the designated planting spot. Don't leave any space between them. If you can nestle them down into the soil an inch or two, all the better.

Allow the jugs to sit in place for a few days, absorbing the heat of the sun and releasing it into the soil. Then plant the seedlings of warmth-loving vegetables such as tomatoes, cucumbers, squash, eggplants, peppers, and melons. They'll be protected from all but the worst frosts. (When extreme cold threatens, prevent damage by throwing a cloth over them.)

SAVVY WITH SEEDS

How Sweet It Is!

▶ Try this method of handling tiny seeds such as snapdragons and carrots, which can be difficult to sow evenly. Mix the seeds with a tablespoon or two of granulated sugar, pinch some of the mixture between your fingers, and sow.

There will be less crowding, less thinning required, and, ultimately, less waste of seeds.

Make Your Point

▶ When planting seeds indoors or out, it's useful to make a tidy hole for each seed or two, especially if you want to get the most from your gardening dollar. You can buy an expensive tool called a dibble just for this purpose, but a pencil will work just as well. Try moistening the eraser by pressing it against the moist soil or a damp cloth, and with a little practice, you can control the number of seeds that will stick to it as you tuck them into the soil. A few weeks later,

Knitting Needles Plus

Put the contents of your knitting basket to good use when starting seeds.

Use old knitting needles to make shallow furrows for planting seeds, to make holes for transplanting seedlings, or to support plastic bags into which you've slipped pots and flats filled with seeds or seedlings.

Once the seeds or seedlings are planted in the ground, use the needles to deter cats and birds that may be attracted to the loose soil. Insert a knitting needle into each corner of the seeded area. Use scrap yarn from your basket to make a giant spiderweb-like maze just an inch or two above the soil. Cats won't want to step into the maze, and birds can't land on it.

Alternatively, use knitting needles and yarn to mark the exact spot where you planted each row by placing a needle at each end of the row and stringing yarn from end to end. Tie a seed packet to one of the needles with a scrap of yarn to make a cute row marker. Just puncture the packet with the point of the needle, thread the yarn through the opening, and tie it to the needle.

Skeins of unused yarn make effective pest traps. Soak the skeins in water and place them next to plants. Lift the skeins each morning and destroy the slugs, earwigs, and potato bugs that are hiding there.

use the pencil point to dig up and separate the seedlings for transplanting.

Wrap Up Your Planting

▶ Planting is a pleasure, but kneeling down to put the seeds in the ground can cause havoc with problem knees and backs. Solve the problem by using a long cardboard tube, such as the type that holds wrapping paper, to help you put the seeds in the ground. Position one end of the tube where you want to plant the seeds and drop the seeds down the chute. No more bending or kneeling!

For rows, just keep the tube moving steadily along the row as you dribble seeds, using your fingers or tapping them from the packet, down into the soil.

Shake Those Seeds

▶ Use empty metal or plastic spice containers to store and plant seeds. Wash each container, and peel off the label. When the container is dry, add the seeds, relabel the container with a permanent marker, and store it in a cool, dry place. To plant, just shake the right amount of seeds into the planting hole.

Alternatively, when you're ready to plant tiny seeds that you've harvested and saved from a previous season, put them in a saltshaker. This will allow you to shake out the seeds evenly in the hole or furrow and will keep any loose chaff in the shaker.

A greeting card makes a perfect tool with which to make a furrow for seeds. Then use the card again to evenly plant tiny seeds along the furrows.

Happy Holidays and Merry Planting

▶ Use an old greeting card to make a row in a flat or other container when planting seeds indoors. Place the folded edge of the card in the soil, opening or closing the card as needed to make the appropriate-size furrow. Then use the folded card as you would a funnel to place small seeds into the soil, if you wish.

Homemade Seed Tape

▶ Space even the tiniest seeds evenly by making your own seed tape using toilet paper and flour paste.

Roll out the toilet paper on a long table. Make a light paste with about 1 cup flour and enough water to create a consistency similar to that of white glue. Mix a small amount of the paste with the seeds. Use a small paintbrush, toothbrush, or even your finger to dab the mixture in a long row along the paper.

Let the paste dry overnight, then roll up the paper and store it until planting time. Once in the ground, the toilet paper will quickly decompose, and the flour paste will provide some starchy nutrients for the sprouting seeds.

On the Grid

▶ When sowing seeds outdoors or planting transplants, let a grid be your guide. Use a section of wire fencing with a 4- to 6-inch mesh to help you distribute seeds in straight lines or space transplants evenly. Lay the fencing flat on the ground and weight the edges with rocks, if you wish. Remove after planting.

Stenciling with Seeds

▶ Minimize thinning and plant seeds more precisely by making a seed stencil for rows outdoors.

Start with a sheet of poster board 2 to 3 feet long and about 1 foot wide. Fold it lengthwise down the center. Cut a series of small V-shape notches, spaced however far apart you want to sow the seeds, along the fold so that when you open the poster board, you have diamonds no more than $1/2$ inch across.

Hold this stencil over a row, keeping it slightly folded, and sprinkle the seeds over the fold. The seeds will fall through the diamonds, exactly in place.

And It Jiggles!

▶ To spread seeds evenly and help keep them moist, make a thick slush by adding small amounts of warm water to unflavored gelatin. Mix in the seeds, place the glop in a squirt bottle (a clean ketchup or mustard bottle will do), and squeeze out a line on the soil in your seed tray.

Polish Your Seed-Starting Skills

▌ Some seeds, such as nasturtiums, peas, corn, and morning glories, have tough seed coats, which slow germination considerably. To help them along, put your old manicuring tools to use. Use an old nail file or emery board (or even a scrap of sandpaper) to rough up the seed coats. This will allow water to penetrate the seeds and result in quicker germination.

A Gourmet Mix

▌ We've all heard of salad dressing in a jar, but how about salad *seeds* in a jar? After planting your spring greens, place any leftover seeds in a small jar. When you have enough seeds for an entire row of greens, plant the seeds. You'll soon have your own custom mesclun (a mix of flavorful and often colorful salad greens).

Milk This Idea

▌ Seeds kept for more than a few weeks need to be stored in a cool, dry place if you want them to germinate well. And believe it or not, the key to keeping them dry and mildew-free may be right in your pantry: powdered milk. Just put a tablespoon or so in a tissue, and fold the tissue into a neat little packet. Secure it with a rubber band and tuck it into an airtight container, such as a jar with a tight-fitting lid or a resealable plastic bag, along with your seed packets. The powdered milk will absorb moisture from the air around it.

CREATIVE SEED-STARTERS

Pots in a Jiffy

▌ There's no need to invest in expensive peat pots. Cardboard egg cartons are perfect for starting seeds indoors. Plant, cartons and all, outdoors without disturbing the seedlings, which is critical for plants such as morning glories, poppies, and others that don't like their roots disturbed. If desired, divide the cells by cutting them apart with scissors. Just be sure to cover all the cardboard with soil when you plant it, or the exposed portion will dry out and wick moisture away from the roots of the plants.

Alternatively, you can use eggshells as seed-starting pots. When you break eggs in half, save the shells. Set each half in an egg carton cell, and plant your seeds. Once the seeds have germinated, plant them outdoors, shells and all. A bonus: The eggshells add valuable nutrients to the soil.

Super Spuds

▌ You can make sure your potato eyes are more likely to sprout if you start them indoors. A great way to do this is to

---

12 Seed-Starting Helpers

Rummage through your kitchen cabinets to find terrific free containers for starting seeds. The best ones are shallow (so you don't have to use lots of expensive seed-starting mix) and either have drainage holes already or are easy to puncture. Here are some items to consider.

1 The bottom portions of cardboard milk or other dairy containers

2 Tin cans

3 Egg cartons

4 Yogurt containers

5 Shoe boxes or other cardboard boxes, trimmed down

6 The bottom portions of plastic milk or juice jugs, bleach bottles, or other large jugs

7 Cereal boxes, with their open ends stapled shut and cut in half lengthwise

8 Disposable plastic or Styrofoam bowls

9 Paper or Styrofoam cups

10 Clear clam-type, plastic produce boxes (A bonus: The snap-on lids help trap the warmth and moisture that germinating seeds love.)

11 Styrofoam, clam-type, take-out containers

12 Chinese take-out boxes

use a cardboard egg carton. Cut one or more potatoes into pieces, each with at least one eye. Place one piece in each cell of the egg carton. Fill with potting soil and keep moist. When the seedlings start to emerge from the soil, plant them outdoors.

An Indoor Salad Garden

▶ Good lettuce can be expensive, especially during the winter months or at other off-season times. But you can grow your own lettuce at home and save.

Set up your "garden" in a large, sturdy, flat container. Possible candidates include one of those flat, plastic boxes used to store wrapping paper or sweaters (punch holes in the bottom) or a flat, corrugated cardboard box (reinforce the bottom with duct tape and any flaps you cut off the sides).

Fill the box with potting soil, and plant your lettuce seeds. They'll germinate in just a few days. Put the box under a grow light or in a very sunny, south-facing window, and you'll have lettuce for salads in a few weeks.

Egg-zactly the Right Container

▶ Save those egg cartons for overwintering small to medium-size bulbs of nonhardy summer-blooming plants. After digging up and cleaning the bulbs in late fall, place one bulb in each egg carton cell. Write the name of each bulb on the carton cover. Stack and store the cartons in a cool, dry place, such as a basement or insulated garage. Don't let them freeze. A temperature of 40° to 50°F is ideal.

WATER, LIGHTS, AND MORE

A Giant Saucer

▶ If you're starting a lot of plants indoors, you may find that each time you water, you end up with water, water everywhere. To prevent leaks, set your flats and pots inside the lid of a large plastic storage box. After a few weeks, when your seedlings are ready to transplant outdoors, you can wash off the lid and return it to the box.

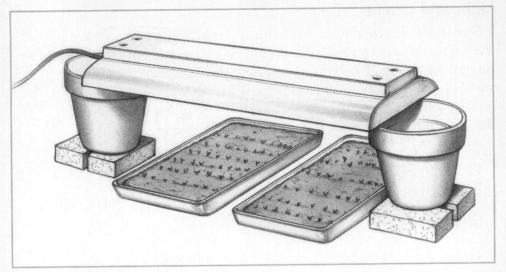

You don't need to buy and install a fancy grow light. Instead, just make two stacks of heat-proof items, such as bricks, to support a shop light over your plants.

Grow, Lights, Grow!

▶ A shop light outfitted with grow or fluorescent bulbs is an innovative way to provide light for seedlings. But finding a way to hang the light can be tricky, especially if your seed-starting setup is in a living area where you don't want to drill holes in the ceiling.

To solve the problem, make two stacks of whatever heat-proof household items you have on hand—bricks, buckets, concrete blocks, clay flowerpots. The distance between the stacks depends on the length of your shop light. Position the light so it rests on the two stacks and is 2 to 3 inches above the seedlings. The closer it is to the plants, the more intense light it will deliver. As the plants grow, adjust the stacks to accommodate the taller plants.

Soak It All In

▶ Peat pots and sphagnum-peat-moss-based growing mixes can dry out quickly and be difficult to moisten again. To avoid this problem, add ½ teaspoon of mild dishwashing liquid, such as Ivory, to 1 gallon of water and use the mixture to water your plants. The detergent acts as a wetting agent, binding the water to the molecules in the soil and moistening it more effectively.

Light and Bright

▶ New seedlings indoors need as much light as possible. Even if you're using a grow light, it's a good idea to use aluminum foil under the seedlings to reflect the light. And if you're putting seedlings in front of a window, wrap aluminum foil around a piece of cardboard and prop it up so the light from the window bounces back on the seedlings.

6 Ways to Brush Seed-Starting Problems Away

Dentists recommend that you replace your toothbrush every 3 months, and that's something for gardeners to smile about. Toothbrushes are great for handling seeds.

1 Use a slightly damp toothbrush to pick up very fine seeds such as lobelias, carrots, or impatiens. Dip the toothbrush into the seed packet, and then gently brush the seeds that cling to the bristles over the seed-starting medium or soil. You'll be able to see and control the amount of seeds you pick up, because the tiny, dark seeds will stand out against the white bristles of the brush.

2 Use a toothbrush handle to make shallow planting trenches in the soil. Once the seeds are in place, you can "sweep" the soil gently over the seeds with the brush.

3 Use the handle to scrape off seeds that stick to your fingers as you brush the seeds onto the soil.

4 To clean mineral deposits, algae, and disease microorganisms from pots, dip a toothbrush into a solution of one part bleach and two parts water, then scrub the pots with the toothbrush.

5 Keep a toothbrush near the sink to clean dirty fingers. The different bristle types—soft, medium, and firm—come in handy for different cleaning jobs, such as knuckles, cuticles, and nails.

6 Use a toothbrush to harvest sunflower seeds. Just rub the flower head with the brush to loosen and remove the seeds.

Forks and More

It seems like such a waste to pitch those plastic knives, forks, and spoons you get with take-out food. So don't.

Use plastic knives to make furrows in the soil, separate seedlings before transplanting, and mark rows (once you label the knives with a permanent marker).

Use plastic spoons to measure organic fertilizers. (Use a teaspoon to calibrate their capacity.) They're also handy as small-scale trowels for transplanting tiny seedlings into the garden.

Use plastic forks to transplant small seedlings. The tines do a superb job of lifting without damaging. Plastic forks also come in handy as miniature spading forks when you mix your own potting soil into small containers. They toss the materials together nicely. And if you want to use the seed packets as flat or row markers, stick the handles of plastic forks into the soil and place the packets in the tines. (Outdoors, the packets will last longer if you wrap them in plastic.)

SEEDLING CARE

Blown Away

▶ To get more use out of your electric fan, pull it out in late winter, not just during the dog days of summer. Use it in the room where your seedlings are located to circulate the air and discourage damping-off, a condition that is fatal to seedlings. Place the fan a few feet away from the seedlings, and run it at the lowest speed for several hours a day to stave off the fungus. An added benefit is that seedlings will grow stockier and stronger.

Milk 'Em for Every Use You Can

▶ The cutoff tops of plastic milk jugs have become popular cloches to protect small tomato plants from late frosts. The best way to use them for this is with their lids off. They'll still provide protection from frosts at night, but the opening allows for air circulation during the day.

After the last frost is past, you can use those milk jugs again as mini-greenhouses to warm the soil for heat-loving seed varieties such as squash and beans. (Seeds are typically planted outdoors 2 weeks after the last frost.) Place the milk jugs over the spots where you'll be planting the seeds. To reduce the time to planting by as much as a week, close the top of each jug with the lid or a piece of duct tape.

Take a Slice

▶ A pizza cutter makes a nifty root slicer when you're transplanting seedlings from a flat, where their delicate roots all tangle together. Use the pizza cutter to section the young plants into small cubes of soil and roots for easier transplanting. The cutter's rotary wheel makes it easy to cut long strips lengthwise and widthwise and thus form chubby planting cubes.

Scat, Cat!

▶ Cats love digging and doo-dooing in the freshly worked soil of a seedbed outdoors. Keep kitty off the bed by topping the area with a single layer of newspaper. Anchor the paper with stones. After a couple of days, remove the paper. The soil will have settled, making it less tempting to felines.

Plant Protective Custody

▶ Until seedlings become established, they are vulnerable to everything from rabbits to frost to hot sun. To provide protection, create a special cage for your tender plants.

A simple cage made of chicken wire and fabric will keep seedlings safe from sunscald, frost, bunnies, and other threats to their well-being.

Simply make a cylinder of chicken wire or scraps of any screening you may have lying around the house. Push the bottom of the cylinder an inch or two into the soil to prevent persistent bunnies from burrowing. Cover the cage with cheesecloth, lightweight or sheer curtains, a pale or lacy tablecloth, an old white sheet, or scraps of lightweight white fabric left over from a sewing project.

Make Them Eat Your Veggies

▌ It's easy to overfertilize seedlings and young plants. To avoid this, give them a light and healthy snack by saving the water left over from steaming or boiling vegetables. Cool this "vegetable tea," transfer it to a clean spray bottle, and spritz it on leaves once a week for a light foliar feeding.

That Manicured Look

▌ Instead of pulling out tiny seedlings to thin them, trim them out instead, so you don't accidentally disrupt the seedlings you want to keep. Most scissors are too big and bulky for the job, but a pair of manicure scissors, complete with a curved blade to get into tight spots, is just the ticket.

When you're done with your nails, thin your seedlings with your manicure scissors. They're perfect for this delicate job.

3 | Instant Cold Frames

Why spend time and money on a fancy cold frame when there are so many easy alternatives right around the house?

1 Arrange four bales of straw to form a large box. Top with a clear plastic shower curtain, anchored with stones or bricks. In the fall, use the straw as a winter mulch.

2 Stack newspaper a foot or two high and bundle with twine. Arrange four bundles to form a box. Top with an old picture frame, glass still intact. If the glass isn't intact, duct-tape and staple clear plastic or acetate (the kind used to wrap gift baskets) over the opening. Compost the newspaper when you're finished with the cold frame.

3 Save those old windows and storm doors. Propped against the south side of a building, they make simple, impromptu cold frames. For extra protection, cover the openings with scraps of plywood or cardboard, held in place with bricks or stones.

Cut That Out!

▶ Once seedlings have started, you often have to "prick them out"—that is, dig up the tiny seedlings and transplant them either into pots of their own or directly into the garden. One of the best tools for this is a plain old dinner knife. Use it like a minitrowel to lift and plant the delicate seedlings.

LABELING SEEDLINGS

A Label That Supports

▶ Those free paint stirrers available at the hardware store make great two-in-one plant labels for tall or vining plants. Just use a permanent marker to write the plant name on the stirrer at seed-planting time. Once the plant has germinated and gained a little height, the stirrer will provide temporary support until you can get a taller, more permanent support in place.

Bleach Bottle Bonus

▶ Empty bleach bottles make the ideal material for seed-starting labels. Unlike some other plastic jugs and bottles, these are made of sturdy plastic, the sides are straight, and the white, slightly rough surface is perfect for writing on.

Use a sharp knife or strong pair of scissors to trim off the top and bottom of a clean bleach bottle, then cut the remaining cylinder into neat strips. If desired, cut the end of each strip at an angle to make it easier to insert into the soil.

If you're really resourceful, you'll use the top of the bottle as a funnel for pouring oil or gas into the mower and the bottom as a plant saucer.

2 Mini–Greenhouses

A number of plastic containers found in most homes make wonderful combination planter/greenhouses. They're excellent for starting plants in the spring indoors, then moving them outside almost immediately so they can get plenty of light—critical for growing strong, stocky plants. Here are two options.

❙ Plastic milk jugs and 2-liter soda bottles. Cut off the bottom 4 inches of each and punch holes in the bottom for drainage. Plant with tomatoes, peppers, or other vegetables. Make several 1-inch vertical slits around the cut edge of the top portion of the jug so it will slip over the bottom portion. In very cold weather, keep the lid on. In warmer weather or on sunny days, take it off for ventilation.

2 Deli or cake trays with clear snap-on covers. Those black plastic trays that veggies, meats, cakes, and other foods are sold in are excellent for planting seedlings. Punch holes in the bottom for drainage, and plant. Then snap on the clear lid. On warm or sunny days, unsnap the lid and set it ajar for ventilation.

STORING AND ORGANIZING SEEDS

Keep 'Em in the Dark

▶ Seeds last longer if you store them properly in a cool, dark, dry place. Your fridge works well.

One way to store them is to tape or clip the packets shut, then put them in a large jar with a lid. Another is to use resealable plastic bags. Divide the seeds into categories (vegetables, flowers, herbs, and so on), then tuck them into small sandwich-size plastic bags. Label each with a permanent marker, then slip them all into a larger bag.

Blowin' in the Wind

▶ Sometimes seeds that you want to harvest emerge and disappear before you have a chance to collect them, either because the wind carries them away or because the plant "pops" its seedpods. To prevent this, use a small paper bag to capture seeds before they fly. When flowers fade and seedpods begin to turn brown, cover the plant with a brown paper bag and secure the opening at the bottom with twine or a large twist tie. When the stems turn brown, cut off the plant, invert the bag, and bring it indoors. Shake the bag from time to time to see if you hear loose seeds rattling around. When you do, remove the remaining stems and store the bag until sowing time.

Minty Fresh

▶ Don't throw away those metal breath-mint tins. Use them as storage containers for seeds. Just wash the tins and thoroughly dry them. Fill them with seeds and secure the lids. Using a permanent felt-tip marker, write the plant name and date on the side of each container. Stack the tins in a cool, dry place. You'll be able to see your entire seed inventory at a glance.

Home, Sweet Home for Seeds

▶ Frustrated by the lack of storage space on your kitchen counters or inside your cabinets? You may discover that stackable sugar and flour canisters you no longer use are stealing some of that precious space. Perhaps they came from your great-grandmother, and you just can't bear to part with them. But who says they have to stay in the kitchen? Put them to better use storing seeds. Be sure to label the outside of each canister with the type of seeds inside. Stack the canisters vertically on a garage or shed shelf until it's planting time.

Picture This

▶ Plastic film canisters with snap-on lids are waterproof and lightproof, making them excellent containers for long-term seed storage. Just make sure the seeds are very dry before you store them, or they may mildew.

Seed Collection Kit

▶ Be prepared to collect spent flower heads at any time, and you'll score some wonderful seeds from the wild or from friends and neighbors.

Make yourself a pocket, purse, or car kit for gathering and labeling seeds. Use a sandwich-size resealable plastic bag to hold a few similar snack-size bags. Tuck in either a permanent marker or a pen and squares of paper on which you can write the seed information.

Note: In the wild, never collect seeds of any plants that may be rare or endangered.

Hold My Mail

▶ Saving your own seeds? The printed envelopes that come with magazine subscription offers and other ads make handy (and free) containers in which to store them.

Look Under "C" for Clever

▶ That old Rolodex address organizer that you no longer use makes an efficient seed packet and label organizer. Just cut a seed packet down to size and tape or glue it onto one of the cards in the Rolodex. (Labels are usually small enough to fit without cutting.) You'll have an alphabetized listing of all your plantings, complete with growing information and full botanical names.

CHAPTER THREE

Cool Tools and Nifty Gadgets

You don't need to go out and buy expensive garden tools or equipment. Some of the best and most innovative helpers are lurking in your kitchen and recycling bin. In this chapter, you'll learn how to garden faster, better, and more easily. You'll also learn about innovative storage solutions, how to water more wisely, and how to clean and store your tools.

NEW TOOLS FROM OLD STUFF

Give Hillsides the Shaft

▌ End those worries about stumbling or losing your footing when you patrol your hilly garden. Rely on an old golf club, found in your garage or at a yard sale, to steady your course as you work on sloped terrain. Simply remove the club head and plunge the bottom of the shaft into the ground as you stride confidently about your garden.

A Thrifty Spreader

▌ Apply dry fertilizer easily and evenly with a plastic jug, such as one used for milk, bleach, or laundry detergent. First, thoroughly clean the jug. Then punch a hole in the lid with a heated nail or other tool. Pour the fertilizer into the jug, replace the lid, and shake the fertilizer where you need it.

Note: Clearly label your repurposed container to avoid accidents.

Alternatively, you can turn a jug into an excellent grass seed spreader for small areas. Clean the jug and fill it with seed. Cut a small piece of mesh from an onion or potato bag, and secure it to the top of the jug with a rubber band. Invert the jug and scatter the seed.

A Close Brush

▌ Don't throw away that old kitchen broom. Keep it handy with your other yard and garden tools. When you sprinkle compost or composted manure over the lawn to feed it in the spring and fall, the broom will do a great job of spreading the material evenly.

The Ultimate Scoop

▌ Clean plastic bleach and detergent bottles make unbeatable scoops. Just cut off the bottom and part of the side, making sure you can still use the handle. Leave the cap on to prevent scoopable materials from pouring out the end. Keep one in that bag of potting soil and one in each bag of soil amendments.

Free Scoops

▶ Save those heavy plastic souvenir cups from amusement parks and restaurants to use as miniscoops for potting soil, fertilizer, gravel, and other yard and garden materials.

Knee-Saving News

▶ Your knees can take a beating when there's a lot of weeding to be done. Keep them healthier and happier by making a simple kneeling pad from folded newspaper and a plastic grocery bag.

Fold sections of newspaper until you've achieved a thickness of approximately 1 inch. Cut open the plastic bag to make it flat, then wrap the paper tightly with the plastic, as though you were wrapping a gift. Seal the open ends completely with duct tape. You'll soon find yourself reaching for

3 New Ways to Use a Walker

Otherwise mobile older gardeners often take walkers outside with them to steady themselves and pull themselves up or lower themselves down. Make these walkers even more useful by turning them into mini–garden centers with a simple adaptation or two.

1 Depending on the design of the walker, you can duct-tape a jelly roll pan or a black plastic tray (the kind cell packs of annuals come in) to the top front of the walker. This is a great place to stash seeds, hand tools, a cordless phone, and much more.

2 Alternatively, you can experiment with a plastic or metal paint tray. If the design of the walker is right, you may be able to hang it so that it protrudes forward to hold light tools and seeds.

3 Many walkers have hooks designed to keep medical tubes and lines in place. Use one of these hooks to hang one of those freebie canvas tote bags that companies are always giving away. Stash garden supplies in the bag while gardening, then hang it by your back door or in the garage when you're done.

this handy kneeling device every time you head out to work in your garden.

No Snow Today

▶ During the off-season, when that long-handled combination brush/ice scraper is doing nothing more than taking up space, use it on your potting bench as a lickety-split cleaner-upper.

7 Clever Hose Guards

You've seen those fancy hose guards in catalogs. You put them in various spots in your yard to protect your plants from the hose as you drag it around. But you don't need to spend your money on those expensive guards. There are lots of items around the house that you can turn into hose guards merely by poking them into the soil in key locations.

1 A length of broomstick or mop handle. If you're worried that the kids might trip over or otherwise hurt themselves on the exposed end, cut a large slit in a tennis ball and slip it over the end.

2 The handle of a broken hammer. It will be more stable if you bury the head of the hammer, too.

3 A croquet mallet with the head still on. Cut off the shaft of the mallet so it's a foot or so long, and bury the head so that a couple of inches of the shaft sticks up out of the ground.

4 A leg from a kitchen chair that's gone wobbly. If you like, paint detailing on the chair leg in a variety of bright colors. Top with a table tennis ball painted an equally bright color or gold or silver.

5 An old curtain rod. Cut each end to about 1 foot, and stick the cut ends into the soil. Fancy finials are especially nice-looking.

6 An old trophy. Bury at least half of the trophy, more if you'd like just the top to protrude.

7 An old doorknob. Mount it on a metal rod, or if the original rod is still attached, leave it on. Insert the rod into the soil.

The brush portion is great for sweeping dirt and debris off your work surface in just one or two swipes. The scraper portion is good for more stubborn spots, like crusted-on mud. Best of all, scrapers clean up with a good hard squirt from the hose.

Doggone It

▎Don't throw out those large, heavy-paper pet food bags. They're ideal for lawn clippings, especially if you set each one in a large bucket or barrel to keep it upright while you work.

When a bag is full, tie it off with string or a rubber band, put it in an out-of-the-way place, and either cover it loosely with dirt or dig a hole and bury it. These pet food bags will break down in 1 to 2 years, depending on environmental conditions.

What a Cutup!

▎Deadheading blooming plants that bear small flowers is easier with kitchen scissors than with traditional pruning shears. The long blades of scissors are easier to maneuver around the flower stems. You'll find that using scissors trims time, too, when you need to shear a lavender hedge, harvest herbs, or trim the grass around the clothesline.

Nail scissors are nifty for very delicate tasks, such as snipping a single spent rose or two from a cluster.

Neatly Clipped

▎Nail clippers are stronger and more precise than hand shears when it comes to removing tough plant parts. Use them to snip off the sharp tips at the ends of yucca leaves to prevent skin gashes when gardening. They also work well for trimming thorns off rose stems.

Fruit Picker

▎One of those cultivators with the fingerlike ends makes a good picker

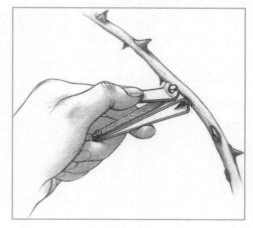

Nail clippers are surprisingly powerful and precise in removing tough, sharp plant parts on everything from yuccas to roses.

for large fruit, especially citrus or any other variety of fruit that won't be hurt by falling. You can use it, for example, to rake oranges off a tree. To extend your reach, attach the picker to a broom handle or any other long, slender object. Secure the picker in place with duct tape.

To harvest more fragile fruit, such as apples or peaches, add a cushioned mini-bucket. Attach the bottom of a 2-liter soda bottle under the head of the cultivator with a screw or wire. Then tuck a sponge into the bottom of the bottle to cushion each fruit.

T-riffic Twine

▶ You can make an excellent-quality garden twine out of an old T-shirt. This will work well for tying up anything from rose canes to light brush.

Lay the shirt flat on a table, and cut it crosswise from armpit to armpit. Discard the upper portion and sleeves. Starting at the bottom of the remaining tube, begin cutting at a slight angle, forming one continuous strip as you cut around and around the shirt. The wider the strip, the sturdier the twine will be.

Give ratty old T-shirts new life by turning them into twine for your garden.

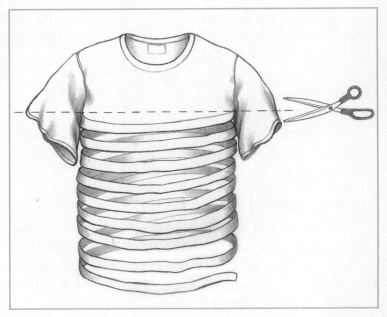

4 Ways a Screwdriver Can Save the Day

A standard screwdriver can be used in the garden in place of various hand tools that you would otherwise have to go out and buy.

1 A tiny screwdriver—the type used to repair eyeglasses—is precisely the right size to clean weeds out of the cracks of walkways and patios. But don't just remove the weeds; use the screwdriver like a chisel to remove loose soil as well. A cleaned-out crevice is less likely to host weeds in the future.

2 A somewhat larger but still small screwdriver makes a strong but lightweight weeding tool. It's excellent for digging those occasional weeds that pop up in groundcovers, including grass that sprouts in your thyme or volunteer plants that invade your Scotch moss. Use the thin blade to avoid damaging the roots of the groundcover.

3 Large screwdrivers do big garden jobs. Auto mechanics use supersize screwdrivers that are 3 to 4 feet long to tighten large bolts. You can use one in the garden as a pry bar to loosen boulders when you dig or to aerate the lawn. Look for patches of clover, a sure sign that the soil is compacted, then use your screwdriver to poke holes in the soil.

4 Any size screwdriver can be used to mark rows when planting seeds.

Once you've got the knack of making twine from T-shirts, you'll find that you can turn nearly any stretchy knit clothing, from pants to socks, into twine with this spiral-cut technique.

The Best Seat in the House

▶ An old bath bench can be used for sitting while weeding, thinning, or picking in the garden. Or if you're kneeling, you can use the bench to push yourself up. Pad it, if you wish, with an old sheet or blanket, folded to fit and stashed in a plastic bag to make it waterproof.

Cushy Work

▶ After a while, all pillows lose their loft. When it's time to put them out to pasture, put them out in the garden instead. They make supercomfy kneeling pads. Simply slip one into an appropriate-size plastic shopping bag and duct-tape it shut. If you like, make a carrying handle by taping a length of heavy twine or light rope to one end of the bag.

Wee Ones

▶ Those small-scale tools you bought for the kids or grand-kids are actually wonderfully functional for adults, too. They're most efficient, of course, if they're made of metal, but even the plastic ones have their place.

That mini–leaf rake is just right for getting around shrubs. A little hoe can do some pretty fancy work around perennials, annuals, and tightly planted veggies. That adorable little snow shovel is amazingly efficient in scooping up remnants of gravel off a sidewalk or driveway. And a small spade makes an ideal tool for digging up perennials in tight quarters.

Give Yourself a Hand

▶ Give torn or punctured rubber dishwashing gloves a second life by doing a quick repair job. A bit of duct tape or a dab of hot glue will usually fix the damage fairly well. The gloves won't be watertight enough to plunge back into a sink of dishwater, but they will be good enough to use in the garden, especially when you're working in the mud. Best of all, they will rinse clean in a flash.

Laundry Basket Redux

▶ When you go out to harvest vegetables, grab a plastic laundry basket or one of those webbed shopping baskets. A retired laundry basket with a few extra holes or damaged webbing is even better. Fill it with produce, and then hose off the edibles right in the basket. The vented design allows the water to drain out. Or you can twirl or gently shake the basket to remove the water quickly. Store the basket outdoors by hanging it from a nail on a post.

Tuck In Those Leaves

▶ You don't need a fancy tarp to collect autumn leaves. Instead, just spread an old sheet on the ground, pile in the leaves, pull up the corners, and haul them away. Sheets are lighter and more flexible than tarps, and you can use the same sheet to protect tender plants from early frosts.

Flour Garden

▶ When designing the garden of your dreams, call on your turkey baster and a cup or two of white flour for help. Fill the baster with the flour, and use it to mark the outlines of your beds and borders. As long as it doesn't rain, the markings will last for several days, while you decide whether

5 More Uses for Milk Jugs

Those plastic milk jugs seem to have a thousand uses around the garden. Best of all, once you've reused a milk jug, you can still recycle it. Just rinse and toss it in the recycling bin. Here are a few suggestions.

1 Fill a few jugs with water and use them to secure plastic sheeting, tarps, and netting over seedlings and berry bushes.

2 Cut the top off of a milk jug, thread some cord or an old belt through the handle, and tie it around your waist, facing up. You've just created a caddy for tools, weeds, or freshly picked vegetables.

3 Make a handy tool holder by cutting a hole larger than your fist toward the top of the jug. Use the jug as a nail bucket or to hold small yard tools. Don't cut off the entire top; leaving it intact makes for a sturdier holder.

4 Cut a large hole in the side of a jug opposite the handle, and use it to hold cut flowers.

5 Trim off the bottom of a jug to create a funnel for filling bird feeders or transferring fertilizer or grass seed into other containers.

that's really where you want to put them. To adjust the outlines, just "erase" the marks with water from a spray bottle.

EASIER PLANTING

Portable Potting

▌ Large paint trays make wonderful portable potting trays. Rather than carry around heavy bags of potting mix, make your own mix in the tray, then carry it to the spot where you need it. To contain the mess, set your pot right in the tray as you fill it. When you are done, leave the pot in the tray and add a couple of inches of water. The water will wick up into the pot, saturating the soil and settling the new plant.

A Garden Guide

▌ Anyone who has a lot of planting to do needs a quick and easy way to measure spaces between seeds and plants. You can solve this problem with a planting guide or two that you can take with you to the garden.

To make one type of guide, cut V-shape notches every 6 inches along one side of a scrap piece of floor molding or

This long-handled measuring tool helps you space plants precisely and avoid unnecessary bending.

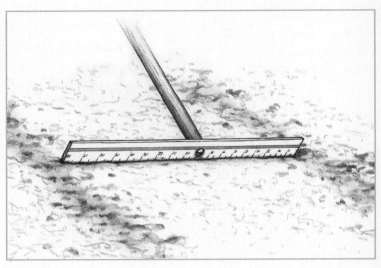

a 1-by-4 board. Press the unnotched side into the soil to create a furrow for your seeds. Use the notches to gauge the spacing of seeds.

To make another type of guide, screw the center of a ruler to the end of an old broom handle. (Use two screws if you can, to keep the ruler from turning on the handle.) By rotating the broom handle, you can "walk" the ruler end over end to measure multiple feet without lifting the device from the ground.

Take a Cue

▌ An old pool cue makes a great planting tool. Without bending over or kneeling, you can use the tapered end to make small holes for pea or bean seeds, for example. Use the larger butt end to make bigger planting holes, such as those for seedlings that come in three- or four-packs.

Potting Table to Go

▌ An old metal ice chest with the lid down makes a handy portable potting bench. Store potting soil, pots, and more inside. The lid provides an excellent surface on which to pot and water plants. Plus, as long as the chest is well built, you can use it as seating when working out in the garden

Dude! Where's My Skateboard?

▌ The next time you have a heavy bag of wet potting soil to move up the driveway or a massive bale of sphagnum peat moss to lug across your yard, borrow the neighbor kid's skateboard. Lift the bag onto the skateboard and push. It makes an amazingly useful little trolley to move heavy objects with ease.

Measure for Measure

Shaving cream caps make just the right size measuring cups for organic fertilizers. Use your kitchen measuring cups to measure out 1 cup, ½ cup, ⅓ cup, and ¼ cup in a large cap, then mark the measurements on the inside of the cap with a permanent marker.

Need to measure out tablespoons or teaspoons? Use a small plastic cup from the top of a cough syrup bottle. Or use one of those semitransparent film canisters. Measure out 1 or 2 tablespoons in a canister, then mark the measurement on the side with a permanent marker.

Improvised Row Covers

▌ The best time to plant or transplant is on an overcast day. But sometimes you can't wait for the perfect time and need to do your planting in the sun. To protect your new plants from the sun's punishing rays, make your own row covers.

Untwist a few wire coat hangers, straighten them with pliers, and shape each into a U. Poke the ends into the ground on either side of a row of new plants, spacing the hoops out as necessary. Drape a dish towel, T-shirt, or other light-colored, lightweight piece of fabric over the hoops. (If you have a long row of plants to protect, a lightweight curtain panel makes an ideal cover.) Secure the fabric to the hoops using safety pins, straight pins, or whatever you have handy. Keep in place for one to three days until the plants adjust to the transplant.

 ## More Uses for Chopsticks

If you like Chinese carryout, you probably have a whole collection of chopsticks cluttering up your drawers. Here's how to put them to use.

1 Use chopsticks to make planting holes for seeds in pots or in the ground.

2 Turn them into supports for mini–greenhouses. When you start cuttings or seeds, stick a couple of chopsticks into the pot, and tent it with a plastic bag. The bag will keep the cuttings moist, and the chopsticks will keep the bag from touching the cuttings or soil.

3 Convert chopsticks into natural-looking stakes for plants that are too small for a stake or bamboo support. Use a chopstick and a twist tie to keep the plant from toppling over.

4 Use these sturdy sticks to aerate soil. Just poke and probe—they're amazingly strong. And if you need to probe a little more, stick a chopstick into a pencil sharpener for a sharper edge.

Smooth Sledding

▶ A child's discarded plastic snow saucer is ideal for moving soil, mulch, landscape rocks, or large potted plants from one area of the yard or driveway to another. The plastic slides easily across the lawn, and the pull rope is located at the right height for maximum leverage. The saucer also works well for moving a tree or shrub with a large rootball from place to place.

Earthmover

▶ When transplanting shrubs or small trees in your landscape, a tarp, drop cloth, or old shower curtain can be your best friend. If you have two cloths, that's even better.

First, dig the new hole, shoveling the soil onto one of the cloths. Then unearth the plant and maneuver it onto the other cloth. Grab two corners of the cloth and drag the plant to the new location. Once it's replanted, drag the soil to the old planting hole and refill it.

This is a back-saving way to move plants from one spot to another, while containing and conserving soil at the same time.

EFFICIENT WATERING

Drink Deeply

▶ When vacation time rolls around, set up your houseplants, container plants, and just about any other plants with a low-tech automatic watering system that's nothing more than a soda bottle.

Heat a very thin nail or very thick needle over a flame and poke a hole in the soda bottle lid. Fill the bottle with water, screw on the lid, and invert. The water should barely bead up and then, after a minute or two, begin to drip.

Nestle the bottle, still upside down, into the top inch or so of the soil next to the plant. Depending on the size of the bottle—a single serving or 2 liters—it will water the plant for days or even a couple of weeks.

2 Uses for a Leaky Hose

There's no need to throw out a rubber or vinyl hose just because it has sprung a leak. Here are two uses for it in the garden.

1 Turn it into a soaker hose. Seal the "male" end of the hose with a cap, available for just pennies at your garden center. Use a nail to punch a series of holes along the length of the hose—or just in the areas you want. Use it in the vegetable garden, or curl it around the base of a thirsty shrub and cover all but the "female" end with mulch.

2 Cut 1-foot sections of hose and lay them wherever earwigs, sow bugs, or slugs are a problem. The bugs will crawl into or under the hose at night, and you can easily collect them during the day. Just drop them into a bucket of soapy water.

Super Soaker

▶If a standard spray bottle aggravates an arthritic hand, sort through your kids' or grandkids' toy box for a less painful alternative: a long-distance squirt gun.

Just a few quick, sliding motions allow you to apply liquid fertilizers, an organic herbicide, or disease and pest controls. Shoot gently or forcefully, as needed.

Use only toys that the kids have outgrown and won't be using anymore. You wouldn't want to expose them to traces of even the organic mixtures.

Catch It

▶An old ice chest makes an ideal mini–rain barrel. Simply position it under a downspout. If you're concerned about it overflowing next to your foundation, bury it at the base of the downspout so that, if it overflows, it will drain away from the foundation of the house.

Note: If you have small children or grandchildren, this might not be a good idea. A child can drown in just a few inches of water.

What U Need

▶ Using expensive irrigation staples to keep your soaker hoses and drip irrigation piping in place? Here's an inexpensive alternative. Unwind a standard wire coat hanger and cut the wire into 6- to 8-inch lengths. Bend each section into a U shape and push it into the ground over a hose. Easy, secure, and free!

Tie One On

▶ To hold ¼- or ⅛-inch drip irrigation lines in place, use those bendable aluminum ties used to secure chain-link fencing to posts. As you push one of these candy-cane-shaped ties into the ground, the hooked end will fit perfectly over the drip line.

Plug a Leak

▶ The next time you're touching up the caulking around your tub or shower, head outside when you're finished. That leftover caulk is great for plugging holes, cracks, and leaks in metal or plastic watering cans and buckets.

You can even use it to plug the drainage holes in plastic and ceramic pots if you want to use them to set another pot inside as part of a double-potting setup to conserve moisture.

Shower Power

▶ Give that old detachable shower wand a new purpose by using it as a water wand outdoors. Even if it's a bit leaky or the settings are limited, it may be just right for watering seedlings and other plants. Connect the end of the wand to your garden hose. Wrap plumbing tape around the connection to prevent any leaks.

Here's the Scoop

▶ To scoop water from your rain barrel, use a plastic milk jug with the top cut off at an angle. And if you want to get really organized, use a scrap of string or wire to tie a loop around the handle. Hang the jug from a nail or hook nearby so you'll always have it handy.

SAVE THE PLANET

Single-Sock Solutions

Our sock drawers always seem to harbor a few socks without matching mates or with worn-through toes. For some reason, we hate to toss them in the trash.

To put some of those socks to use, snip off the feet of worn or mismatched, knee-high, cotton socks. Put these socks on your forearms to protect your skin against nicks from rose-bushes, as well as dirt and grass stains, when you weed and plant in your garden.

Children's socks are great for slipping over the ends of hand tools to help prevent blisters and absorb perspiration.

5 Great Stakes

Why spend a lot of money on fancy stakes for your veggies and flowers when you have an assortment of options lying around the house? The following all make great stakes, and if you spray-paint them dark green (for plastic items, use paint specially formulated for plastic), they'll be nearly invisible.

1 Freebie yardsticks and paint stirrers
2 Curtain rods
3 Table and chair legs
4 Spindles from wooden beds
5 Scraps of wood flooring

Saucepan Supreme

▶An old saucepan is a surprisingly useful tool to have around the garden. Use it to dip water out of a rain barrel, birdseed out of a bag, or potting soil out of a bin. It's also helpful for watering a potted plant. Fill it partway with water and then set the pot in it for a good, deep bottom soaking.

A Can of Rain

▶Turn a small tuna or cat food can into a rain gauge. Wash it well and place the empty can in the center of your garden bed or screw it onto a wooden stake with a rubber washer to seal the connection. These cans are typically about 1½ inches deep, but if you want an exact measure, make a permanent mark at 1 inch on the inside of the can.

Easy Rain Gauge

▶ A straight-sided jar or drinking glass makes an inexpensive rain gauge. Simply mark off inches on the sides with a permanent marker or, if you really want the marks to last, dabs of dark fingernail polish. Position it atop a post by finding a lid (perhaps the one that came with it) that the jar or glass will fit into. Nail the lid to the post, and insert your new rain gauge.

Bottoms Up

▶ Make a fairly accurate in-ground rain gauge (and spend not a penny) by recycling one of those sturdy, straight-sided, clear plastic glasses that fancy Italian sodas come in at upscale coffee shops. Using dabs of nail polish, mark off inches on the inside of the glass. Then sink the glass into the lawn or set it in another place where tall plants, eaves, or the side of a building won't block the rain.

Pitch Weeds instead of Tents

▶ You may have one of the best weeders in the world right in your own backyard: a metal tent stake. Tent stakes have a sleek design that allows them to pierce the soil easily. Use duct tape to wrap a piece of foam or a folded dishrag around the blunt end of the stake to make a comfortable handle. Then use the long, fluted end to remove those deep-seated taproots.

SUPPORTS AND STAKES

Shocking Savings

▶ The next time your radio, toaster, or other electrical appliance goes on the fritz, salvage the cord by trimming it off with a sharp knife or scissors. Trim off the plug as well.

Use the trimmed cord as is or split it in half down the middle with a paring knife to create two more slender cords.

These cords have dozens of uses around the garden such as tying sturdy plants to stakes and tying up bundles of brush. Use your imagination!

A Sunny Outlook

▶ An umbrella without the fabric makes an amazingly attractive plant support. Lock it into the open position, and then insert the handle several inches into the soil so it's steady. If needed, anchor it by stacking stones at its base. Plant your favorite annual or perennial vine at the base. The vine will grow up the handle and spread out along the metal ribs, creating a pretty parasol effect.

Turn a broken umbrella into a striking support for your favorite climbing plants.

How Pretty!

❱ Hair scrunchies make fast, soft ties for plants on stakes. They're especially good for plants that need to be tied to a single stake, such as delphiniums, lilies, and glads.

CLEANING AND CARE

Foiled Again

❱ Those scraps of aluminum foil we're all so fond of saving come in handy in the toolshed. Lightly crumpled, they're excellent for scraping mud and other gunk off metal tools. They'll even sharpen the tools slightly.

And if you're doubly clever, you'll save the box the foil came in. Use it to store those small pieces until you need them for tool cleanups.

Blade Aid

❱ Has your garden hose seen better days? Don't throw it out. Cut a chunk of it off to use as a blade protector for your pruning and other gardening saws.

With a serrated knife or garden shears, cut a section of hose as long as the blade of the tool you want to protect. Then cut a slit in the hose and fit it over the sharp blade. No more dinging and damaging the blade, and no more sharp edges to cut fingers.

Supersized Scrub Brush

❱ Once that broom is no longer any good for sweeping the kitchen floor, give it a second life as a heavy-duty scrub brush. If the broom has a plastic

A length of old hose will protect the blade of your pruning saw—and protect your fingers as well.

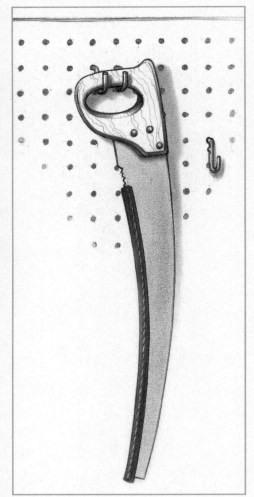

handle, you can simply unscrew it. If the handle is wooden, you'll need to saw it off. Then take out a pair of shears and cut the tired bristles to just 3 to 4 inches long. Now you can use the brush to scrub muddy spades or knock off caked-on grass.

SOS

▶ Those steel wool soap pads made for pots and pans are also convenient for cleaning tool blades. Whether the blades are plagued by a bit of rust or something sticky, you can clean them quickly with warm water and one of those pads. Be sure to dry the tools thoroughly to prevent further rust.

Slick Trick

▶ If pine or cedar pitch gums up the blade or handle of your pruning shears, put a bit of vegetable oil on a rag and rub it off. The oil will dissolve the pitch and lubricate and protect the metal and wood besides.

Wipe Out Mud

▶ If you live in a region with snowy winters, you may rejoice when spring arrives. But don't put your windshield scraper into a drawer or on a shelf when the snow melts. Put it to work year-round, especially during the rainy spring months, as an excellent boot scraper. Hang it on a nail by the back door to get the worst of the mud off your boots or shoes before coming indoors.

The Brush Off

▶ That steel or copper wire barbecue grill brush also comes in handy when cleaning up in the garden. The stiff bristles

3 More Panty Hose Ideas

Panty hose have many uses in the garden. Here are just three.

1 Panty hose make some of the best plant ties around. Just cut the legs crosswise to make little rings, then cut each ring to make a strip. These ties are soft and stretch with the plant as it grows.

2 Scrunch up the toes or panty portion and secure with a rubber band or two. Use it as a scrubber to clean off muddy tools under the hose.

3 The feet of panty hose are great for storing bulbs over the winter. Tuck the bulbs into the panty hose with a label and tie them off. Hang them in a cool, dry place or put them in a cardboard box with foam peanuts as packing material.

are excellent for scrubbing mineral deposits off pots and are also ideal for scrubbing caked-on mud and grass off the underside of a lawn mower. Plus, the metal scraper often found on the end of barbecue brushes makes even the toughest, crustiest clean-up jobs a snap.

Roll Out the Barrel

If changes in trash collection rules have made your old garbage can obsolete or you simply have a spare can, put it to good use collecting rainwater. A 32-gallon plastic trash can is ideal for this, and if it has wheels, you can even move it as needed.

The easiest way to turn a garbage can into a rain collector is simply to tuck it underneath a gutter with the downspout removed and fill 'er up. You can get a little more efficient by positioning the downspout so it goes into the can. Keep debris out of the rain barrel by cutting an opening in the lid a bit larger than the downspout and feeding the downspout through the hole.

To prevent mosquitoes from making a home in the barrel and to keep even small leaves out, stuff an old pair of panty hose into the gap between the downspout and the lid.

For more convenience, install a plastic spigot, available at home improvement stores, in the barrel. Drill a hole in the side of the barrel at least 12 to 18 inches above the ground—high enough to set a watering can underneath. Install the spigot according to the product directions.

If you want to get really high-tech, add an overflow barrel. Find a piece of leftover tubing of nearly any sort. Cut a hole in the side of the garbage can a few inches from the top; make sure the tubing fits very snugly in the hole. If you're worried that water might seep out around the tubing, caulk it with some leftover exterior or bathroom caulk.

Set a second garbage can (this one doesn't have to be quite as large) next to the first one. Cut a hole in its side an inch or two lower than the hole in the first can, and push the tubing through.

What a Doormat

▶ When your rough plastic doormat is done, give it a whole new life as a tool cleaner. Nail it to the side of your garage or toolshed so that you can wipe muddy tools on it. Position it so that the rain will wash it off or so it's close to the hose.

Smooth Move

▶ Are the wooden handles of your tools or wheelbarrow getting splintery? Prevent a painful splinter in your palm with this nifty trick. Rub old candles or leftover paraffin into the wood, then buff with a piece of waxed paper.

If the wood is very splintery or porous, light a candle and allow the wax to drip onto the wood. Slip on a garden glove to protect your hand, and smooth the wax with a warm piece of aluminum foil, heated for 5 to 10 minutes in a 175°F oven.

Bumper Sticker
Bumper Crop

▶ So you've been given yet another bumper sticker? If you have no interest in putting it on your bumper, put it on the handle of a wooden tool to protect hands from splinters and (if the bumper sticker is brightly colored) make it easy to find the tool in the garden even when it's lying in tall grass.

First make sure the tool handle is clean and oil-free. Wash it and then clean with a rag dipped in rubbing alcohol to remove all traces of dirt and oil. Let the handle dry thoroughly.

Then peel off the protective backing from the sticker and wrap the sticker carefully around the handle, smoothing it as you go.

PASS IT ON

A New Home for Tools

The next time you're going to upgrade that mower or purchase a better weed whacker, consider giving away your good-quality old tools to a worthy organization.

Give a call to your local battered women's shelter, residential home for troubled youth, homeless shelter, or a halfway house for those with alcohol and drug problems. Many of these places keep up their landscapes themselves, and good-quality tools can help.

Just be sure that the tool is in good working condition and that, if possible, you pass along the owner's manual and other documents.

Rust Away

▶ You just completed a major garden chore in your backyard. A week or so later, you discover your favorite hand tool barely visible in deep grass. A close look confirms your worst fears: The rust invasion has begun. Don't worry, but don't wait. Get rid of the rust by immersing the stainless steel portion of the tool in a bucket of cider vinegar for 24 hours. Then take a clean, dry rag and wipe away the rust effortlessly.

Girly-Girl Tools

▶ Sure, it's wonderful if you take the time to paint all those tool handles bright red so that you can spot them when they end up hiding in the grass.

But what's even easier is to raid your daughter's or granddaughter's room for colorful castoffs to mark tools.

Put a hot pink scrunchy around the handle of a trowel. Tie a sparkly turquoise hair ribbon around your garden shears. You can even use a large, glittery barrette to clip together seed packets or plant labels so you'll never, ever have to wonder where you laid them again.

SMART STORAGE

Extend Your Reach

▶ Getting a bit creaky in the knees? Extend your reach by using duct tape to attach an old broom or mop handle to your handheld weeding tools, and save on some of that up-and-down action.

The Purrfect Bucket

▶ Many brands of cat litter now come in sturdy square buckets with handles and attached lids. Use them to store potting soil, lug small tools, collect pulled weeds, haul water, protect birdseed from rodents, dump dirt in when you sweep the patio, carry biodegradable materials to the compost pile, and sit on as you're working in your garden beds.

Hose Holdup

⚫ A 5-gallon bucket makes a clever hose holder. Just nail or screw the bucket to the side of your house near a spigot. Wrap the hose around the bucket, and store watering accessories, such as spray attachments, inside.

A Cheesy Trick

⚫ That empty Parmesan cheese shaker makes a handy storage container for certain soil amendments, such as kelp meal and other finer materials that you sprinkle on the soil. Clean out the shaker (a little salt shaken around inside will help remove the last bits of cheese). Fill the container with the help of a funnel, then label it clearly with a piece of masking tape.

A Fountain of Fertilizer

⚫ The kids are gone, and with them the need for that giant insulated drink cooler, complete with a handy spigot. Put the cooler to new use—storing a premixed organic fertilizer or compost tea. (To make compost tea, simply fill the cooler with water, add a cloth bag full of compost, and let it steep for a few days.) Label the cooler clearly so that no one thinks he's pouring iced tea instead of fertilizer or compost tea. Whenever you need to give your plants a nutrient-rich snack, just fill your watering can from the cooler.

Gardening to a Tee

⚫ Did you know that you can put old golf equipment to new use in the garden? That wheeled golf bag is an ideal garden tote, easy to move about, pick up, or stand upright on the grass. It maneuvers on slopes and steps beautifully. Pack

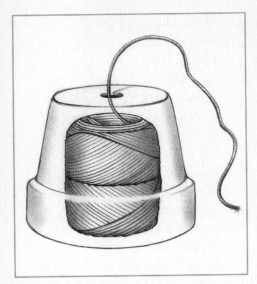

Slip a clay pot over a ball of twine to give you easy access and prevent the twine from tangling.

the main compartment with long-handled garden tools such as hoes and spades. There's also plenty of room in the outer pockets for other gardening aids, including a water bottle. The shoe compartment is ideal for garden clogs, while another pocket is handy for holding gloves and shears.

A Pot of Twine

▶ A ball of sisal or jute twine can be of great value to the gardener, but it can be messy, too. It always seems to unwind and get tangled up with tools. A 6- to 8-inch terra-cotta pot is the perfect solution for keeping twine tangle-free.

Place the ball or cylinder of twine on a shelf or table. Turn the pot upside down, and feed the end of the twine through the pot's drainage hole, from the inside out. Position the pot over the twine. When you need a length of twine, simply pull the protruding end and snip it off. The ball will unwind inside the pot, and the end will always be handy. Be sure you draw the twine vertically out of the pot. If you try to pull it out at an angle, the pot could end up on the floor, shattered.

Rake Rack

▶ What can you do with a broken garden rake? Turn it into a useful rack for holding your gardening hand tools.

Attach the rake head to your garage or shed wall so that the tines stick out at a 90-degree angle. You can hang tools from the tines by a cord or position them upright between the tines.

Hang 'Em Out to Dry

▶ Garden gloves are never where you want them, but you can use an old-fashioned wooden clothespin to keep them handy. Simply nail or screw the pin to a garage wall, by the back door, or wherever is most convenient. Then clip the gloves in place.

If you have several pairs of gloves, use a wire coat hanger outfitted with several clothespins. Put the hanger on a nail in a handy place, and clip up to a half-dozen pairs of gloves in place.

Pipe Dreams

▶ Keep hoses high, dry, and neat with an easy-to-make hose hanger fashioned from leftover plumbing parts.

Gather leftover lengths of threaded pipe—galvanized or copper are the best-looking—and fashion them into an L shape using a 90-degree elbow. Make the lower part of the L about 12 inches long and the upper part of the L about 14 inches long.

Hang this L by attaching a round, galvanized flange to the wall or fence where you want to store your hose. Screw the longer length of pipe into the flange, and cap the other end with a hose cap.

CHAPTER FOUR

Container Gardens with a Twist

Look around the house, up in the attic, and down in the basement. You'll find dozens of common household items that will make your container gardens better, cheaper, and more beautiful.

NOT YOUR ORDINARY CONTAINERS

Hats Off

▶ Old straw and other beat-up or out-of-fashion hats make fun plant containers. Line each with black plastic cut from a garbage bag, make a few slashes in the bottom for drainage, and plant.

You can also turn a hat into a hanging basket. Run fine wire through the crown, and then loop it around the crown for support. Poke three long pieces of wire through the crown and twist into place, using both the material of the hat and the wire around the crown to anchor the wires. Twist the wires together, and fashion them into a closed loop to hang from a hook.

These hat planters are especially effective when hung in groups of three or more for visual impact. If you have old jewelry or gloves, make them part of the container by draping them from the sides or fastening them to the fabric.

Depending on the hat and climate conditions, a hat planter will last anywhere from a single growing season to several.

The Gift That Keeps On Giving

▶ Have a pretty decorative gift box or two that you can't bear to part with but haven't yet managed to reuse? Forget about putting a present in it. Fill it with a plant instead.

Protect its interior by lining it with clear plastic wrap or a section of a black garbage bag. Hot-glue, tape, or staple the liner in place.

Tuck a potted plant into the box, slipping a plastic saucer or margarine tub underneath the pot to further

ONE MAN'S TRASH

Rust Bonanza

On walks, drives, and, yes, visits to the landfill, you come across an amazing array of tin cans, hubcaps, and other pieces of metal, especially in desert areas. Often these objects are beautiful in their decay. The rust and dings give them a sense of age and a patina you can't re-create with paint or sandpaper. Collect these metal treasures to use as planters for succulents or for gray-leaved plants, which look fabulous against a rust-color background.

Turn the seat of an old chair into a charming planter for a one-of-a-kind container garden.

protect the box. Then conceal the pot by tucking in some green floral moss, dried floral Spanish moss, or brightly colored, shredded, crinkled paper (the kind sold as a packing material for gifts).

Don't limit yourself to decorative boxes. Water-resistant gift bags can make clever cachepots, too.

By the Seat of Your Plants

▶ Wooden or metal chairs without the seats can be remade into planters by attaching fine wire mesh where the seat was. Drape the mesh so it forms a planting pocket, staple it in place, and trim off any excess. Line the pocket with green sheet moss, add planting mix, and plant.

If you like, play off the style of the chair by planting, for example, peppermint in a metal ice-cream-parlor-style chair, succulents in one with a southwestern flair, or Johnny jump-ups in a child's chair.

Pet Plants

▶ Those large buckets that pet food or cat litter come in make terrific plant containers. Just punch a few holes in the bottom of each for drainage (a Phillips screwdriver heated over a flame works well), then paint them with a spray paint for plastic. You could also decorate the containers by hot-gluing small stones or flat marbles to the sides in creative patterns.

Cooking with Herbs

▶ Old baking pans—round, square, or rectangular—are great planters for tabletop succulent, cactus, or herb gardens. Punch a few holes in the bottom of a metal baking pan with a hammer and nail. For a ceramic dish, drill holes with a power drill outfitted with a diamond-head drill bit. Add a thin layer (¼ to ½ inch deep) of gravel to the pan. Fill with soil, plant, and enjoy.

Paint the Garden Red

▶ Or white. Or purple. Or any other color you happen to have hanging around your basement or garage. All that leftover paint from interior and exterior projects, as well as spray paint and craft paint, can help you brighten up or unify your collection of pots and containers.

"Age" brand-new clay pots by soaking them in water and then dabbing on a bit of white paint with a rag. The white paint looks like mineral deposits. If you have any brown or green paint, dab some of that on as well, mimicking moss and soil. If you apply too much, use an old scrubber sponge to remove it.

Or use leftover paint to unify a hodgepodge of containers so they all match the trim on your house. Even if you have nothing but tin cans, a fresh coat of paint can make them look smashing.

School Composition

▶ An old, metal, school lunch box can make a whimsical plant container. Keep small plants in their original plastic pots, and place them in the lunch box. (A collection of herbs would make an ideal arrangement.) Hide the pots and fill in the empty spaces with moist sphagnum peat moss. The lunch box will corral the plants into a pleasing composition and contain the excess drainage.

Can You Say "Hypertufa"?

If you have some large foam containers left over from purchasing a tree or shrub or have some shaped like a box, you can make a natural-looking container with hypertufa (pronounced hy-per-TOO-fuh).

Hypertufa is a mixture of cement and other materials that is used to make very lightweight containers resembling aged carved stone. To make hypertufa, combine two parts sphagnum peat moss, one part sand, and one part dry portland cement in a wheelbarrow or bucket. Add just enough water to moisten it thoroughly.

Make drainage holes in your container, inserting wooden dowels through the holes to keep them open. Using your hand, spread a 1- to 2-inch-thick layer of hypertufa on the container. It will dry in a day or two, and you can proceed with planting.

Purse Planters

▶ That collection of outdated purses can make a fine container garden on your patio or deck. Just line each purse with a section of a black plastic garbage bag, being sure to punch a few drainage holes in the plastic. Add soil and plants, tucking in a bit of dried floral Spanish moss as needed to help hold the soil in place and cover the plastic and soil.

Hang the purses from a porch ceiling or rafters, deck railings, or cup hooks attached to fences or wooden buildings. Or just set them on the porch steps. Depending on the material and your climate, they'll last 1 to 3 years.

Basket Redux

▶ Don't throw out that grungy or broken wicker basket. It can make a darling in-ground planter. Just bury the basket ½ inch or so in the soil and line, if needed, with sphagnum peat moss or even scraps of black plastic garbage bags or brown paper bags.

Don't pitch it—repurpose it! Partially bury a badly damaged wicker basket for use as a wonderful in-ground container.

This is a great way to grow any plant that needs the excellent drainage provided by a raised bed. It also will contain plants that are slightly invasive.

Canned Idea

▶ Collect 2-pound coffee cans to make perfectly shaped hanging containers for a fence, wall, or trellis. Cut the bottom out of each can, then step on the bottom end of the can to press the sides together. Secure them in place by crimping with pliers, almost the way you would with a piecrust. Or use a hammer and nail to punch a row of holes and "sew" up the seam with wire.

A coffee can with one end flattened and crimped makes an excellent hanging planter to brighten fences, walls, and trellises.

Punch two holes on each side of the can near the top, and insert a wire coat hanger for the handle. Decorate the can with paint or by gluing pretty objects to the front, then tuck some panty hose, crumpled newspaper, or used coffee filters into the bottom to keep the soil from washing out when you water. Fill the can with potting mix, plant with annuals and trailing vines, hang up, and enjoy.

Herbal Themes

▶ If you like to grow herbs and smaller edibles that suit a certain cuisine, grow them in containers that reflect that theme.

Do you make a mean spaghetti sauce or other Italian favorite? Grow your basil, thyme, oregano, and parsley in those beautifully labeled Italian tomato cans.

Or perhaps Mexican is more your style. Grow cilantro, oregano, and hot peppers in cans with Spanish wording that previously held Mexican staples such as seasoned tomatoes, mole (a spicy chocolate-based sauce), or peppers.

Give 'Em the Boot

Gardening truly is good for the sole! Give old boots new life by turning them into a creative collection of plant containers.

Cowboy boots, leather work boots, bright yellow rain boots, high-fashion go-go boots, and others can be nailed, singly or in pairs, to a wooden fence or wall and filled with potting soil. Poke drainage holes in the soles with a nail. Sedums and succulents such as hens-and-chicks may live for years in a pair of leather boots. A bonus: As the leather slowly decays, it releases nutrients to the plants.

Or use the boots as pot holders, setting plastic pots of geraniums, herbs, or trailing plants into the tops. Add foam packing peanuts or wadded-up newspaper, if necessary, to keep the pots on top.

Chinese and Asian food fans can have fun growing spring onions, cilantro, or hot peppers in waxed cardboard carryout containers. A few spare chopsticks, stuck in trellis- or tepee-style, complete the theme.

Dressed to the Vines

▶ An old dresser makes a cute container garden for your backyard. Use as is, or give it a coat of paint in a fun color suiting its whimsical new life, such as deep purple, magenta, or cobalt blue.

Drill drainage holes in each drawer. Open the drawers partway, making sure the bottom drawers are pulled out farther than the top ones. Place black plastic pots turned upside down in the back of each drawer so you don't have to use so much soil. Then fill each drawer with soil and add plants, preferably including at least a few trailing ones.

Set more plants on top of the dresser. If there's a mirror still attached, tap in a few finishing nails around the frame. Run monofilament fishing line around the mirror, wrapping it once around each nail. Plant ivy at the base so it grows up around the mirror.

Get Cracking

▶ Most of us have heard of or seen a broken clay pot lying on its side with a blooming plant "spilling" out. Why not expand on this idea with chipped or cracked ceramic containers from inside the house? Check around for an old pitcher, vase, cookie jar, decorative box, or other item that you've been wanting to replace and repurpose it for a cute little garden vignette.

Clean 'n' Green

▶ Ever notice how laundry supplies often have a retro, June Cleaver-esque appeal? Up-to-the-minute garden designers on the coasts certainly have. They sell vintage laundry and cleaning product containers for big bucks. Lucky you can capitalize on these products and their often-colorful designs for free by turning cleaning containers you already have into a themed container garden.

A large detergent bucket or box (they're usually waxed for durability) makes an excellent container. Or cut off the top of an empty fabric-softener bottle and turn it into a planter. Go for an assortment of shapes, sizes, and heights.

To really carry the theme to the limit, use plants that are reminiscent of cleaning: soapwort and mint, for example. Just make sure to clean the detergent containers thoroughly before planting.

Stack 'Em High

▶ Make the most of limited garden space by creating a vertical garden with old Styrofoam coolers, wooden boxes, or kitchen drawers left over from a kitchen remodeling project.

Simply stack them four or five tall to make a strawberry tower or vertical garden. Make a hole in the center bottom of each item that is large enough to accommodate a piece of old hose or pipe. Cut the hose a few inches longer than the height of the tower. Punch or drill holes along the hose for watering the center. If you're using wooden drawers, line them with plastic so they will last longer.

Give new life to old Styrofoam coolers by turning them into a vertical garden.

Stack the containers, setting them one on top of another at an angle. Insert the hose, then fill the containers with 6 to 12 inches of potting soil. (If the containers are deep, fill the bottoms with foam packing peanuts so you don't have to use a lot of potting soil.) Plant in the corners of the lower containers and all of the top one.

A Freebie Strawberry Jar

▶ Turn a no-longer-used but attractive plastic wastebasket into a strawberry-jar-inspired planter. Using a paring knife heated over a flame, cut holes about 3 inches across into the wastebasket sides, spacing them at least 4 inches apart to allow for plenty of root growth. Also cut a small drainage hole in the bottom. Fill the basket with potting mix and add your strawberry plants.

Water the Watering Can

▶ A leaky metal watering can makes a fun container for planting. Just fill with soil and plant!

You can also use a cracked plastic watering can. If necessary, drill or punch a few drainage holes in the bottom and get planting.

A Birdbath Reborn

▶ The next time your birdbath goes to pot with a leaky basin or broken pedestal, turn the basin into a nifty planter. If it's concrete and cracked, there's no need to do anything. Just plant (alpines and sedums especially love this environment). Metal or other watertight basins will need a few drainage holes drilled in the bottom.

And that pedestal? If it's still intact and suitably designed, put it on your porch or tuck it into a flowerbed and put a flowerpot on top.

Lovely Lamp Shades

▶ Before you discard that broken lamp or light fixture, take a good look at the shade and see if it might make a nice planter. Just turn it upside down and line it with a black plastic garbage bag cut to fit. Staple the plastic in place along the sides, and make a few slits in the bottom for drainage.

Metal hanging lamp shades work best. They have a clean, dishlike design and need only a peat hanging basket liner or a little landscape fabric (or even regular fabric) draped inside to hold the soil.

Toys on Parade

▶ After the kids have left home and you have all their wonderful toys stashed in the attic or elsewhere, collect them and turn them into a little botanical remembrance of some of your favorite people.

Start with the toy box, which will make a terrific planter. Fill it to the brim with soil and plants. Then position an old dump truck, a small wagon, or a miniature baby buggy at its base to use as a smaller container garden. Use an old baseball bat as a plant support inside the box, making sure you plant it deep enough to keep it steadily upright.

Use plastic dolls, building blocks, trains, and other assorted toys as accents in and around this child-inspired garden.

Tower of Flower

▶ Those oversize cardboard tubes, such as the kind carpets come shipped in or wrapped around, make attractive vertical container gardens. Cut holes in the tube with a sharp knife, then sink the bottom foot or so into the ground, deep enough to keep it stable and to create the height you want.

Plant as you would a strawberry pot. Good candidates include ivies, trailing geraniums and lantanas, moss roses, and other drought-tolerant trailing plants.

4 Uplifting Ideas

Clever retailers sell decorative "pot feet" to keep pots up off decks and patios, where they can stain or rot the building material. You can have all the benefits of these little feet without the expense by scouring your house for appropriate, noncorroding materials.

1 Chipped or otherwise unusable saucers

2 Old custard cups

3 Plastic jar or jug lids, such as those for peanut butter jars or liquid laundry detergent bottles

4 Leftover ceramic tiles, stacked a few tiles high

A Hot Look

▶ Don't need that brass firewood holder anymore? Turn it into a planter. If it can contain soil easily, just punch some drainage holes in it, and you're ready to go. Otherwise, place some soil in the bottom of a black plastic garbage bag, tie the bag shut, and set it on the holder. Punch holes in the bag, then plant your seeds or insert your plants in the holes.

If you have a poker, anchor it in the planting bag and wire it to the holder's handle as a trellis for small vines and ivies.

HANGING CONTAINER IDEAS

Bagged Plants

▶ Have an assortment of fabric bags you don't know what to do with? Turn them into planters! Simply fill each halfway with empty plastic soda bottles or foam packing peanuts and top with potting soil. Then add your plants. Hang the bag from the rafters (two hangers work better than one) or on a wall or fence.

You can loop one handle over a fence post and let the other one hang loose, or loop both handles over for a tidier look. Or attach cup hooks to a fence or wall and hang several bags from the hooks. Line them up vertically for a stunning effect.

Hanging Surprise

▶ Hubcaps make the ultimate hanging planters. Drill some drainage holes in the center of a hubcap (the "cap" part) and fill it with soil and plants. String three or four lengths of lightweight chain or wire coat hangers through the "spokes," and hang the planter.

Wired Up

▶ Before you give away or sell a mirror or framed item, remove the picture wire from the back. When hanging a plastic basket, replace the plastic hanger with the wire. It's much less obtrusive than the plastic.

Excellent Drainage, for Sure

▶ You can turn an old colander into a hanging basket. Line it with landscape fabric, panty hose, or a thin layer of sphagnum peat moss before putting in your soil and plants. Hang it up using raffia, scrap galvanized wire, or old baling twine.

Bowl Me Over

▶ A bowl, especially a pretty ceramic one, can make a beautiful hanging planter. Use a diamond drill bit (designed for drilling holes in ceramic tile) to drill a drainage hole or two in the bottom. Then carefully drill three holes along the rim, and thread strong twine or wire through the holes, twisting it together at the top and making a loop for hanging on a hook. Or opt for a "cradle" of twine or wire (rather than drilling holes) to suspend the bowl.

Swing 'Em High

▶ An old swing set can be the basis of a delightful hanging garden. Keep the original paint job, or give the set a coat of spray paint. Then deck it out with a variety of hanging baskets. Hang them not just from the horizontal poles and ladder rungs but also from the swing chains (use S hooks, if needed). Bolt a pot to each seat of the glider (drill a hole in the seat and run a long bolt with washers through the pot's drainage hole). Set a pot with long trailing blooms (a 'Wave' petunia is ideal) atop the slide.

SOIL SOLUTIONS

Sunny Side Under

▶ Crushed eggshells are high in calcium and great for most container plants. They not only provide nutrients but also prevent soil from washing out of the drainage holes. Save eggshells in a container in the freezer. Before planting a new container, crush a handful of shells and place them in the bottom of the pot.

Simply Crushed

▶ Even if you're a careful recycler, sometimes recycling centers won't take crushed aluminum cans. Use them in the bottom of large pots and planters to save on potting soil and improve drainage.

Yes, We Have No Bananas

▶ There seems to be a never-ending supply of brown-spotted bananas in most households, so try this tip the next time you're planting just about anything in a container. Plunk an overripe banana into the bottom of the pot (you may need to cut it up into a few chunks). It will break down quickly, providing valuable organic matter for the plant.

Pack It Up

▶ These days, it seems that every item you buy is packed in those annoyingly planet-unfriendly Styrofoam forms. Get at least one more use out of them by putting them in the bottom of plant containers to improve drainage and keep soil from washing out.

Trashy Reading

▌ Persuade yourself to give up those tattered paperbacks or old magazines you've been hoarding by putting them to use in the bottom of planters and pots. These items are biodegradable and will eventually break down, but for at least a couple of years, they'll prevent soil from washing out. Also, in large planters and pots, they take up space so that you don't have to use quite so much precious potting soil to fill the pot.

Slug Plug

▌ Want to prevent insects from creeping into your container plantings and soil from washing out? Just cover the drainage hole with a piece of panty hose. Tuck it into the hole for a firm fit. It will prevent slugs, centipedes, sow bugs, and other dark- and moisture-loving insects from moving in.

Give paperbacks a second life by using them to line a planter. They reduce the need for potting soil and will eventually add nutrients to the soil.

Liner Notes

▌ Save leftover plastic tubs and containers from cottage cheese, margarine, and other products to use inside baskets or other delicate containers, or even metal containers that might discolor. Simply place a tub in the container, fill the tub with potting soil, and plant. If the tub is visible, tuck in some dried floral Spanish moss or green floral moss around it.

Fabulous Filters

▌ Furnaces, dehumidifiers, and window air conditioners often have flexible mesh, foamlike filters that need to be replaced periodically. Save the old filters and use them to line plant pots or baskets to prevent the soil from washing out.

Peanuts to You

▶ Foam packing peanuts have become a popular item for lining pots and planters, replacing the traditional gravel and clay shards. The problem is that when you remove the soil from the pot, those pesky peanuts go flying everywhere. Solve this problem by pouring them into a net produce bag—the kind potatoes and onions are sold in—and close the bag with a twist tie before placing it in the pot.

Alternatively, tuck the peanuts into a pair of panty hose or an old pillowcase and tie it shut.

Fridge Salvage

▶Before the movers come to collect that old fridge, salvage any parts you can for your garden. Drawers and ice cube trays make great containers or flats for seed starting once you drill or punch some holes in the bottom. Plastic or metal shelves are good for holding smaller containers when starting seeds. Cut off the electrical cord and plug, and use the cord to tie plants. Even the copper tubing used to run water to the icemaker can be twisted into an abstract trellis for a container.

Pot Magic

▶Do your potted plants suffer from slowly disappearing soil? If so, save old fiberglass window screens to cut into squares and place over the drainage holes in your pots. The soil will stay in place, and your patio will stay clean.

Window Box Wonder

The secret to keeping window boxes colorful all year round is to continually "change out" the flowers so that when they start getting ratty-looking, you can replace them with something new.

It's a pain to keep pulling out and replanting, so try this trick. Recycle 1-gallon nursery pots by planting them in your window boxes, sinking them so that their rims are level with the soil.

Plant ivies or any other continually fresh and green-looking plants around them. Slip pots of pansies into the nursery pots in the spring, annuals such as marigolds or salvias in the summer, and mums in the fall. You can even insert holly or evergreen branches for the winter.

If the pots sink too low, toss in a few handfuls of foam packing peanuts or some wadded-up newspaper to keep them level with the box.

WATERING WONDERS

Suck It Up!

❱ If your turkey baster is gathering dust in a kitchen drawer, store it with your garden supplies instead. It's the perfect tool to use on the deck, porch, or indoors when watering plants. If the saucer underneath a plant is in danger of over-flowing, pull out the baster and suck up the excess water. This is especially helpful with large containers, where it would be difficult to lift the pot and dump the water.

Hose for the Hoses

❱ Don't you hate it when you turn the spigot too far and water comes blasting out, spraying soil and mud every-where? If that happens with your hose or if you have trou-ble regulating the pressure on your spigot, try this. Use old panty hose to diffuse the spray and deliver water where you want it without disturbing loose soil.

Cut off the bottom 4 inches or so of one leg of the panty hose. Attach it to the end of your garden hose with a strong rubber band. (The kind that comes around broccoli and other produce is ideal.) Leave ½ inch or so of the panty hose at the end for "give."

The foot from a pair of panty hose, fastened to the end of your garden hose, is a terrific water tamer, diffusing the flow so it doesn't blast soil out of your containers.

When watering, be sure to hold on to the panty hose so the "filter" doesn't slip off. The water will flow more gently and cause less distur-bance to your container plants.

Watering Jug

❱ Keep an assortment of plastic milk or other jugs filled with water near thirsty plants that always seem to need watering but are a pain to reach with a hose. Keeping the jugs handy not only reminds you to give them a drink, but it also makes watering a breeze.

A Better Bucket

You can turn a 5-gallon bucket, or any large, strong plastic or metal container that you might otherwise throw away, into a handy pot with its own self-watering system.

Start by drilling a line of holes 1 to 1½ inches apart and 5 to 6 inches from the bottom of the bucket.

Measure off about 6 yards of strong nylon twine and cut it. Wrap the ends with masking tape to make threading the twine through the holes easier. Tie one end to the bucket through two of the holes. Weave the twine back and forth across the bucket to make a sort of hammock.

Next cut a piece of old garden hose or rigid pipe 2 inches longer than the bucket's height. Cut the bottom at a slant so that even when it's resting on the bottom of the bucket, it won't block the water flow. Insert the hose or pipe into the bucket, positioning it so that the twine holds it in place.

Lay landscape fabric or old panty hose on top of the twine and extending up the sides of the bucket. Poke a small hole in the center of the fabric, and insert a piece of nylon twine several inches long through the hole. The twine needs to be long enough to touch the bottom of the bucket but also to extend 3 to 4 inches above the fabric. Knot the twine just above the hole to hold it in place.

Fill the bucket with soil and plant. Use the hose or pipe to fill the reservoir below the "hammock" with water. This container will be able to last without additional water for weeks.

If you don't need the reminder but do need the easy access to water, tuck the jugs behind a nearby shrub or other screen.

What a Sponge

▶ Don't throw out those old bath and scrubber sponges. Instead, use them to conserve water in container plantings. When planting, tuck a wet sponge directly below the plant's roots. Later, when you water, it will hold the moisture rather than letting it run out the bottom.

A Wet Suit for Pots

▶ Before you go away on vacation, make a wet suit for your clay pots to keep the soil cool and moist while you're gone. Just cut old T-shirts, towels, or all-cotton sweats into strips. Soak the strips in water, and then wrap them around the pots. They should cling of their own accord, but, if not, secure them with rubber bands or twine. Then wrap the pots with plastic bubble wrap, securing it in place with duct tape.

Even better, you can reuse these wet suits every time you go on vacation.

Temporary Mulch

▶ If you are leaving for a weekend trip and are concerned about your container plants drying out, try this unconventional trick. Give them a thorough soaking as usual, then soak sections of an old T-shirt or a few rags in water. Wad up the dripping fabric and place it on the soil. When you get

Self-Watering Wonder

Create a self-watering system for smaller pots using a strip of panty hose and a well-washed margarine tub large enough to set the pot on. It's ideal for any small container that tends to dry out quickly or for a plant-watering solution when you're going to be away from home. It's also great for plants that prefer to be watered from the bottom, such as African violets or other plants with slightly fuzzy leaves.

To make the system, first cut a wick hole in the center of the tub's lid. Then cut a second hole along the edge of the lid for filling the tub with water as needed.

Thread a strip of old panty hose through the center hole, making sure it's long enough to rest on the bottom of the tub but also can be inserted an inch or so up through the pot's drainage hole. Insert the panty hose into the drainage hole, using a chopstick or other tool as necessary. Put the lid back on the tub and fill it with water.

back, the fabric should be reasonably dry. Shake the rags out and give 'em a good washing for use another day.

Wagon Waterer

❥ Rushing to get out the door on vacation? Grab your child's or grandchild's little red wagon to help water your plants. Toss an old vinyl tablecloth or large plastic garbage bag into the wagon. Add a few inches of water and set your plant containers and hanging baskets in the shallow water to keep them well-watered for several days.

A Nice Soak

❥ Finding just the right place to soak smaller indoor plants, such as cyclamens, African violets, and orchids, which need to be thoroughly watered, can be a challenge. One solution is to use a plastic salad spinner. Fill a spinner with water (mesh colander and all), then add a pot or two—or even three, depending on the size of the pots and the spinner. Let the pots soak, then lift out the mesh colander to remove the plants without damaging the leaves or stems.

Use your salad spinner to give potted plants a thorough watering.

CLEAN AND CARE

Pot Spa Treatment

▶ If you like pots that look like new, give them a bit of pampering. First, soak them for a few minutes in a good old-fashioned bubble bath, created by adding a little dish-washing liquid to very hot water. Use a scrub brush to remove stubborn dirt.

If the pot has whitish mineral deposits on it, put it in a bath of 2 gallons water and 1 cup white vinegar. Let the pot soak for at least an hour (or up to a day), then take a scrubber sponge to it. Finally, soak the pot for at least 10 minutes in a mixture of 2 tablespoons bleach per 1 gallon of water. This will kill any harmful bacteria that might attack new plantings.

A Waxy Solution

▶ Have problems with plant stems rotting where they touch the rim of a clay pot or planter? Try this trick that African-violet growers swear by. Coat the rim with melted paraffin.

For small pots, the easiest way to do this is to heat an oven to 200°F. Put a few handfuls of chopped paraffin in an aluminum pie pan and place in the oven for about 5 minutes, or until melted. (*Note:* Watch carefully, and remove the pan as soon as the wax is melted. If it's overheated, it can catch fire.) Invert a clean clay pot over the tray, and dip the rim into the wax to coat evenly. The wax will harden almost immediately.

For larger pots, melt the paraffin in a small saucepan, then dribble or brush it on the rim. An old paintbrush works well here.

Quick Cover

▶ In Zone 7 and colder, clay and sometimes even concrete pots must be taken indoors for the winter so they won't crack. However, if a pot is just too heavy to move, try this. Slip a black plastic garbage bag over the pot. It will keep out rain and snow and increase the pot's chances of surviving the winter.

If you can, remove all or even part of the soil in the pot. The soil will contribute to cracking as it freezes and expands.

In the Doghouse

▶ The best place to store clay pots for the winter is indoors, but if your basement and garage are overflowing (and

 Ways to Water Strawberry Jars

A long-popular—and effective—method of keeping even the centers of strawberry jars watered is to insert a length of PVC (polyvinyl chloride) pipe, drilled all over with holes, into the center at planting time. Just pour the water into the pipe, and it will be more evenly distributed throughout the pot.

But every idea can be improved on. Here's how.

1 Fill the pipe with gravel, foam packing peanuts, or crushed seashells. This will keep out debris so that the water can flow through freely.

2 Instead of the PVC pipe, use a length of copper pipe left over from a remodeling or plumbing project. It should be long enough to reach the bottom of the jar and also to extend a few inches above the soil surface. Punch holes all

over the pipe. Extending the pipe above the soil not only prevents debris from washing into it but also provides a decorative opportunity. You can top it with an old lamp or curtain rod finial, an outrageously large piece of costume jewelry, or a pretty stone.

3 Knot a pair of panty hose along the entire length to make one thick "rope." Plant it vertically in the center of the pot, allowing at least an inch to protrude above the soil. This material will wick moisture down through the pot.

4 Cut a hollow plastic or wooden curtain rod long enough to reach the bottom of the pot and extend a few inches above the soil surface. Drill or punch holes along the length of the rod. Top with the original finial for a decorative touch.

whose isn't?), you might want to look to that empty dog-house you never managed to get rid of. It will protect the pots from the elements, and a larger house can handle even the biggest pots.

USEFUL ACCESSORIES

A Clear Solution

▌ Those clear plastic lids from shortening, oatmeal, and other food containers are ideal and unobtrusive saucers for pots. Keep them on hand in a variety of sizes and depths so that you will always have just the right saucer for any container, inside or out.

Booster Seat

▌ An empty margarine, yogurt, or cream cheese container can be used as a "booster seat" for container plants. Use one, turned upside down, to elevate an already potted plant that would otherwise sit too low in its outside container or cachepot.

Books and Blooms

▌ Don't pitch that old bookcase. Instead, move it outside onto a porch or patio, or even up against a fence or the wall of a building. It makes a great staging area for all your potted plants, especially those that spill or drape. (If the shelves are bowing a bit, trying turning it upside down to compensate for and correct the bow.)

Warm and Toasty

▌ To capture the warmth of the day when evening temperatures dip below 50°F, encircle a container plant and its pot in a bubble wrap cocoon. The pockets of air capture the warmth of the soil and the pot, provide insulation, and can even stave off a light frost. Be sure to wrap the container loosely enough that you don't crush the leaves and stems. Use a couple of pieces of tape to keep the cocoon closed.

Freewheeling

Use an old children's wagon, wheelbarrow, or cart of any size to hold or move plants, indoors or out. For a wagon too decrepit to move, paint the outside a bright color to match your garden decor and plant directly in the wagon to create a garden focal point. Use a very light potting mix, and this wagon planter will last for several seasons.

Plant It High

▶An old high chair makes a cute plant stand for a large fern or any large pot. Just set the container on the seat. If you want, put smaller plants on the tray (or remove the tray altogether). Use the high chair as is, or spray-paint it a color that will complement your favorite flowerbed or your porch or patio.

Get a Move On

▶That abandoned baby walker can be a handy pot mover. It's highly stable and has wheels that are just perfect for the job. Simply heave a larger pot into it, and wheel it to its new spot.

Handy Helmet

▶ Immortalize your favorite football player by digging his old helmet out of the attic and planting a trailing vine in it. You can even hang it by the mouth guard. If you want to plant directly in the helmet, line it with part of a black plastic garbage bag before adding potting mix. You can also set a pot directly in the helmet.

Building Blocks

▶ Cement blocks make sturdy planters. Fill the slots with soil, and they're ready to grow. Pile the blocks as high as you need for cascading plants. Get innovative and create a planting pyramid, a block wall (turning alternate blocks so the slots face outward), or a living cube.

Mini–Compost Bin

▶ An important part of keeping a collection of container plantings looking nice is deadheading, which keeps those pretty plants blooming. But if you're like a lot of gardeners, a handful of spent blooms is hardly worth carrying over to the compost. An easy solution is to keep an empty popcorn or other tin tucked in with the pots. Just treat it like a mini–compost bin, and toss the blooms in there. When it's full, you can make that trip way over to the compost heap.

Bloomin' Luminarias

▌ Everybody loves luminarias, those neat Mexican-style lanterns made from tin cans. You can create luminaria-inspired containers in your garden. They're free, they allow you to recycle cans you'd otherwise throw away, and they look pretty atop a deck railing or clustered on a step.

Using a nail, punch holes in the bottoms of a variety of tin cans. Fill the cans with potting soil, and plant as you would any other container.

PLANT-PERFECT CONTAINERS

Planted to a Tea

▌ An old teakettle that has done its service on the stovetop is ideal for moving outdoors as a container. Punch a few holes in the bottom, and plant it with mint, which grows rapidly and, come to think of it, makes an excellent tea. Set the kettle in a sunny spot, or sink it an inch or two into the ground in your herb garden. Mint is so invasive that it needs to be contained, and this clever container is just the way to do it.

Care for a Sedum?

▌ To recycle an old metal or wooden serving tray with sides an inch or more high, drill drainage holes in the bottom, line with old fiberglass window screening or a layer or two of newspaper, and fill with potting soil. Plant succulents such as sedums or other highly drought-tolerant, shallow-rooted plants in the tray. It's perfect for the top of a picnic table or other outdoor table in full sun.

Into the Frying Pan

▌ Searching for a way to hang your staghorn fern? Mount it in an old frying pan or any other long-handled pan. The fronds will soon cover the pan, and the handle makes hanging a breeze.

Got Milk Crates?

▶ When your plastic milk crates and laundry baskets have outlived their usefulness, recycle them as planters. Break off a corner section of each by hitting it with a hammer or cutting it with a knife heated over a flame. Then nail it to a wall, line it with sphagnum peat moss, and plant it with a staghorn fern.

Blooming Baskets

▶ Vanda orchids and other aerial plants, such as some bromeliads, thrive when grown in produce baskets with loosely woven bottoms. The holes allow optimum air circulation for the "roots."

PROBLEM-SOLVING DECORATIVE TOUCHES

Pretty Up a Container

▶ Instead of tossing that old oilcloth or vinyl tablecloth, use it to cover cheap plastic pots, especially those that are a mishmash of styles and colors, and coordinate them nicely.

Set a pot in the middle of the cloth, and draw a circle large enough that when the ends are brought up, they reach slightly above the rim of the pot, not unlike the foil covers that florists use with potted plants. Cut out the circle, and bring up the material around the pot. Use a rubber band to hold the cloth in place, then cover the rubber band with a scrap of ribbon or a strip cut from the tablecloth.

Petals with Metal

▶ Group metal garbage cans together on a patio or deck for a funky, industrial look. Large garbage cans can hold small trees, smaller cans (including the metal liners from trash cans with pop-up lids) can hold shrubs, and even smaller metal wastebaskets can hold flowers.

5 Salvaged Plant Shelves

You've seen elaborate shelving systems for potted plants in garden shops and catalogs. However, there's no need to invest a small fortune to display container plants. You can create a highly functional and attractive shelving system with materials from around your house and garage.

Depending on how much you have of a various material, you can build these shelving systems customized to your space in a variety of heights and configurations—and do so in minutes. Some ideas to get you started:

1 Weathered brick supports combined with weathered boards

2 Cinder block supports combined with scraps of corrugated metal, rusty or in pristine condition

3 Galvanized metal pails for supports combined with scrap lumber painted white

4 Milk crate supports combined with scrap lumber painted different, bright colors

5 Brick supports combined with slabs of limestone or slate left over from a landscaping project

Rusty or dented metal cans also can be put to work. All it takes to hide their flaws is a can of spray paint. Use black or silver paint to keep your trash can garden contemporary and hip, or spray each can a bright primary color for a funky look.

Old tools and scrap metal parts add to the look. Use long-handled tools or copper piping to form a tepee for growing a vine in a can.

Splatterware

❱ Turn clean, metal, 1-gallon paint buckets into a cute hanging garden. Use the dripped paint that inevitably collects on these for inspiration by spattering paint all over them. Use just one color, or do color themes: Cream, dark green, light green, and brown have a natural-looking, almost camouflage effect that works well outdoors. Primary colors create a playful mood.

Poke several drainage holes in the bottoms of the buckets, and hang them from an old stepladder or extension ladder, either propped up against the house or hung horizontally from the rafters of a porch. Screw the ladder into the rafters, or hang it with hooks and chains. You can even add four tall vertical supports and place the ladder on top to create a small pergola, perfect for supporting vines.

RESOURCEFUL MULCHES

Pop a Cork!

▌ Recycle corks from your favorite bottles of wine by using them as mulch for potted plants. Corks allow water to pass through but provide insulation from heat and cold. You don't even have to chop the corks into smaller pieces. Merely layer whole corks around plants for a rich and interesting texture.

You Want Ketchup with That?

▌ Those 2-inch plastic containers with snap-on lids that restaurants use for salad dressing, dipping sauces, ketchup, and other take-out condiments are just right for growing miniature plants. Just punch a drainage hole in the cup and use the lid as a miniature saucer. They're especially nice grouped together on a tray.

Pop Your Top

▌ Those pop-off metal bottle tops from beer and soda bottles might seem useless, but they can actually make a cool mulch for your container gardens. Collect a few handfuls, the more colors and designs the better. Press them gently into the soil surface at planting time. The glint of metal provides a nice contrast to the plant material spilling out from the pots.

Dish It Up

▌ The remnants of your grand-mother's china, or just about any assortment of broken dishes, can be the basis of an adorable "mulch" that suppresses weeds and conserves moisture while it adds charm to any container garden. After planting the container, arrange bits of chipped and broken china on top of the soil. If you have room, tip a teacup on its side, pack it half full of soil, and plant it with baby's tears or another plant that will spill out of the cup. Tuck in a portion of a plate for a vertical accent.

Remnants of Grandma's china make a terrific mulch and decoration for larger container gardens.

Marble Mania

▌ Has little Johnny moved away from home but left his marble collection behind? Put those marbles to good—and attractive—use as mulch in plant containers. Arrange them at least one marble thick over the soil. They'll be prettier and more effective, though, if you add a couple of layers so that the top ones can catch the light.

A Fishy Idea

▌ That old or unused aquarium gravel makes a fine mulch for containers. Coordinate the colors of the gravel with the blooms of the plant.

And if you also have a spare aquarium decoration or two, tuck it into the container, too. Ivy never looked so good as it does spilling out from around a tiny pirate ship!

CHAPTER FIVE

Getting Organized

Ever feel that walking into your garage is like taking your life in your hands because of all the yard and garden stuff threatening to topple? Or that you can never find what you need? We've got dozens of ideas for organizing your favorite hobby and reusing things you have lying around the house in the bargain.

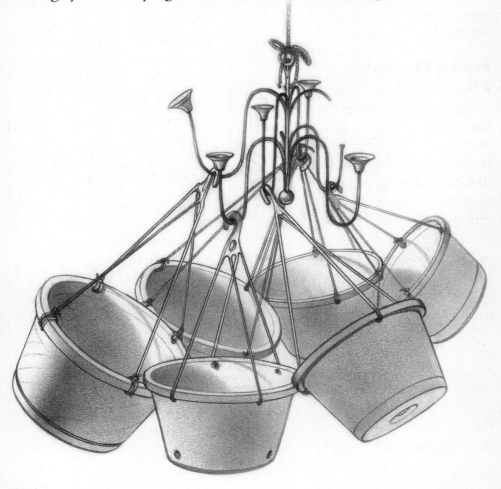

TOOL AND SUPPLY STORAGE

The Sole of Organization

❱ That old-fashioned shoe bag might not be the best for holding shoes (they never seem to fit in securely), but it's great for holding garden supplies. Nail it to the wall in your garage, shed, or back entry to hold small tools, garden shoes, labels, pens, and more.

Just Hanging Around

❱ An old chandelier that's on the fritz makes a superb hanger for empty plastic hanging baskets. Just suspend the chandelier from your garage or shed ceiling, and hang up to a dozen baskets on it.

Feeling Flattened

❱ Waxed-cardboard milk cartons are useful for starting seeds and slipping over small plants for frost and pest protection. But if you have a collection of cartons, they can take up a lot of room. Solve the problem by taking a serrated knife and cutting off the top of each carton. Then cut the bottom panel along three sides, leaving one side connected. The entire container will now fold flat for storage. If you want to fill it with soil, just tape the bottom shut with duct tape.

It's in the Can

❱ An old coffee can or small oatmeal canister with a plastic lid makes a terrific twine dispenser. Cut a hole in the lid just barely large enough for the twine to feed through but not fall

3 Things to Do with a Fast-Food Bag in the Garden

The next time you resort to drive-thru, save the paper bag the food comes in. These bags are wonderfully handy to have in the garden.

1 Keep one in your garden caddy or on your potting table to hold the bits of trash you inevitably collect around the garden.

2 Keep one on the kitchen counter to simplify composting. Collect potato peelings, onion skins, and more. Then take the whole thing out to the compost heap and pitch it.

3 As long as a bag is clean, store tender bulbs such as cannas and glads in it. Add some sawdust or vermiculite, staple it shut, and label.

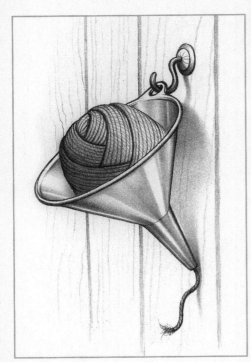

An old funnel makes an excellent string dispenser, preventing tangles.

back into the can. Pop the ball or spool into the can, attach the lid, and store it on a shelf. When needed, just pull out the desired length of twine and snip.

Funnel Effect

▶ An old funnel, either plastic or metal, also makes a super string dispenser. Hang it from a cup hook on the wall or just nail in place. Set the ball of string in the funnel. Thread the string through the opening, and you're good to go.

Cord Corral

▶ Electric power tools are wonderful, but dealing with all those cords can feel like fighting an army of octopuses. Use a long, narrow, cylindrical cardboard tube—the kind some potato chips and powdered drink mixes are sold in—to create a nifty cord holder.

Cut off the bottom and remove the plastic snap-on lid. Then wrap the cord of your tool into a roughly 2-foot-long loop, and slide the cardboard tube over the cord. Now when you store or carry your power tools, you won't have that long cord to worry about. Plus, the cardboard tube is much quicker to remove and replace than a traditional plastic cord tie.

Get Tubby

▶ If you no longer have a use for that big, round plastic or metal tub—the kind shaped like a bushel basket—convert it to a hose caddy. If it's not already leaking, punch several large holes or make a number of large slashes in the bottom. Bury it up to its rim in the ground where you want to store the hose, being sure to add a couple of inches of gravel or sand underneath the tub to facilitate drainage.

Because it's below ground, the tub is held steady as you coil the hose in it. Also, since it's nice and low, the coiling process is easier.

Meds and More

▶ The next time you redo the bathroom, save that old metal medicine cabinet. It's a great storage space for garden supplies. Mount it on a wall or fence, especially at the end of a path, where the mirror can cast a long reflection and add the illusion of space or an interesting opening in the fence.

Terrific Totes

▶ Those canvas tote bags that companies give away as promotions come in handy inside your garage or toolshed. Just nail them to the wall for storing various items.

Turn giveaway canvas totes into useful wall storage for garden tools and supplies.

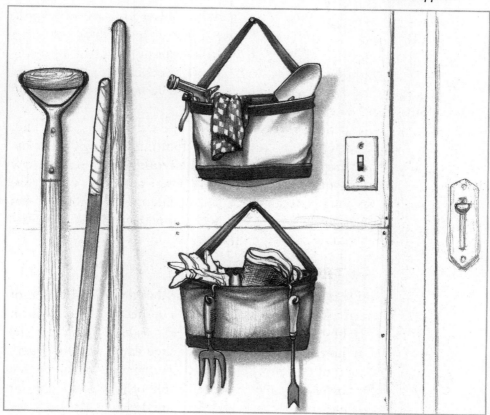

A Place for Everything

Turn a 5-gallon bucket into a portable garden center in just minutes. Start by tying an old leather or canvas carpenter's apron around the bucket. It's great for holding smaller items. If needed, secure the apron in place by punching holes around the rim of the bucket and using a length of wire to thread through the apron to secure it in place.

Leave the bucket empty for more tool storage or to collect weeds until you get them to the compost heap. Finish off this garden helper with a padded seat so you have a comfortable, portable perch to use while working or resting in the garden. Cut a circle the size of the lid from an old foam pillow. Then cut a piece of wood about 4 inches wider than the lid. Cut a piece of an old oil-cloth or plastic tablecloth 4 inches wider than the wood. Stretch the material over the foam and wood, then staple it to the wood. Drill a hole through the center of the foam, wood, and plastic lid. Align the holes and attach the seat to the lid using a locking nut, washer, and bolt (nut on the wood side). Don't make it too tight—a dimple in the center is ideal.

For each bag, hammer a nail into the wall and hang one handle on the nail. Drive five or more nails through the top of the wall side of the bag and into the wall. Leave the other handle hanging and the bag open. Add an S hook or two for hanging small hand tools and other assorted supplies. If you have more than one tote bag, position them one above the other to create a column of storage on the wall.

Alternatively, hang a bag near your favorite spigot to hold watering accessories, such as spray nozzles.

What's Cooking?

▶ If you have one too many kitchen aprons, or you simply don't use one anymore, put it to use in the garden. It's great for those times when you don't have your gardening clothes on but want to move a heavy container or pot up a few plants. The pockets in the front can hold seed packets, small tools, a cordless phone, tissues, and other small items.

No Need for Matching Shoes

▌ Stash all your essential small gardening needs—trowel, pruners, sunblock, whatever—in an old handbag. Hang it by the back door so you're always ready to garden at a moment's notice.

Wall o' Tools

▌ Recycle plastic-coated wire shelving that you've torn out of your home by installing it in a garden shed. You can

 More Uses for Milk Crates

Ever since college students started using them in their dorm rooms in the 1970s, milk crates have found hundreds of uses. Here are just four that are helpful in the garden.

1 Stack crates inside your garage or toolshed, with the bottoms to the wall and the openings facing out. Use these cubbies to hold garden supplies. You also could stack them outdoors in a protected area. Just drape canvas or oilcloth over the stack to guard against the weather.

2 Nail crates to a wall or fence, with the bottoms of the crates against the vertical surface. Stack small clay pots, hose attachments, small watering cans, and other gardening supplies inside the crates. Arrange three to five crates along a fence or wall at different heights to create an interesting design.

3 Use crates to store bags of potting soil or soil amendments. The crates will protect the bags from ripping and keep them upright for easy access.

4 Stack crates, open ends out, then stack wood in them, ends facing out. The logs won't roll and topple when you remove a few for a fire. Plus, the crates make convenient log carriers. Just grab a crateful and bring it inside.

always install it the way it was previously, but if you don't need any more horizontal shelves, try turning the shelves so they are positioned vertically, up against the wall, not unlike a ladder.

Equipped with plenty of inexpensive S hooks, the shelves will come in handy for storing hand tools and plastic grocery bags filled with bulbs, seeds, and more—all the items that often get lost in a jumble on a traditional shelf.

Showy Storage

▶ Those seed packets that come in the mail in the spring are so pretty, why hide them? Keep them on hand for planting by tucking them into canning jars and lining your kitchen windows with them. Sort by type (veggies, flowers, and so forth) and by planting time (10, 8, 6, or 4 weeks before your region's last frost date).

Don't have canning jars? Choose some of your nicer regular jars and spray-paint all the lids with chrome paint for a zinc-plated look.

Waste Not Want Not

▶ Don't pitch those old wastebaskets. Take them out to the garage, where they'll have plenty of uses. Keep one near your potting bench so you'll always have a place to toss old labels, small pots, and other detritus. Wastebaskets also work nicely as caddies to hold bags of potting soil and other soil amendments. (Storing these bags in wastebaskets protects them and keeps them upright.).

Good Hang Ups to Have

▶ An old free standing coat rack, having outlived its usefulness in your front hall, makes a handy place to store tools in the garage or tool shed. The hooks that once held coats and scarves are an ideal place to hang hand tools and jackets or sweatshirts you reserve just for the dirty business of gardening.

If the coat rack has a spot that once held umbrellas, use it to stow long-handled garden tools or to hold bags of potting mix.

A Better Box

❱ Fertilizers, bulk seed, birdseed, and other garden supplies are often sold in bags that don't hold up very well, especially if they get wet or the weather is humid. With the help of a funnel, transfer these materials to clean, dry laundry detergent jugs, bleach bottles, or milk jugs. Label each clearly, or cut out the original label and instructions and attach it to the jug with lots of clear mailing tape.

The Gift Bag That Keeps on Giving

❱ Those cute little gift bags that once held presents are good to have in the garden. Choose bags that are a bit too battered for recycling for further gift-giving but are still sturdy.

Use larger gift bags for reinforcement and support for bags of potting soil or soil amendments. Use the smaller bags to corral seed packets, plant labels, gloves, or other garden supplies. You can keep the bags standing upright on your potting table, or hang them on the wall for space-saving storage.

Slurpy Storage

❱ Those oversized, durable plastic cups seem to come from everywhere—fast-food places, sporting events, convenience stores, and more.

Rather than pitch them, use them to store garden supplies. Simply nail them onto the garage or toolshed wall with a couple of nails. They're perfect for holding lighter-weight hand tools, seed packets, gloves, and just about anything else.

2 Uses for a Plastic Bucket

Don't kick the bucket. Find a new use for it instead. Here are yet more ways to use a plastic bucket with a handle.

1 Bury it up to its rim in the soil behind or among shrubs for a nearly invisible composting stash. Drill some holes in the bottom for drainage and be sure to position it so that no one might step into it and get injured. Collect small weeds, deadheaded blooms, and more in the bucket. When the bucket is full, dump it in the main compost bin.

2 Hang the bucket from a tree branch for easy access and quick storage of garden tools and gloves. High up, the contents will be protected from your sprinkler system. Plus, the bucket will be out of the reach of small children.

If the cup has a snap-on lid, use it outdoors. Nail it onto the siding of a building, wooden fence, or fencepost for watertight storage. This is a great way to store, say, vegetable seeds near your vegetable garden.

Tab It

▶ Those square plastic tabs that hold bread bags shut come in handy as garden book and magazine markers. Just slip one onto any page that you want to mark.

You can make the tabs more permanent by taping the tabs just on the edge of the page. If desired, mark the topic with a permanent marker.

Forget the Sweaters

▶ Those flat plastic sweater boxes are supreme plant carriers and soakers. They are perfect for holding freshly divided perennials until you can plant them. They're also great for holding that assortment of potted plants awaiting—and awaiting—planting. And best of all, since they collect

Plastic sweater boxes are just right for holding, toting, and watering plants.

rainwater (or hold water you've added), they're ideal for bottom-watering large numbers of plants.

After Fido Has His Fill

❱ Heavy-paper pet food bags come in handy around the garden. They're sturdy and decompose. Use them to collect thorny rose prunings and other branches, which will compost right in the bag. Or set torn bags of potting soil or soil amendments inside larger pet food bags for reinforcement.

THE ORGANIZED POTTING TABLE

String 'Em Along

❱ Garden stuff tends to pile up, especially in the spring. Keep things organized—and charmingly so—by stringing a length of thick yarn or ribbon across a wall of your porch or shed like a clothesline. Use wooden or bright plastic clothespins to display seed packets, garden gloves, and even plant labels to help you organize for the busy spring planting season.

A Better Mousetrap

❱ Mouse problem solved? Use that old mousetrap as a surprisingly strong clip on your garage wall. Simply screw the wooden portion to the wall. The spring mechanism is strong enough to hold plant care sheets, magazine pages, potting instructions, and so on. Rat traps can hold heavier objects, such as gloves.

Pots Are Perfect

❱ Some of the best items for organizing your potting bench or garden supply shelves are there already—pots! Just wash out used clay pots and label each with a black permanent marker: seeds, old labels, plant ties, hand tools, and so on.

You can label black plastic pots with masking tape. Just tear off a length of tape, stick it on the pot, and write on it with a pen. Place the pots on a shelf in your work area, or nail one or more to the wall for hanging storage.

An old dresser, with a little retro-fitting, can be turned into a really wonderful potting table.

Dressed to Thrill

▶ Don't throw out that old dresser or nightstand. With a some paint and a few embellishments, you can turn it into a whimsical storage center cute enough to sit on your front porch or covered patio.

Remove any knobs and use an enamel spray paint to cover damaged wood and stains. Be creative! Paint each drawer a different color using leftover paint. Set a garden theme by replacing the old knobs with metal or ceramic ones that have a floral or hand tool design. With a drill and long screws, you may even be able to convert an old trowel or hand rake into a drawer pull.

Next create places for convenient tool storage. Screw in cup hooks, add nails, attach clips—anything for hanging tools, your garden calendar, or a ball of twine. A wooden or plastic clothespin nailed to the side is perfect for garden gloves.

Finish off the top, if you wish, by stapling or nailing in place a large plastic place mat or an old vinyl or oilcloth tablecloth.

Terrific Trellis

▌ That pretty bit of trellis—the part that didn't break or otherwise deteriorate—can find new life as a garden organizer, either inside or outside your garden shed. Add a few inexpensive S hooks, and hang garden gloves, hats, and tools from it. Add a few bunches of dried flowers, and you'll have storage that is as attractive as it is useful.

An Edgy Look

▌ Do you have a low wire fence or faux picket fence once used to protect garden beds? If so, hang a section of it on the wall of a porch or garden shed. Rusty, peeling, or damaged fencing adds a touch of shabby chic. Now clip or tack your seed packets, brightly colored cotton gloves, and new trowel to the fence for a wall display that also acts as storage.

More Shelves

▌ Mounting old kitchen cabinets in garages and work sheds has been a time-honored tradition. They make for top-notch storage. But if you don't want to go to the time or trouble of mounting the whole cabinet, or you don't have the right space or wall, you can still put the shelves to good use.

The next time you remodel your kitchen or bath, save any loose shelves from those kitchen cabinets. They're ideal for tool and garden supply storage. Just stack them with the help of bricks or concrete blocks.

Shut It Up

▌ Prevent potting soil from drying out, or other materials in plastic bags from spilling, by recycling household objects to keep 'em shut. Options include old clothespins, chip clips, and even large, spring-type hair clips.

Nifty Nail Polish

▌ Use nail polish for labeling everything from plant markers to storage

Rummage through your hair supplies for a spring-type hair clip to keep a plastic bag of potting soil closed.

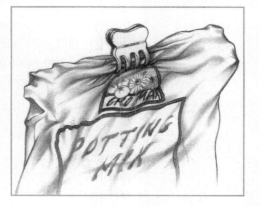

3   Fast, Free Potting Benches

You don't need to spend hundreds of dollars and lots of weekend time crafting a potting table for your garage or backyard. You probably have the makings of a very serviceable storage/potting area around the house. Try one of these ideas.

1 An old desk. Top with shelves made from stacked bricks and scrap boards.

2 Old cabinets. Are you or your neighbors remodeling the kitchen? Save a chunk of kitchen cabinet with the counter still attached, and anchor it to the garage or toolshed wall. If you have any upper cabinets left over from the project, mount one of them directly above it.

3 Stacked milk crates. Stack six crates, on their sides, into two towers of three crates each. Wire them together for sturdiness. Top with a piece of scrap lumber bridging the towers.

boxes outdoors. Unlike permanent marker, it almost never fades or wears off.

A Box Made Better

▌ Plastic shoe boxes are invaluable for storage, but there's no need to go out and buy them. Instead, turn a cardboard shoe box into a waterproof storage container for the garden. Slip the bottom of the box into a plastic bag and fold the excess bag inside the box. (Secure it with duct tape, if desired.) Do the same to the lid. These boxes can hold everything from muddy garden clogs to seed packets and weeding tools.

A Vacation from Varmints

▌ Old suitcases and footlockers make great animal-resistant storage bins inside a garden shed. Place organic fertilizers (especially bloodmeal and alfalfa meal) inside suitcases or footlockers to keep out pesky squirrels, skunks, and raccoons. Use smaller overnight bags to store birdseed so that mice, raccoons, and other marauders don't get into it.

Make Organization a Picnic

❱ Have an old wooden picnic table you no longer need, now that you've upgraded to lighter-weight, splinter-free patio furniture? If so, move it into the garage or a protected place and use it to store stuff. Place bins to store potting soil and other supplies under the table. Use the top as a potting and work surface. Cover the table with an old oilcloth or vinyl tablecloth, stapling it in place, to make it easy to wipe clean after you've finished a project.

Diapers No More

❱ Long after your kids have outgrown diapers, you can put that changing table to good use as a potting table. The bins that once held baby powder and wipes can now hold potting soil and hand tools. And the top couldn't be easier to wipe clean after potting a few flowers.

Trash to Treasure

❱ All those plastic cell pots and other plastic pots seem to multiply like magic during the planting season. Use a simple cardboard carton from the grocery store or elsewhere to collect them neatly as you plant over a period of several days or weeks. When the box is full, take it to your local greenhouse or garden club, or put it on the curb with a Free sign attached.

Metal for Petals

❱ Have a couple of metal garbage cans on your hands? You or a neighbor may be stuck with them when

Fruitful Ideas

Keep an eye out for useful storage containers when you're strolling through the produce aisle of the grocery store. You're likely to find a variety of crates, flats, bins, and baskets that are usually thrown away. Just ask the produce manager if you can have them.

You can use wooden fruit boxes and oblong plastic berry baskets, for instance, to store hand tools, plant markers, plant ties, small pots, and other garden essentials. Crates with handles are ideal for lugging pots and dug-up plants.

your garbage service changes to special plastic containers. Why not turn them into a make-it-in-minutes potting table? Just remove the lids, then lay a sturdy board across the tops. The cans themselves are perfect for storing bulky garden items, especially those you don't use very often.

4 Ways to Use Scraps of PVC Pipe

Many gardeners have sections of PVC (polyvinyl chloride) pipe left over from home improvement projects. Here are some uses for bits and pieces you may have saved.

1 PVC pipe can be used to create tool storage in a garbage can. If the pipe is wide enough, cut it into 18-inch sections and stick them into a few inches of sand poured into the can. Insert the long handles of tools into the pipes, and they will stand upright for tidy storage.

2 Short sections of pipe are perfect for wall-mounted tool holders. Cut a few 6-inch sections. Drill a hole or two in the side of each and hang it from a nail (positioning the pipe vertically) on a wall. Use it as a holder for long-handled tools.

3 PVC pipe also makes a nifty boot rack. Place 1-foot-long sections upright in a large flowerpot. Drape damp garden gloves over the pipes, or prop your wet boots on them. For heavier boots, you may need to add gravel to the bottom of the pot to steady the pipes.

4 A short, chunky piece of PVC pipe can be turned into a twine caddy. Drill a hole in the pipe—anywhere will do. Place a ball or cylinder of twine inside the pipe and thread the end through the hole. Hang the holder and prevent the twine from slipping out by slipping the pipe over a large (3- or 4-inch) nail hammered partway vertically into a windowsill or other horizontal wooden surface in the garden shed. You'll be able to pull the twine out of the hole with one hand. Tie no-longer-used school scissors to the nail for handy cutting.

Everything *Including* the Kitchen Sink

▶ Don't throw away an old sink. Instead, put it by your outdoor faucet and use it as the basis for a handy produce-washing and pot-watering station.

Build a simple base around it, using rot-resistant wood such as cedar, so the sink is waist-high. Put a large bucket below the drain to catch the water (which you can use to water your garden).

If you want to avoid any muddy messes below and having to empty the bucket, create a gravel drain pit. Simply dig a hole 2 feet across and at least 2 feet deep under the sink. Loosen the soil at the bottom of the hole and add 8 inches of sand. Top with gravel or small stones.

MORE PLANT LABELS

Rock Solid

▶ Collect flat stones from the beach and hikes, or save the interesting rocks you find when digging in your garden. Use a permanent marker to write plant names or even care instructions on the surface of the stone.

Gone to Pots

▶ Small clay flowerpots turned upside down and placed on a stake (metal curtain rods or café rods work well) make cute labels. To make the pots stay on the stakes, wad up used aluminum foil and stick it inside the clay pot. Then turn the pot upside down and insert it on top of the stake and stick the stake into the ground.

Par for the Course

▶ Score more yardage from old or damaged golf clubs by turning them into plant markers. Insert the handle of a golf club into the ground, then slip a seed packet over the club end. Or make your own label, tape it to the club, and cover it with a plastic sandwich bag. You can even make laminated labels and tie them to the club.

In the Pocket

▶ Hang onto those old pool balls. They make colorful plant markers and garden ornaments. Use paint or a permanent marker to write a plant name on each ball, then place the ball at the base of the plant.

Pool ball plant labels look especially cute when you recycle tall pool sticks into a tepee to support vines. Use the triangular ball rack to corral the pool cues and give them support.

Thirst-Quenching Plant Labels

▶ From time to time, fast-food restaurants offer promotional plastic drinking cups. Save these cups to make durable plant labels. You can get a dozen labels by cutting a 20-ounce plastic cup into strips from top to bottom.

Labels Out of Lids

▶ Plastic lids come in all colors and sizes. Turn them into fun and easy-to-see plant markers by cutting each lid into a rectangle and then writing the plant name on it in permanent marker. Staple the label onto a craft stick, and insert the stick into the ground.

Shell on a Stick

▶ Those craft sticks come in handy for another type of label—one made with a seashell. Just hot-glue a shell atop a stick, and write the plant name on the shell with a permanent marker. (Scallop shells work especially well.) Insert the stick into the ground so only the shell shows.

Original Packaging

▶ Turn a seed packet into a durable plant label. First, make a squared-off, U-shape support with an 18-inch length of a

Long after the pool table is gone, pool balls can serve as whimsical plant labels.

wire coat hanger. Then slip the seed packet over the wire. If you tore or cut the packet at the top, just tape it shut and cut open the bottom so that you can slide it onto the wire. Cover with clear mailing tape to make it weatherproof and to secure it to the wire, then insert the two prongs into the ground. You'll not only remember the plant name but also have all the growing information instantly handy.

Clip 'n' Save

▶ Clothespins make cute plant labels or row markers. You can use either the old-fashioned clip type or the more modern spring type. Just write the name of a plant in permanent marker on a clothespin and stick it into the ground.

Strengthens and Lengthens

▶ Wooden plant labels are terrific, but they tend to weather and splinter by season's end. To help them last longer, coat them with clear fingernail polish after writing the plant names on them. If you don't have any clear polish on hand, use colored polish to paint just the bottom part of the label (the part that's inserted into the ground). That's usually the first part to go.

Long-Lasting Label

▶ Commercial aluminum labels are wonderful but expensive. You can save yourself some money by making your own at home for free.

Just cut and shape a portion of a wire coat hanger into a squared-off U about 6 inches long and 1 inch wide. Then cut two long rectangles from a disposable aluminum baking dish, such as a pie pan, making each about 4 inches long and 1½ inches wide. Staple the two pieces over the U-shape wire. (Having two pieces helps stabilize the label. If you can cut the aluminum so that you can fold the label in half over the top, it will be even more stable.)

Use a ballpoint pen to write information on the label. Even in the coldest regions, it should last for a couple of years.

4 Ways to Keep Pots from Sticking Together

Larger clay and plastic pots have an annoying habit of sticking together when you stack them, forcing you to waste time and effort prying them apart. And if the weather is cold, clay pots are especially brittle and may crack if handled too roughly. Here's how to prevent all that.

1 Keep a bag of old panty hose handy, and tie one leg around the rim of each pot before stacking.

You can reuse the panty hose as needed.

2 When you stack pots, tuck each one into a plastic grocery bag.

3 Fold squares of newspaper so they're about ½ inch thick. Put a square in the bottom of each pot before stacking.

4 Rip the flaps off cardboard boxes. Fold them in half and tuck one into each pot before stacking.

An Abrasive Aid

▶ Save those small scraps of sandpaper left over from household projects. You can use them to roughen up the smooth surface of plastic plant labels so that permanent marker will better adhere and endure the weather.

TOOL CLEANING AND CARE

Smooth Operators

▶ Use a drop of olive or vegetable oil to lubricate the joints of your metal cutting tools. If you have any wooden-handled tools, rub a little oil on the handles, too. It will seal and protect them. Just dribble some oil on an all-cotton rag and wipe away.

Corncob Scrubbers

▶ Next time you have a sweet corn feast, don't throw out those old corncobs. Instead, set them aside to dry thoroughly, then collect them in an open container in your garage or potting shed. They're the perfect tools for cleaning your dirty garden tools. Use them to scrape off crusted soil and debris, then toss them on the compost pile.

Spuds to the Rescue

▶ If you lose the cap to your lawn mower's gasoline can, use a small potato or potato half to keep the can closed. It will temporarily prevent the gas and fumes from spilling out until you find another cap. Don't use it for more than a day or two, as it will start to decompose.

Glad Rags

▶ We all know that keeping our tools clean prolongs their lives. Make it easy by keeping an old T-shirt or rag doused with just about any kind of oil on a hook by your toolshed or garage door. And while you're at it, keep a clean rag on a hook next to the door so you can wipe your hands in case you have to dash into the house to answer the phone.

Get a Handle

▶ Save those handles from old window sashes, dressers, and other furniture. They come in handy in the garden, making things easier to lift and slide. Screw a handle onto your wooden compost bin, for example, for easy, splinter-free lifting.

An empty tissue box is just right for collecting bits of trash that you find as you weed and water.

OTHER ORGANIZATION IDEAS

Trash Begone

▶ Ever notice how when you garden you always seem to find little bits of trash—a shard of glass, a faded label, a piece of string? Save an empty tissue box to tuck into your garden caddy or to keep handy while you garden. You'll never have to figure out what to do with those bits of debris again.

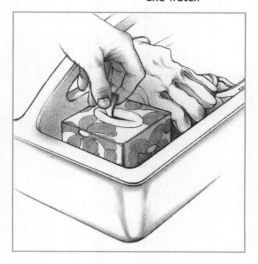

Garden First-Aid

▌ Turn a large margarine or other plastic container into an outdoor first-aid kit that you can carry in your garden caddy. Tuck in adhesive bandages, disinfecting cream, anti-itch cream, lip balm, and whatever else you might need. Use a bit of red fingernail polish to make a cross on the container to designate its contents.

A Shoe-In

With seemingly everyone organizing their closets these days with sleek custom systems, old-fashioned shoe racks are falling out of favor. You see these on curbs or at garage sales for pennies or free. You may even have a spare one languishing in your attic.

Give a shoe rack new life in your garden shed or on the back porch. Use it horizontally on the floor, or experiment with nailing it to the wall for more efficient storage. It's an ideal way to air-dry, and even store, wet garden gloves. You're able to see which glove is the right and left, and because they're upright, they're less likely to attract nesting spiders and bugs. Plus, you might actually want to use the remaining portion of the rack as somewhat intended—to store garden clogs and work boots.

Clean Up

▌The next time you pick up your dry cleaning, take the clothes into the house, but leave a bag or two in the trunk of your car. When you head to the garden center, you'll always have a disposable, moisture-proof liner to protect your vehicle from water and soil when buying flats of annuals or bags of compost.

Fast Fertilizing

▌Container plants benefit from frequent "snacks" of liquid fertilizer, but mixing up small batches as you need them is a hassle. Save time and aggravation by preparing big batches and storing them in large, plastic, laundry detergent bottles. Stash them somewhere near your plants. Depending on the fertilizer, the mixture should keep for a couple of months.

Portable Pavers

▌Whether you're trying to work along a muddy path or you just need a protective landing pad to stand on while you work in a flowerbed so that you don't compact the soil, you'll love having a set of four or five pavers that go where you go.

Pizza boxes can be used as pavers in muddy parts of your garden or in your flowerbeds to help you avoid compacting the soil.

You can use scrap lumber, old wooden drawer fronts cut in half, or any bits of wood that are flat and measure about 2 by 2 feet. Nail a length of rope or heavy twine to the top of each paver to make a nifty handle.

Set several pavers in a row to make a path over muddy ground. Or use just one or two, tucked into a large flowerbed, to stand on while you work.

For an instant and disposable alternative, hold on to those take-out pizza boxes and use them instead.

Spray 'n' Feed

▶ Many organic foliar fertilizers and organic pest controls need to be mixed with water before using. But if you use a large, conventional sprayer to apply them, you may be wasting money by having to dump the remainder of one mixture when you need to use the sprayer for something else.

The answer is to have multiple bottles in which to mix and store these solutions. Empty spray cleaner bottles are perfect for mixing smaller amounts. Just label each clearly with a permanent marker. Check the package directions, but you should be able to store these solutions for a month or two without any loss of potency.

Roll On Over

Keep an eye out for old microwave or television carts on wheels left out for the garbage collector. Just about any small rolling carts, especially those with open shelves, are great places to store gloves, trowels, small fertilizer containers, spray bottles, labels, plant ties, clogs, and other items that you use throughout the garden. And if you feel that the cart looks too out of place in the garden, give it a coat of deep green paint to make it seem more at home.

Red Flag

▶ If you've ever gone out into the garden and felt overwhelmed because there are seemingly a thousand different areas that need attention right this second, use this tip to create a sort of three-dimensional "to do" list.

Save several of those colorful flags utility companies always seem to be poking into your yard or your neighbor's yard. With a permanent marker, write numbers 1 through 10 or so on the flags in big numbers. Then go out into the garden and put the flag marked with a 1 where the most urgent task lies. Then mark the second most urgent with a 2, and so on.

In much the same way a paper to-do list would, this method helps you stay focused on the task at hand and gives you a sense of accomplishment as you work through each chore.

JOURNALS AND RECORD-KEEPING

What Day Is It?

▶ Save one of those freebie calendars you get at the end of the year, and turn it into a garden calendar for the upcoming growing season. Record frost dates, planting dates, unusual weather, fertilizing dates, mower and other power tool maintenance dates, and so on. Use the blank spaces that are often in the back for further notes.

A Recipe for Recycling

▶ Recycle a recipe box by using it to file seeds by the date when they need to be planted. Those new snack-size resealable plastic bags make great airtight seed holders. Clip them to a recycled index card to make them easier to file.

Garden Grocery List

▌Just as a grocery list saves you time and money at the supermarket, a garden list can help you save at the garden center. Create one that you can hang outside in a protected spot so that it's always handy—just the way your grocery list is in your kitchen.

Start with a plastic or metal clipboard, if you have one, and fill it with several sheets of paper. (You might as well use up some of that paper that's been used only on one side.)

If you don't have a clipboard, use a bullnose clip or other strong clip attached to a piece of corrugated cardboard. Protect the paper with a waterproof cover made from an old plastic binder. Tie a pencil to the clip with a length of string. (Pens tend not to write in damp conditions.)

Now you can jot down notes, sketch ideas, and make "to do" lists when the ideas come to you as you work in the garden. As you head to the nursery, just grab a page from your list.

A Different Kind of Garden Center

▌At the end of the school year, just in time for the high gardening season, think about recycling your kids' school supplies into a convenient garden record center.

Snatch an old backpack to hold everything. That partly used spiral notebook can become your garden journal, with the pockets making handy storage areas for magazine articles and catalogs. A zippered or rigid pencil case can hold old seed packets and plant labels you want to keep for reference. And the garden book or two you're always referring to will fit nicely in the pack as well.

Hang the backpack from a hook in your garage so it's always handy. During the winter, tuck it into a closet so you can grab it for some off-season planning by the fire.

Those old school supplies can be converted into a mini-office, organizing all your garden paperwork and information.

A Journal Where You Want It

▌ A garden journal can easily get wet or dirty if you're using it outside—the best place to use it, of course. Solve the problem with a large resealable plastic bag. Slip the journal into the bag with a pen or pencil.

Now your journal will stay nice and clean, come rain or shine. And if you find yourself using it only outdoors, you can even keep it right on your favorite garden bench in all types of weather.

Plants with Extra Baggage

▌ Waterproof luggage tags, often given away free by travel agencies, make sturdy plant tags for trees and shrubs. The belt and loop meant to attach the tag to your luggage can just as easily be used to hang each tag from a tree branch or shrub for easy viewing.

A Sharing Book

▌ How many times has a friend admiring your garden said, "Oh! I want some of that," and you never quite remember to give her some when it's time to divide?

Solve the problem with a sweet little sharing book. Simply make a book cover out of wallpaper scraps or heavy wrapping paper, and fill it with sheets of paper stapled in place between the covers.

Keep the book, along with a pencil, in your garage or on your porch, and have friends write down what they want so you'll be able to refer to it when you divide perennials. A bonus: If you have them date their requests, you'll also have a nice reminder of which plants look their best when.

Write This One Down

▌ How often, while working in the garden, do you wish you had a pen and paper handy to jot down plant names or notes to yourself? One of those tall cardboard containers that powdered lemonade or iced tea come in is the solution. Those canisters are perfect for storing pens and pencils, a small notebook, and sticky notes. If you want, toss in a pair of scissors for cutting open seed packets. Keep the canister handy in your garden caddy so that paper and pen will always be at your fingertips.

Express Storage

▶ Metal mailboxes are commonly found in gardens for storing hand tools where and when gardeners need them. But these mailboxes are also great for storing your garden journal, planting notes, "to do" lists, and other garden paperwork. Position a mailbox on a pole near your favorite garden sitting spot, and you'll be more inclined to keep up with your garden record-keeping than if you have to trot back into the house to retrieve the paperwork.

Hold the Milk

▶ Index cards are a time-honored way of keeping track of information in the garden. But you can save money and get slightly sturdier stock by cutting cards out of cereal boxes. Just keep them with a "real" index card so that you always have a template to cut out more.

In the garden, you won't even need a hard surface to write on because the cardboard is rigid enough. Also keep a supply of these planet-friendly cards in a folder tacked to your garage wall, along with a pencil on a string, and you'll always have the means to jot down that quick memo. Then, if you want, file them away in a recipe box.

On-the-Spot Records

▶ A length of scrap lumber can help you keep better track of what's going on in your garden. Just stick the wood into the ground next to a plant. Using a fine-point permanent marker, keep track of relevant information, such as planting time, bloom time, and pest problems and treatments.

In the fall, just pull up the markers and take them inside. You can tuck them into a box to refer to next year. Or during the winter, when you have more time for such matters, record the information in a more traditional way, such as in a journal.

Picture Perfect

▶ Turn a giveaway calendar into a useful record of bloom times. Once or twice a month, take your camera out into the garden (using the date function on the camera, if needed, to help keep track) and photograph plants that are in full bloom. Once the photos are developed, tape or glue them over the existing picture for that month. Now you have a lovely visual record of which plants bloom in your garden each month.

CHAPTER SIX

Trees and Shrubs

Trees and shrubs are the bones of any garden, lending height and drama to the landscape year-round. Get new additions to your yard off to a vigorous start and keep your existing plantings at their best with the smart reuse of everything from newspapers to cut-up T-shirts to ice cubes.

STARTING OFF RIGHT

Cutting Remarks

▶ Pull out that aquarium that has been in the basement since the fish died. It's ideal for starting cuttings from trees and shrubs.

Take cuttings several inches long of new wood from your favorite trees and shrubs. Strip off the lower leaves and dip the ends in rooting hormone to promote faster rooting.

Fill the aquarium with several inches of perlite or potting medium. Water lightly, being sure not to overwater, since there is no drainage. Insert the cuttings and cover the top of the aquarium loosely with a plastic bag.

When the cuttings show signs of sprouting roots—you can gently push away some of the medium to check, or you may even see them against the glass—remove the plastic and put the aquarium outdoors in a sunny spot. Once the roots are an inch or two long, remove the cuttings and plant them in the ground.

An aquarium that hasn't seen a fish in years can be recruited as the perfect climate-controlled container in which to start trees and shrubs from cuttings.

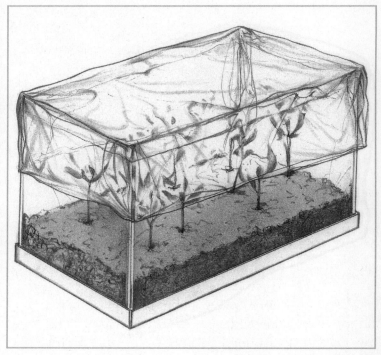

Wondrous Waterer

Tree-watering bags, sometimes called "gators," have been adopted in many cities because their slow, steady delivery of water to the tree's roots at planting time increases its chances of survival. When planting a tree or large shrub with a deep root system, you can make your own slow-leak watering bag with a 20-gallon watertight garbage bag.

Dig the planting hole extra large to accommodate a full bag of water. Position the tree in the hole. Then put the bag in next to the tree and fill the bag with water. (Filling it while it's in place will reduce the chances of its ripping.) Tie the bag closed with a twist tie or rubber band. Prick a few holes near the bottom of the bag with a pin or needle. You want to have just enough holes to barely allow the water to escape. The goal should be for a 20-gallon bag to empty in about 3 hours, watering more deeply and slowly than you ever could with a hose. Fill in around the tree and the bag so that the soil is level with the surrounding soil.

Later in the day or the next morning, remove the empty bag and fill in with soil. Water the area around the tree to moisten the new soil and the top layer of soil that the water from the bag may not have reached.

Hedge Your Bets

▶ Start an entire evergreen hedge for just a few dollars by taking cuttings and recycling an old drawer or two.

Prepare a place in which to start the cuttings by taking an old, fairly deep (at least 6 inches) drawer and drilling a few holes in the bottom. Fill the drawer with sand and position it in a sunny spot.

In the spring, take bushy cuttings of new wood from your favorite evergreen (columnar yews are particularly easy). Strip the lower leaves and dip the ends of the cuttings in rooting hormone. Use a pencil to poke holes 4 to 6 inches deep in the sand and insert the cuttings. (The holes will prevent the rooting hormone from rubbing off.) Keep the cuttings well-watered. By late summer, most of them will have rooted and be ready for planting.

Save a Seedling

▌ If you're lucky, a tree worth keeping will sprout in your yard, reseeded from a nearby parent. Protect the tree by surrounding it with edging fashioned from an old tire. Use a sharp knife or box cutter to slice off the top part of the tire, then place this ring around the seedling. The low, sleek, circular edging will keep mowers and string trimmers away from your prize.

Where There's a Willow, There's a Way

▌ Willows contain a hormone that makes them insanely easy to root. Just cut off a branch and stick it in loose, moist potting soil. You can take advantage of that same hormone when rooting softwood cuttings of other trees and shrubs.

3 Great Ideas for Rooting Cuttings

Cuttings of trees and shrubs need to be rooted in containers that can accommodate their long, slender shapes. Also, since gardeners often try to root more than one at a time, it's nice if the container can squeeze in a crowd. Here are some ideas for deep, generously sized containers.

▌ An old dishpan. Just use a steak or paring knife to make drainage holes in the bottom of the dishpan. Then fill it to within an inch of the top with your favorite planting medium.

2 A plastic newspaper bag. Fill with a moist potting medium. Use a plastic bread bag tab or a twist tie to close the top, then cut holes in the side of the bag for the cuttings. Poke a couple of drainage holes in the bottom with a pencil.

3 An old window box. It may be too battered to mount under a window, but it's unbeatable for starting large cuttings.

Cut a long stem from any type of willow, choosing one that's 4 feet or so long. Cut it into thumb-length pieces and toss them into a stockpot of boiling water. Remove from the heat and let the pieces steep overnight to make a willow tea. Store the tea in clearly labeled, clean plastic milk jugs for up to 1 month. Use it to water cuttings of any tree or shrub. Not only does the tea encourage rooting, but research at Ohio State University shows that it prevents damping-off as well.

Waxing Eloquent

▶ When making a graft on a tree, there's no need to buy fancy grafting wax to seal the graft to the main branch. You can get the same results by using melted candle wax.

If the angle of the graft lends itself to it, just drip the wax directly from the lit candle, tilted horizontally, onto the graft. Otherwise, cut a candle stub into ½-inch chunks and melt them in the top of a double boiler. Use a Popsicle stick or dinner knife to apply the melted wax to the graft.

BUYMANSHIP BASICS

Chill Out

▶ How often have you purchased container trees or shrubs, only to have them sit around by your back door forever, awaiting that magic moment when you can plant them? Meanwhile, they dry out easily. And once they dry out, the soil shrinks away from the sides of the pot so that when you try to give them a thorough drenching, the water just runs quickly out of the bottom without ever really soaking the soil.

Solve this problem by tossing a handful of ice cubes into the container each morning. The ice will

A handful of ice cubes tossed into a large pot delivers water slowly and efficiently to parched soil.

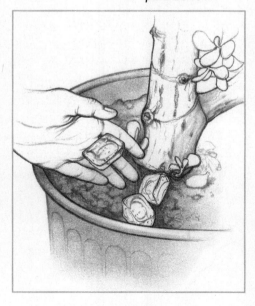

melt slowly and soak down into the soil. And with a little water each day, the trees and shrubs will thrive.

Old Blankets to the Rescue

❯ Keep a couple of thin blankets or old sheets in your trunk to use when buying trees and shrubs at your local nursery. Place them under pots to keep your trunk or car seats clean. And if you're buying a tree or large shrub, you can wrap an old sheet or blanket around the top to protect it from the wind if the tree will be poking out of your car window, trunk, or truck bed. (Make sure to tie the tree or shrub in place with string or a bungee cord.) If the weather is hot and the drive will be more than a half hour, dampen the blanket or sheet first to keep the plant from drying out.

PLANTING TIPS

The Kindest Cut

❯ A razor-edge box cutter comes in handy when planting a container tree or large container shrub. Use it to slice apart the pot with minimal disturbance of the plant's roots. First, slice off the bottom of the pot. (Be sure to wear heavy gloves to prevent cuts to fingers; those box cutters are sharp!) Next place the tree or shrub in the planting hole and position it, making sure it is straight. Slice up the side of the pot and remove it. Now you're ready to backfill the hole and water.

Using this method keeps the rootball intact while you maneuver the tree and keeps the roots protected from drying out for as long as possible.

Compost to Go

❯ Fill paper bags (recycled fast-food bags are ideal) with bits of kitchen or garden waste. Keep these mini–compost bags on hand near your compost pile—they'll last for months. Use them to toss into the bottom of a planting hole each time you plant a tree or shrub. A small hole might accommodate just one or two bags, while a large hole will benefit from several.

Tree Transport

▌ Don't like where you planted your young tree? There's no need to call for a bodybuilder to relocate it. Simply dig beneath the rootball and move it back and forth until it is free from the soil. Position a large, sturdy piece of cardboard (perhaps one you saved from your last major house move) under one edge of the rootball. Bending from the knees, pull the tree onto the cardboard. Now you can slide it easily to the new location.

Gimme Shelter

▌ The ideal time to plant a shrub is on an overcast day, so the hot sun doesn't stress it. But sometimes you don't have the luxury of waiting for perfect weather. The next time you find yourself having to plant a small shrub on a sunny day, provide some fast, easy shade by grabbing a laundry basket. Position it upside down over the shrub and leave it there for 2 to 3 days, until the shrub has the chance to get a bit more established.

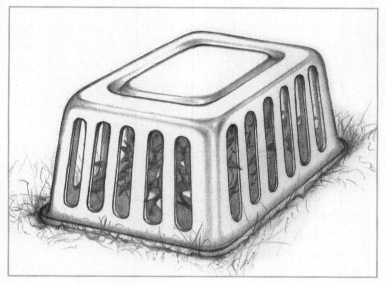

Provide instant shade for a newly planted shrub by tipping a laundry basket over it. The basket will prevent the shrub from wilting in the sun and heat.

9 Ways to Protect Tiny Trees and Shrubs

Little trees and shrubs are so vulnerable to damage—from everything from a footstep to a car tire to a string trimmer. Try positioning some of the following items around your tree to lessen the chances of its getting injured.

1 A lamp shade frame, with or without the fabric

2 A 5-gallon bucket with the bottom cut out

3 A cardboard oatmeal container with the bottom cut out

4 An old wastebasket with the bottom cut out

5 Brightly colored gift ribbon wrapped around paint stirrers stuck into the ground in a circle

6 An old tire

7 The rim of an old springform pan

8 A large black plastic pot with the bottom cut out

9 A tomato cage, cut on one side if needed to fit around tree.

Wetter Longer

▶ When planting a tree or shrub, help the roots stay moister longer by draping several layers of newspaper over the sides of the planting hole. Dampen the paper with a hose to keep it in place. Position the tree or shrub atop the paper and backfill as you normally would. The paper will slow the flow of water away from the tree for months, until it decomposes, adding organic matter to the soil.

PLANTING AFTERCARE

Fit to Be Tied

▶ You don't need to buy twist ties or special material to tie trees and shrubs to stakes. Your dresser drawers likely hold plenty of material suited to the job. Try nylon hose, strips of old T-shirts, legs from stretchy tights, knee-high socks, and even old neckties. You may end up with the best-dressed trees in the neighborhood.

Tree Time Capsule

▌ Labels on permanent plantings such as trees and shrubs always seem to fade or get lost. But they're such useful reminders, right down to information on pruning and mature size, that you'll want to hang on to them for years. One way to do so is to tuck each label into one of those little metal breath mint boxes and to bury the box just beneath the soil at the base of the tree, so that the top of the box is level with the ground. Cover the box with mulch. When you want to open the box and retrieve the label, just brush the mulch aside. The box is too large to get lost, and it's durable enough to protect the tree label for years.

A Place for Place Mats

▌ Stained or faded fabric place mats make top-notch weed mats for newly planted small trees or shrubs. Cut a hole in the center of a mat large enough to accommodate the trunk or crown of each plant. Then cut a line from the hole to the outside of the mat. Slip it around the base of the plant and cover with grass clippings, wood chips, pine needles, or other mulch to prevent weeds from rearing their ugly heads.

WINTER PROTECTION AND WRAPPING

Cage Your Trees

▌ Just about the time you're pulling up your frost-felled tomatoes is when new plantings of trees and shrubs need a little extra protection. Put those tomato cages to use during the winter months by inserting them around small trees and shrubs to protect them from getting tramped on or snapped off by snow and ice. You might also want to line the tomato cages with newspaper and fill with

Tomato cages are perfect for providing winter protection for small trees and shrubs. Just line them with newspaper and fill with leaves.

leaves or shredded newspaper to protect the plants from low temperatures.

Button Up Your Overcoat

▶ Azaleas, boxwoods, and other small evergreens can be severely windburned when a winter storm blows through, especially during the first winter after they are planted. Save those past-their-prime windproof jackets, raincoats, jean jackets, and other light jackets to use as winter protection for these plants.

Bag Your Trees for Winter

▶ Wrap the trunks of young trees with brown paper grocery bags to shade the bark and prevent sunscald until the canopy of leaves can provide adequate shade and the bark can toughen. A grocery bag wrap also deters wildlife from gnawing on the bark.

A bit of leftover paint applied to tree trunks is just the ticket for protecting smooth bark from splitting and the resulting insects and diseases.

To make a wrap, cut a bag into continuous strips and wrap it, bandage fashion, from ground level up to the tree's first branches. Secure the wrap in place with masking tape or twine.

Goodbye, Old Paint

▶ Use any leftover white or light-colored latex (not oil) paint on the sunny side of young tree trunks to reflect the winter sun and keep the sap cold during warm spells. If the sap freezes at night and expands during the day, the bark may split, giving insects and diseases easy access. Some people paint the whole trunk, but that isn't necessary. Painting the south half of the trunk from a few inches off the ground to just below the first branches is sufficient.

Winterize a Tree

If you want to overwinter a small tree that's only marginally hardy in your zone or want to grow a frost-sensitive tree, such as a palm or banana, in an area where it is likely to experience a few frosts, you can bundle it up for the winter with all that bubble wrap you've been collecting from mail-order packages.

First, protect the trunk. Tie or tape chopsticks, knitting needles, pencils, or a few twigs next to the trunk to promote air circulation. Then wrap the trunk with bubble wrap, securing it with duct tape or string.

After the trunk is taken care of, work on the top of the tree. If possible and practical, cut back the limbs to minimize the amount of foliage that needs to be covered. Then put a small blanket or old sweatshirt over the tree and "cap" it with a large plastic pot to keep out moisture that could freeze and expand. You may need to stuff newspaper into the pot to keep it stable and prevent movement in the wind. If so, keep the paper in place by stretching duct tape across the bottom of the pot.

If you can't cut back the top of the tree, wrap it as best you can with old sheets, blankets, or clothing. Drape the top with more bubble wrap and tie it into place, creating as waterproof a canopy as you can.

If the tree is in a container, wrap the container in bubble wrap, too.

This technique adds as much as 6°F to the area around a tree—which may be just enough to get the tree through the winter.

T-Shirts or Tree Shirts?

▶ You can recycle old T-shirts into excellent winter protectors for trees and shrubs. Simply cut them into strips, wrap the strips around the trees you want to protect, and secure them in place with string or twine. To protect small evergreen shrubs from extreme cold and wind, just slip a T-shirt over each shrub for instant insulation. Be sure to use a light-colored shirt to let in as much light as possible.

MORE TREE AND SHRUB PROTECTION

Good Fences

▶ If you have snow fencing to help you with drifts or winter winds, you probably put it away in the garage or shed in the spring. But don't put it too far away. If you have any summer projects afoot—building a deck, fixing the driveway, repairing the pool, digging utility trenches—you can put your snow fencing back to work.

Construction jobs, even small ones, threaten mature trees, even though it's not obvious. Most trees' roots are in the top 18 inches of soil and reach way past the outermost branches. Your project, which is likely to consist of digging, parking vehicles, and piling lumber, can damage your most valued trees unless you protect them. Position snow fencing in a circle 2 to 4 feet outside the dripline (the imaginary line created by the tree's outermost branches). It's a useful physical reminder to you and any worker that this is an area to avoid.

Don't have any snow fencing? Pull out those lengths of chicken wire you use as temporary rabbit protection in the garden. They're an effective second-best solution.

Pallet Protection

▶ Shingles, drywall, and other building supplies are often delivered on pallets, also called skids. There are many outdoor uses for them, but an excellent one is as a rock-solid snow shelter for foundation plants. Just screw in two hinges along the edges of two pallets and use them as a V-shaped shelter over a shrub. This will protect the shrub from snow falling off the roof.

PROTECTION FROM CRITTERS

Muy Picante!

▶ Protect your tree trunks from rabbits and deer by painting them with a fiery concoction that will discourage nibbling.

Mix together 1 cup vegetable oil, ¼ cup Tabasco sauce, and ¼ cup cayenne pepper. Rub the solution into the bark, using rubber kitchen gloves to protect your hands. Reapply once every month or so, more often if it's been raining a lot.

Pesky Wabbit!

▶ You know all that washed aluminum foil you're always saving? Use it during the winter months to protect your fruit trees from nibbling rabbits. Wrap a collar of foil 1 foot high around the base of each young tree, then tie it in place with strips of panty hose.

Ban Bugs

▶ Keep ants and other insects from climbing fruit trees by smearing petroleum jelly thickly around the trunks a few inches from the ground—just high enough to prevent mulch and grass clippings from sticking to it. Make the barrier about an inch wide to prevent crawling insects from gaining access to your tree.

Caution: Do not use petroleum jelly on thin-barked trees. Petroleum-based products may cause swelling and

A thick ring of petroleum jelly around the trunk of a fruit tree will trap crawling insects before they can do any damage.

cankering on thin-barked trees. If you're unsure if your tree is thin-barked or not, take the precaution of first wrapping duct tape around the trunk and topping with a layer of petroleum jelly.

Protect New Shoots

▶ Deer love to nibble the tender new shoots of trees and shrubs. A sharp poke in the nose will make them think twice about munching on your trees.

Loosely twist scraps of medium-gauge wire (thick enough to maintain a sturdy edge, but thin enough to twist easily) around the ends of the branches, with the wire tips protruding out at least 3 inches. When the deer move in to take a bite, their noses will make first contact with the wire. This might be just the discouragement they need to move on.

Protection from Pets

▶ When you plant a new tree or shrub in your yard, pets feel compelled to mark their territory by urinating on the newcomer. Make your mark first and encourage canines and felines to take their business elsewhere.

Fill several plastic milk jugs with water (to keep them upright) and place them in a circle around the plant you want to protect. The operating theory here is that any pet that tries to spray on these will be soiled by rebounding urine, an unpleasant enough experience to make him stop and go away.

PRUNING POINTERS

Tie a Yellow (or Red or Orange) Ribbon

▶ Pruning is as much art as science, and it's tough to decide which branches to cut and which to leave. To help you along with your artistic decisions, tie a bit of scrap gift ribbon on the branches you'd like to cut. Leave it for a day or two to help you visualize what the tree would look like without those branches.

Wake Up Your Shrubs

Everyone loves rhododendrons and azaleas, but they do best in cool, temperate climates with moist, acidic soil, such as the Pacific Northwest and some regions of the South. You may not be able to control your garden's temperature and rainfall, but you can create the right soil by enriching it with large amounts of coffee grounds and tea leaves. They're highly acidic and help retain moisture.

The ideal is to work in 2 gallons or more of coffee grounds or tea leaves at planting time. Alternatively, work 1 to 2 cups of coffee grounds into the soil surface at the base of the shrub once a month during the growing season.

Ask around at coffee shops to see if they'll give their used grounds to you. Or use your own and save up. Toss coffee grounds or tea leaves into a brown paper bag. Toss in the coffee filter or tea bag, too, if you wish. Leave the paper bag open in a warm, dry place (a pantry or closet is ideal) so that the contents dry out. Work the material into the soil—still in the filters or bags, if desired—but do make sure that it's covered with soil so that it will break down faster.

Rake It In

▶ When pruning a tree or large shrub, toss an old sheet or blanket under the area you're trimming. It will catch all those tiny twigs and sticks that are such a pain to rake up or gather, especially if they fall into a ground cover or annual bed. Just pull up the corners of the sheet and haul away the collected debris.

This tip works especially well near hedges, where frequent trimming creates lots of little bits and pieces.

Sweet Solution

▶ When you're pruning or deadheading certain shrubs, such as rhododendrons, sap leaves your hands sticky. Give your

A pasta fork makes a handy tool for deadheading spent rhododendron blooms.

hands a shot of nonstick cooking spray or rub them with a little olive oil and sugar. The sugar helps dissolve the sap and the oil distributes it evenly—and softens your hands in the process.

Easier Deadheading

▶Remove the spent blooms from your rhododendron with the help of a pasta fork—the kind that has several prongs and is normally used to toss noodles. To extend your reach, duct-tape the pasta fork to a broom handle, and you'll be able to deadhead even really tall rhodies.

Giving Direction

▶Sometimes branches of young trees and shrubs start to grow in the wrong direction or cross over one another. Set them on the correct growth pattern by weighting down the ends.

Cut a thin strip of panty hose and push it through the loop on a lead fishing weight, using a pencil or metal skewer. Tie the hose near the tip of the wayward branch, leaving plenty of growing room for the branch, to direct it into the correct growth pattern. Every 2 to 3 months, remove the weight to see if the branch is growing properly yet.

WATERING MADE EASY

Heavy Drinkers

▶ Azaleas, kalmias, and hydrangeas are thirsty shrubs that never seem to get enough water. You can help them stay amply hydrated by planting them along with some underground watering aids made with clean plastic milk jugs.

Dig the planting hole a little wider than usual. Then punch a couple of small nail holes in the bottom of three milk jugs. Plant them, evenly spaced, around the shrub so that the necks of the jugs protrude just ½ inch above the ground (top the necks with a stone to disguise them).

When you water the shrub, fill the jugs as well. The water will slowly drip out of the holes in the jugs' bottoms, delivering water more deeply to the plants.

Deeply Thirsty

▶ Arborists use a metal probe and a watering wand to get water down to a tree's roots, targeting the dripline (the circular area around a tree that marks the outermost branches). It provides water where the tree needs it without wasting any water in the upper layers of soil.

You don't need to buy a commercial root-watering wand. Just use a crowbar to poke four holes a foot or two deep evenly spaced around the tree, being sure not to force it in too hard and injure any roots that might be in the way.

Now insert the hose into a hole and let the water run slowly—just a drip—for at least an hour. Repeat with the other holes. The tree roots will reach out toward the moist soil, encouraging vigorous root growth, and you won't waste water.

TREE AND SHRUB PROBLEM SOLVERS

Show Some Glove Love

▶ Did a baking snafu leave your favorite oven mitt a greasy mess or burnt? Don't toss it in the trash. Instead, give it a new purpose—outside, to stake a newly planted tree and prevent the rope from rubbing the tree's bark.

String a rope through the mitt by using a scissors to make a small hole in the tip of the thumb. Make another on the other side of the mitt, where your wrist would be. Run the rope through these holes. Fit the mitt against the tree and finish staking the tree.

A Tuna Timer

▶ Use a clean small tuna (or similarly shaped) can as a low-tech timer for your sprinkler. It's roughly 1 inch deep, just the amount of water your newly planted tree or shrub should receive each week. Nestle the can into the soil near the tree or shrub, then run the sprinkler. When the can is full, you know you've applied an inch of water to the plant and it's time to turn off the sprinkler.

Gaps Gone

▶ When a hedge loses a shrub or two, creating a gap in your otherwise neat row of plants, don't be too quick to buy a replacement. Instead, use the gap as a unique decorative opportunity.

If your hedge has developed a gap, fill it artfully with a salvaged door or window.

Erect an old screen door in the gap and train a vine up it (or use a wooden door for a more solid filler). Simply screw the door into two posts and sink the posts into the ground a couple of feet. To steady the door further, hammer in 2-

foot-long stakes, one in front and one in back, spacing them at least 1 foot apart.

You could also mount a window, mirror, or picture frame on tall posts. Sink the posts 2 to 2½ feet deep to keep the window from tipping over. If desired, train the vines up the posts and plant a perennial or small shrub underneath.

Deep Thoughts

▶ While you have that yardstick out there to measure how wide and how deep you're digging a hole for planting a tree or shrub, put it to further use once you have the tree or shrub planted. To make sure you have a tree or shrub positioned at the right depth, simply lay a yardstick across the planting hole after you've placed the rootball in the hole. Most trees and shrubs should be planted at the same depth as they were in the container. A ring around the trunk should indicate that depth. The yardstick should line up with the ring, letting you know if you've dug the hole too shallow or too deep.

If a yardstick isn't handy or isn't long enough, a broom handle—even with the broom head still attached—also will do the job nicely.

Pull Out the Rug

▶ Newly planted trees will take off nicely as long as they don't have too much competition from surrounding weeds or turf. An easy, thrifty way to prevent even bermudagrass from encroaching on your planting is to tuck a small scatter rug around a tree, creating a thick layer of mulch that not only will halt encroaching plants but also will protect your tree from mowers and string trimmers. Nearly any type of rug will work as long as it isn't moisture-proof—you want rain and other water to be able to get to the tree's roots.

Cut a slit from one edge of the rug to the center and slip the rug around the tree. You may want to trim the edges of a rectangular rug to create a round mulch. Top with no more than a couple of inches of wood chips (too much mulch isn't good for a tree) for a more natural-looking effect.

Bark Rx

▶ The next time a storm breaks off a branch and leaves a nasty ragged cut that's too short to trim off with a traditional saw, head for your toolbox (or your kitchen). The solution to healthy healing may be within easy reach.

First, use a box cutter or paring knife to score a clean cut through the bark. Then use a hammer and a sharp chisel to knock off high points from the wound. Finish with a wood file to create a cleaner, smoother wound that will heal more quickly and cleanly, making it less likely that insects or disease will invade.

CHAPTER SEVEN

Fantastic Flower Gardens

When growing everything from astilbes to zinnias, there are dozens of ways to reuse things around the house in your flower garden. Whether you're getting your seedlings off to a strong start with plastic cups, using paper bags to thwart heavy reseeders, or lending a little support to downed daffodils with chopsticks, you'll have your prettiest flower garden ever—without spending a penny!

FLOWER PLANTING TIPS

Heat Things Up

▶ Marigolds, vincas, salvias, impatiens, and other annuals that love heat and warmth often suffer in the spring. Even after your region's last frost date, the time for planting these seedlings outdoors, the soil is still a little too cool, especially in the northern third of the country.

Get your warmth-loving annuals off to a stronger start with the help of clear plastic disposable cups, the largest ones you can find. Just cut out most of the bottom of each cup for a vent. Slip the cup over the newly planted annual and nestle it slightly into the soil. Leave the cup in place for 1 to 2 weeks. It will trap warmth and get your flowers off to a faster start.

SAVE THE PLANET

Bags o' Black Gold

We've all seen the planting bags that you can hang from fences and trees. But here's a new twist on an old idea—one that makes it possible to grow moisture-loving shade annuals underneath mature trees with shallow roots that rob other plants of moisture.

Fill dark garbage bags with compost or high-quality soil. (Bonus points if you use bags that have already been used once. It doesn't matter if they're a bit gooey or leaky.) Tie them shut and make a few slashes in the bottom of each for drainage. Arrange them, flattened, in a ring around the tree, placing them at least a foot away from the trunk to prevent moisture-based pest and disease problems.

Make a number of slashes in the top of each bag for planting. Tuck in impatiens, begonias, and other annuals.

In the fall, empty the bags onto your vegetable garden, spread the quality soil lightly on the lawn to fill low spots and improve the soil, or simply spread the soil out around the base of the tree.

A bonus: The cup will protect the plant until it's large enough to be less attractive to rabbits.

Extra! Extra!

▶ When you prepare to plant perennials, get them off to a better start by adding something a little extra to the hole: yesterday's newspaper. Simply dig a hole 2 to 3 inches wider and deeper than usual for your perennial. Then take a page of newspaper, wet it thoroughly, and wad it up into a ball. Place the wad in the hole and plant the perennial. You'll be amazed at how well the newspaper keeps the roots moist, thus spurring better and faster growth.

KEEPING FLOWERS WATERED

Soak It In

▶ If you plant a lot of flowers, you know how those flats of annuals tend to hang around on your deck or patio for days, waiting for you to get a spare moment to plant them. Keeping these small plants well-watered is a must, but it takes time and patience to make sure each little cell gets its fair share.

Solve the problem with the help of a plastic sweater box—the kind you can stow under the bed. Add a few inches of water to the box and set the flat inside. Let the flat soak for a half hour or so, and each cell will be perfectly saturated.

Catch It If You Can

Keeping up with the watering needs of moisture-loving perennials, such as astilbes and ligularias, can be difficult. Solve this problem by creating a minibog under each plant with a plastic or metal tray or other container from the house. Good candidates include aluminum pie pans, TV dinner trays, or the bottom quarter of a plastic milk jug—whatever you can find that will hold an inch or two of water and is several inches across.

Next time you're planting or dividing a particularly thirsty perennial, place the container in the planting hole a few inches below where the roots will be at planting time. Plant as you would normally. The container will collect water and prevent moisture from draining too freely away from the plant. This is an especially good solution in sandy soils where even plants with moderate moisture needs suffer from too much drainage.

6 Flowers That Benefit from a Water Tower

A number of annuals go downhill fast if allowed to dry out. Solve this problem at planting time by creating small reservoirs near each to ensure a slow drizzle of water that soaks down deep for longer-lasting moisture.

Remove the label from a 2-liter soda bottle. Cut the bottle in half horizontally. Make a tiny hole in the cap with a sewing needle, knitting needle, or slender nail—whatever it takes to allow barely a drop to drip from the bottle every few minutes. Nestle the bottle, cap down, several inches into the soil (it will be low enough to be fairly unobtrusive), then fill with water as needed.

For larger plantings, create several of these reservoirs. Good flowers to plant with water towers include the following:

1 Annual lobelias
2 Fuchsias
3 Impatiens
4 Ligularias
5 Small hydrangeas
6 Astilbes

A Taste for Tea

▶ Plants that bloom all summer, such as geraniums, repeat-blooming roses, marigolds, and zinnias, need a lot of nutrients. Perk them up by watering them with leftover tea—herbal or traditional, iced or hot (of course, you'll need to let it cool to room temperature first). Different types of tea provide different nutrients, but nearly any flowering plant will be perked up by the small amount of organic matter tea contains.

Shady Character

▶ The ideal time to plant is on an overcast or rainy day, but the weather doesn't always cooperate with our busy schedules. Sometimes your only choice is to go ahead and plant on a sunny day.

When this happens, grab an umbrella (the more battered and broken, the better; that way, you won't mind getting it a little dirty). Open it and position it over a new planting. You can either poke or bury the handle in the soil so the umbrella is upright or position the umbrella so it lies on the ground. (If there's any wind, you'll need to put two or three stones around the base to prevent it from blowing away or may even need to add a stake and tie the umbrella securely to the stake.)

The umbrella will provide shade but also allow plenty of cooling ventilation. Remove it after the sun goes down.

GENERAL FLOWER CARE

A Plant Parasol

▶ Baking sun and heat are often the death of hanging baskets in sunny locations, especially if you're going to be away and can't water once or twice daily. You can buy yourself a day or two by providing some shade for a basket. Just open one of those small collapsible umbrellas and secure it to the hangers with twine.

Keep Her In Check

▶ Lady's mantle is a lovely perennial, but it can reseed a bit too prolifically if you don't deadhead it promptly and thoroughly. But the flower stems are all tangled up in the beautiful leaves, making them difficult to trim easily.

Try this trick, using twist ties, to corral a number of stems at a time. Gather a handful of blooming stems —easier than snipping them individually—and secure them with a twist tie. Then cut just below the tie.

Time this operation for right before the moment that the blooms fade and go brown, and you can hang the minibouquets upside down to dry and enjoy later indoors.

Second-Hand Rose

The next time you're dividing perennials and you find you have too many to place elsewhere in your garden, check in with a local daycare center or residential facility for the elderly.

These organizations often are delighted when you pass along your favorite flowers (especially if you're willing to do the planting) to brighten the days of small children and senior citizens.

A Pole Saw Pronto

▌ If you're trying to prune the top of a tall plant with slender branches, such as a wisteria or honeysuckle, give the following makeshift pole saw a try. Simply duct-tape a serrated knife to the end of a broom or mop handle. With a little luck and persistence, you'll be able to reach up and saw off those branches.

FLOWER MULCHING TIPS

Wipe Out Weeds

▌ When planting warm-season annuals such as marigolds and petunias, it's smart to wait at least a couple of weeks after planting before mulching. This allows the soil to warm up.

If weeds are notorious for sprouting early in your garden, however, create a light layer of mulch to keep them at bay until you can lay down a more substantial layer. Just place a single layer of paper towels over the area you'll be planting. Sprinkle with the lightest possible layer of soil—barely enough to conceal the towels. Cut holes in the towels and plant the annuals in the holes.

In a couple of weeks, the paper towels will be mostly broken down, and you can add a layer of grass clippings, wood chips, pine needles, or other type of mulch up to 2 inches thick.

A foam tray or two at the base of a clematis will help keep its roots cool, ensuring a healthier plant and more blooms.

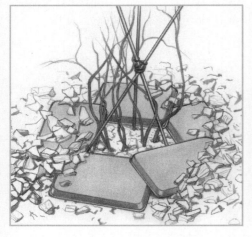

Cool Clematis

▌As the saying goes, clematis like their feet in the shade and their heads in the sun. You can keep their roots comfortably cool with an insulating layer of plastic foam. Use hot soapy water to thoroughly wash one or two of those flat foam trays that meat comes on. Set the trays at the base of a clematis and cover them with mulch. They will insulate the plant nicely against the heat.

SMART FLOWER SUPPORTS

Daffodils Salvaged

❱ Don't you hate it when a late-season snowstorm or ice storm leaves your daffodils bent and broken or your Dutch hyacinths get top-heavy and flop over? You can do a little repair work by getting out there with some of those chopsticks that come with carryout Asian food. Use just one stick per stem to prop it up.

If necessary, sharpen one end of the chopstick with a paring knife and push it gently into the base of the flower, then push the other end into the soil. There's no need to secure the stem further to the chopstick.

Light Up Your Life

❱ Give a young vine support and create outdoor evening lighting at the same time by digging out some of those spare exterior Christmas tree lights (dark green is the least conspicuous). Weave the lights through a trellis or up an arbor. The lights will provide the vine with additional "traction" for climbing. And once you plug them into an outdoor GFIC (one that won't shock even outdoors) outlet, they will add to your evening enjoyment all year round.

It's Curtains for Flopping Flowers

❱ Delphiniums, lilies, and monkshood grow tall and slender in a hurry, setting them up for some serious flopping. To prevent this, you can create a stake that grows with them.

Insert an old expandable curtain rod into the soil next to the plant. Secure the plant to the rod with a strip or two of panty hose. Over the next several weeks, as the plant grows, gently extend the rod to accommodate the taller plant and tie with additional panty hose strips.

New Life for an Old Chair

❱ Turn an old chair into an adorable support for tall flowers such as delphiniums, tall phlox, tall asters, and lilies. Remove the rush or wooden seat from the chair. If you want, give it a coat of paint. Position the chair over one or more plants when they are a foot or two high, just tall enough to tuck through the seat. As the plants grow, the seat will provide them with much-needed support.

Cool Copper

▎ The next time you get a new fridge or freezer or repair the tubing on the one you have, save the old copper tubing to create a modern-looking spiral support for tall plants such as delphiniums, foxgloves, and hollyhocks. Cut off the tubing with a pipe cutter or simply with a large wire snips (the ends will be crimped, but that's okay). Gently work with the coil of the tubing to create a spiraling support and cut to the desired height. Insert the bottom 6 to 12 inches into the soil to keep it upright.

Give damaged long-handled tools new life by using them to create an adorable three-legged tepee to support an annual flowering vine.

Tool Trio

▎Turn long-handled tools with weathered or damaged handles or blades into clever plant supports. Simply collect three of these tools— such as shovels, hoes, or rakes—and insert the handle ends into the soil near any flowering vine that doesn't exceed 8 feet in height. Bind the tools together with twine.

This tool trellis provides ideal support for scarlet runner bean, hyacinth bean, or black-eyed Susan vine. It also works well for a climbing or long-caned tall rose.

Light Support

▎When your floor lamp goes on the fritz, don't pitch it. Use it as an unusual way to get some height in the center of a flowerbed. Cut off the cord (save it to tie stuff later on) and then position the lamp, shade and all, in your flowerbed. Cut away any fabric or stiff paper from the shade, leaving the wire frame. Anchor the base with a few stones, or push it down slightly into the soil. Clematis, shorter morning glories, and hyacinth bean are just a few of the flowering vines that would look gorgeous climbing up your new support.

Put Out Your Antennas

▶ If you break off a car antenna, use it as a garden stake. A plant with a single tall bloom, such as a yucca, is wonderfully supported by this individual stake. Plus, the telescoping antenna can grow as the plant does.

Rake Them In

▶ Tall blooming shrubs such as hydrangeas and rose mallow, as well as lanky daisies and ambitious roses, can spill over into pathways by the end of the summer. But you can use a damaged rake to keep them in their place. Just saw off the bottom half or so of the rake and pound the handle into the ground. The rake will act almost like a comb, holding stray stems up and out of the way.

An old car antenna makes the perfect telescoping plant support for a tall, slender flower such as a delphinium.

Spring in Your Garden

▶ An old box spring (just the metal part, not the wooden frame) makes an effective and offbeat flowering plant support. Just lean it upright against a garden shed or fence and plant honeysuckle, sweet pea, clematis, or other vines at the base. By late summer, you'll have a flowering wall.

Pedals for Petals

▶ An old bike, either rustic and rusty or painted to match your garden color scheme, can be a portable, temporary

Boxed In

In colder climates, some roses, especially hybrid tea roses, need reliable winter protection. Those white foam cones have fallen out of favor because they're not particularly effective. And old-fashioned wrapping in burlap can be awkward and time-consuming. If you live in Zone 6 or colder, try this easy, inexpensive, and earth-friendly way to protect smaller roses.

First, mound several inches of compost or topsoil over the crown of each rose to prevent cold damage. Remove the top and bottom of a cardboard box large enough to slip around the rose. This cardboard "collar" should surround the bottom foot or two of the plant. (Cut back the rose as little as possible; the more stems and foliage it has, the more likely it is to make it through the winter.) Fill the collar with autumn leaves that you've run over with your mower. Your rose will be toasty warm until early spring, when you can remove the box, leaves, and soil.

support for floppy dahlias, daisies, or roses that begin to encroach on your garden pathway. Just park the bike in the flowerbed, adding extra support, if necessary, with a few stakes near the tires. If the bike has a basket, use it to display small pots of flowers. After the blooming season, it's easy to cut back the flowers and roll away the bike.

Raise the Bar

▶ Lilies have such tall stems and large flowers that staking them can be difficult. Corral them instead by removing the seat from an old bar stool and setting the stool on top of the lilies just as they emerge in the spring.

Framed!

▶ You can mount an empty metal or wooden picture frame on a garden fence or stump to help annual vines go vertical. Just weave your climbing nasturtium, sweet pea, or black-eyed Susan vine under and through the frames to support its growth and frame its flowers.

RAVISHING ROSES

A Hot Tip

❯ Wear oven or long-armed barbecue mitts on your hands instead of garden gloves when handling thorny or prickly plants such as roses, cacti, hawthorns, or hardy orange. Thicker and longer than most gloves, the mitts offer better hand and arm protection.

Thorns No More

❯ An old grid-type potato masher makes a good de-thorner for cut roses. Just push each stem through a hole, then pull it out. The thorns will come off easily.

Put the Tweeze On

❯ Tweezers of all sizes come in handy in the rose garden. Use them to squish small green worms, pull off side rose-buds (called disbudding) to encourage bigger blooms, and hold back thorny stems while you cut. Store them outside where they'll be handy in a moisture-proof plastic bag to prevent rust.

Approach with Caution

❯ Cleaning up around your roses in the spring can be a painful chore complete with scratched arms and thorns embedded in fingers. Make the chore a little less traumatic by hauling out those fireplace tongs— the ones you use to turn and adjust logs. They're great for reaching into the center of a rosebush and pulling out dead leaves and debris.

Save your arms and fingers from scratches and thorns by using a pair of fireplace tongs to reach into rosebushes and pull out early-spring debris.

MORE AND BETTER BULBS

No-Strain Planting

▶ Time to pitch your dish drainer? Use it as a planting cage for tulips, hyacinths, and other spring bulbs that mice and other critters like to munch.

Just dig a large planting hole at the appropriate depth for the bulbs and position the drainer in the hole. Add a spadeful or two of soil and position the bulbs at the recommended planting depth (6 to 8 inches for most daffodils, tulips, and hyacinths; 2 to 4 inches for most smaller bulbs, such as crocuses and grape hyacinths). Top completely with soil and rest assured that you'll have a pretty show of bulbs come spring.

SAVE THE PLANET

A Tisket, a Tasket

You can foil a variety of bulb-nibbling pests by planting your bulbs in protective little cages made from plastic berry baskets.

If moles, voles, and other burrowing animals have been a problem in the past, plant each bulb inside a berry basket planted right side up. The mesh is wide enough to accommodate the roots reaching outside the basket, but small enough to protect the bulb from hungry critters.

If squirrels, dogs, and other animals have been digging down from the soil surface, place the berry basket upside down on top of the bulb to protect it from above. With larger bulbs, such as tulips and hyacinths, you'll need to cut a hole 1 to 2 inches across in the bottom of the basket to allow the plant to grow through it. Crocuses, snowdrops, and smaller bulbs can grow right through the mesh.

If both burrowing and digging animals are a problem, create a little cage for your bulb to *really* protect it. Position the bulb in one basket and fill the basket with soil. Then top with another basket and secure it in place with a twist tie or two. Fill the top basket with soil and finish planting.

Rack 'Em Up

▶ Old wire racks from ovens and grills are useful to keep on hand for bulb planting. Squirrels and chipmunks love to dig up bulbs right after they've been planted, but you can foil them by tossing one of these racks on top of the planting spot. Leave it there for a month or so until the soil settles and the bulbs have a chance to sprout underground, making them less attractive to the bushy-tailed critters.

Give old wire racks from ovens and grills new life by using them to protect freshly planted bulbs from squirrels and chipmunks.

Know the Drill

▶ Use your cordless hand drill with the widest auger you have to drill holes in the ground for quick and easy bulb planting. It's a welcome alternative to hacking holes into hard, dry autumn soil.

While you're at it, slip on a smaller drill bit and aerate compacted areas of the lawn, such as the spot where you step off the deck or the space underneath an arbor.

Screen Out Squirrels

▶ Save that window screen, whether it's in the form of a busted screen window or just some pieces of screen cut from a window or door about to be repaired. This is great to place over newly planted bulbs to prevent squirrels from digging down and uprooting the bulbs. If desired, cover the screen with leaves to disguise it and leave it in place until spring. In the meantime, it will also serve as a reminder not to dig in that spot.

X Marks the Spot

▌ It's easy to forget where you planted bulbs when adding other plants or bulbs to the garden. Golf tees make convenient bulb markers, but drinking straws, pickup sticks, Popsicle sticks, and knitting needles work even better. Stick them into the soil above the bulbs, leaving an inch or two showing. They won't be easily dislodged or lost.

Tiles for Tulips

▌ Use leftover tiles from a kitchen or bath project to mark where you've planted tulip or other bulbs and prevent their being disturbed when you work in the rest of the garden. Use a permanent marker or a paint pen to write the name of each bulb on a tile and perhaps to make a nice border around the edge. Lay the tile on the ground, nestling it slightly into the soil. This works best with smaller tiles (5 inches across or smaller), since larger tiles will block the growth of emerging foliage.

No More Ruined Bulbs

▌ Have you ever dug a planting hole in late summer or fall, only to find you just dug into a tulip bulb you forgot was there? You can avoid this problem by using inexpensive plastic clothes hangers to make bulb markers.

Cut the two rounded ends from a plastic hanger. When spring bulbs are blooming, insert one of these markers behind the plant. Later in the season, you'll know that a tulip or daffodil is located right in front of the marker. You can even match the color of the hanger with the color of the flower.

Saved by Shavings

▌ Use little piles of that shaved-wood packing material that comes in bags of summer- and spring-blooming bulbs to mark planting spots. Toss a handful or two of the shavings onto each spot, then press the shavings firmly into the soil to prevent them from blowing away. The color and texture of the shavings are different enough from plant material to alert you that something is underground, and you won't accidentally dig up or plant over the bulbs.

Seal in Freshness

▌ Those foil bags that chips and other crispy snack foods come in can be used for overwintering tender bulbs such as glads, dahlias, and cannas. Wipe clean the inside of the bags, then fill them with sphagnum peat moss. Add the bulbs, cover them with a bit more moss, and label the bags with a permanent marker. Leave the bags open for air circulation and store them in a cool, dry spot over the winter.

Baggy Bulbs

▌ Mesh onion and potato bags are handy for overwintering dahlias, tuberoses, cannas, and other tender bulbs. Keep the bulbs from touching, thereby preventing rotting, by putting them in the bags layered with sphagnum peat moss or foam packing peanuts. Hang the bags in a cool, dry place.

Tuck Them In

▌ In many parts of the country, if you want to save your dahlias from year to year you need to dig up and store them for the winter. In Zones 6 and 7, you can skip this laborious process with the help of an old plastic table-cloth or shower curtain.

In the fall, cut back the dahlias to ground level. Cover the entire area with the tablecloth or shower cur-tain, weighting down the edges with

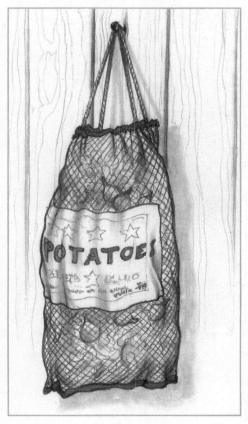

Mesh produce bags, such as those used for potatoes and onions, are well suited for overwintering bulbs.

stones or soil. If aesthetics are a concern, cover the table-cloth with autumn leaves and a few branches, both of which will help insulate the soil further.

The waterproof barrier will protect the bulbs from cold winter rains, which promote rot. In the spring, before new shoots start to emerge from the soil, remove the protective covering.

FLOWERING VINES

Clip It

▶ When training a vine to cling to a trellis or support, a plastic hair clip can get the job done nicely. Simply clip a tendril to the support. The hair clip's tension should be slight enough not to damage the plant. Check on the vine after a day or two, removing the clip when it's no longer needed.

Down to the Wire

▶ Clematis and other flowering vines look beautiful climbing up a light post, but there's nothing on the smooth surface of the post for the plant to cling to. To solve this problem, use a scrap of heavy-gauge wire to create an excellent support.

First, attach the end of the wire to the screw or lateral extension at the top of the post. Then coil the wire down around the post and insert it into the soil.

To protect perennial vines in cold climates, untwist the wire and, with the vine attached, gently push it to the ground. Mulch over the vine for the winter months. In the spring, gently pull the wire up and reattach it to the top of the post.

Drape Your Vines

▶ People often throw out old curtain rods, but you can turn them into a highly functional trellis for a fence or the side of a wooden building.

Attach two rods horizontally to the side of a house, shed, or garage, using the original hardware, if you can. Or screw cup hooks into the building to hold the rods in place. Attach one rod near the ground and the other one several feet above the first one.

Every 6 inches or so along the bottom rod, tie a length of monofilament fishing line. Stretch it straight up to the top rod and tie it in place. Your trellis is just the right size for a row of annual flowering vines.

Next time you change your window treatments, save the curtain rods. Teamed with lengths of fishing line, they make a strong and efficient trellis.

Hang Them Out

▶ Clip vines to their supports with spring-type clothespins. A vine fits nicely into the notch where the clothespin usually attaches to the clothesline. This technique works especially well with lattice.

You can make the clothespins less noticeable by painting them the same color as the support or background. Or add

Gone Fishin'

Don't waste all that wonderful vertical growing space along a wooden fence in your garden. Instead, plant it with vines.

Whether you have just a 6-inch strip of soil along the fence or a whole flowerbed, the key is to provide sturdy support up the fence. Most vines won't grow with nothing more than, say, wood panels to support them.

Solve the problem quickly and cheaply with monofilament fishing line. Just tap a few galvanized nails into the fence with a hammer, making a zigzag pattern up the fence. Then tie with fishing line; it's almost invisible.

In fact, fishing line is an inexpensive substitute for a trellis just about anywhere. Create matching, slender invisible trellises up either side of a front or shed door, up and around your garage door, or up and around a favorite window. The possibilities are endless!

a splash of color to a leafy vine by painting the clothespins a vivid or contrasting color.

Flair with Floss

▶ If you run out of string or twine for a climbing vine, use dental floss instead. It's wonderfully slender and seems to disappear, giving the illusion that the vine is climbing up into thin air. Unflavored, waxed floss stands up best to the weather.

Trailing from a Tree

▶ Use fishing line to create a pretty trellis suspended from the branch of a tree. Tie the fishing line to a low branch and then run it to the ground, tying it to a stick or rock and burying the anchor. Plant a twining annual vine, such as cup-and-saucer vine, at the base of the line. Since the fishing line is invisible, when the vine reaches the branch, it will appear to be growing down from the tree rather than up from the ground.

Reel It In

▶ Give an old fishing rod a new lease on life by turning it into a support for a climbing plant. Simply push the handle end securely into the ground at a slight angle. Pull out enough line to reach the ground and tie the end of the line around a stick or rock. Bury this anchor in the ground.

Alternatively, you can insert the rod straight into the ground and simply allow the line to twist around the rod for additional traction for vines.

Plant a moderate-size vine, such as black-eyed Susan vine or a smaller clematis, at the base of the line.

Vines Away

▶ When it comes time to paint your house, you'll need to get in behind that flowering vine. To keep the vine away from the house gently and securely, carefully pull the vine away, then use a leaf rake to prop up the vine so it doesn't snap off or get otherwise damaged. If the vine is tall, duct-tape a broom handle to the rake handle to lengthen it.

Step by Step

▶ A wobbly stepladder that can no longer support a person will do nicely in the garden, supporting flowers instead. Give it a coat of paint or leave it alone to let it weather to a neutral gray. Position it over a tall rose with sprawling canes, weaving the canes in and out as desired or tying them to the ladder with soft twine.

Or use the ladder as a flower tower, training annual flowering vines up its steps. If the paint tray holder is still sturdy, top it with a pot or two of pretty trailing flowers for even more color.

FLOWER GARDENING ACCESSORIES

Wire Plant Hoops

▶ Rather than buy expensive wire plant support hoops, make your own from wire coat hangers.

Use pliers to untwist four wire coat hangers and then straighten them out. Make a large C-shaped hook on the end of three of the wires. Shape the fourth into a circle, making small hooks at the ends so they are able to connect securely.

There's no need to buy expensive wire plant supports. Turn wire coat hangers into homemade versions.

Push the three straight wires into the ground around the plant. Encircle the plant with the fourth wire and connect the ends. Now insert the circle into the hooks on the three straight wires. If you need a larger support, twist two wires together to form the circle and add an additional "leg."

Simple Stepping-Stones

▶ Stepping-stones are convenient to have throughout your flowerbeds to give you handy "landing pads" as you weed, water, and groom your garden without compacting the soil. The ideal stones may be lurking in your basement or garage, either leftovers from installing new tile or remnants of tearing out old tile. Large (at least 1 foot across) terra-cotta tiles are ideal. But even smaller ceramic tiles can be turned into pavers. Just cut a piece of weather-resistant plywood to accommodate four or more tiles. Attach the tiles to the board with leftover mastic and grout just the way you would attach them to a floor or wall.

From Perch to Plant Stand

▶ The next time a step stool or bar stool goes wobbly on you, give it a new role in the garden as a plant stand. Position the tall seat in the back of a flower border and top it with a large pot. You'll add instant vertical interest to your garden and a bit of character besides.

END-OF-SEASON HELPERS

Do the Twist

▶ Late summer is the best time to dig and divide irises—when they're no longer blooming. But often you can't remember what they looked like. Next year, use twist ties to leave a clue for fall. In the spring, while the irises are still in bloom, gently loop a twist tie in a similar color at the base of one of the tall, slender stalks. For a pink iris, twist a red and a white tie together. If it's a blue and yellow iris, attach both a blue and a yellow twist tie.

Croquet, Anyone?

▶ When you're not knocking balls through those croquet hoops, the hoops can come in handy in the garden. Place a couple of hoops over a tender, newly planted flower. If you're concerned about a late frost, slip a clear plastic bag over the hoops, making slashes in the bag to act as vents. If you're concerned about rabbit or deer damage, slip a mesh potato or onion bag over the flower, securing the ends with soil or stones.

CHAPTER EIGHT

Growing Your Own Fruits and Vegetables

What could be nicer than growing your own fruits and vegetables with minimal expense and effort? Whether it's harvesting high-up berries with the help of fireplace tongs or preventing rot on melons by growing them in a milk jug cradle, we have lots of ways to put everyday or throwaway items to new and inventive uses.

PLANTING POINTERS

A Hoe That Plants

▌ Turn your hoe into a double-duty tool with a scrap of slender PVC (polyvinyl chloride) pipe or any other rigid piping or tubing. Cut it to the length of the hoe handle and attach it to the side opposite the blade with a series of strong rubber bands. This long, slender tool is excellent for dropping seeds into planting holes, a major help to gardeners with problematic backs or knees.

Flat Out

▌ Save those webbed plastic flat trays that annuals come in. They make an easy protector in the veggie garden for newly planted seeds and seedlings.

Simply lay one over seeds and seedlings to protect them from animals. Hold it down with a rock or two. Cats, dogs, and bunnies won't be able to get to the plants, but sun and rain will.

If the trays are too wide to position over your rows, cut them lengthwise into thirds and nestle the two outside portions together to make a longer, narrower webbed tray.

Board Up Your Beans

▌ Crows and other large birds love to pluck bean seeds from the loose, freshly planted earth. Foil them in their attempts with an old trick from farmers. Toss a wooden plank or two on top of a row of beans.

If you don't have any planks handy, just cut an old shower curtain into narrow strips. Or fold newspaper into long strips. Secure the ends with bricks or stones. Check the

---

ONE MAN'S TRASH

Planting Space Cubed

The next time you see some dinged-up, beat-up storage cubes—the modular kind that you stack on top of one another to form shelves—on the curb waiting for the garbage guy, grab 'em You can turn them into excellent planters for edibles. They're an ideal size for patio tomatoes, miniature fruit trees, strawberries, and more. Depending on the type, you may even be able to stack them. Their gridlike design makes them easy to work into a vegetable garden or use to turn a corner of a deck into a garden of edibles.

rows every few days and remove the protection once the beans have sprouted.

Screen Them Out

▶ Keep a collection of screens, such as wood- or metal-framed window screens or old screen doors, in your garage or stacked in a corner of your garden. No matter how ratty they are, they're useful for tossing over new plantings of vegetable seeds for a week or so to keep out everything from cats to birds to squirrels. They may even deter children who would otherwise be tempted to walk over the newly planted bed.

Bottomed Out

▶ If you have an old window box that has rotted out on the bottom, set it in the vegetable garden and plant heat lovers such as peppers, tomatoes, and eggplants in the box. The sides form an instant raised bed that warms up quickly in

Those old, broken-down window boxes have life in them yet. Use them as small raised beds in the vegetable garden to create ideal conditions for plants that need thoroughly warm, well-drained soil to thrive.

Hill on Wheels

Those old auto tires make convenient mini–raised beds for plants that need warm, well-drained soil to get a vigorous start in life. Cucumbers, melons, zucchini, squash, pumpkins, and beans all need to be planted after the soil warms adequately, usually about 2 weeks after your region's last frost date.

For decades, gardeners have planted these veggies in "hills" of mounded soil. You can take the technique one step further by creating mini–raised beds. Just lay a tire on the ground and fill the center with high-quality soil and/or compost. Allow the soil to warm up for a day or two before planting.

Potatoes also are well suited to planting in tires. Plant them the same way you would the other vegetables. When the green growth starts to poke through the soil, top the tire with another tire and fill it with soil. When the growth starts to poke through once again, repeat the process with a third tire. These tire planters can be created with up to five or even six tires.

This tire-planting technique provides your potatoes with the loose, well-drained soil they love. Also, it causes the potato vine to grow longer and therefore produce more potatoes than it would with traditional planting methods. And this method allows you to harvest potatoes just as you need them, without digging up and thereby destroying the whole potato plant.

the spring. If you have lots of window boxes, line them up to make a creative and highly functional garden border.

Don't Kick the Bucket

▶ When planting a new fruit tree, it's important to keep it well-watered during the first few months. You can achieve this by using a 5-gallon plastic bucket. Punch a small hole in the bottom of the bucket with a nail heated over a flame. Plant the bucket alongside the tree, so that only the top 2 to

An old garbage can on wheels makes an ideal container for growing a tropical fruit tree in a borderline climate. The wheels make it easy to move the tree into a protected spot for the winter.

3 inches are showing. Fill the bucket with water, which will drip slowly down to the roots of the tree, where it needs moisture most.

Leave the bucket in place for a month or more, using it as needed to keep the tree well-watered. Then pull out the bucket and fill the hole with soil.

Tropicals on Wheels

▶ That garbage can on wheels makes the perfect oversize pot in which to grow tropical fruits in decidedly non-tropical conditions.

Cut off the top half of the garbage can to make an appropriate-size planter and punch a few holes in the bottom. Plant a tropical fruit tree, such as a banana, lemon, lime, orange, or fig tree, that otherwise wouldn't survive the winter in your climate.

In late fall, before the first frost, wheel the container into any spot that won't dip below freezing, such as a garage, porch, or breezeway. If the area has natural light and the tree continues to grow, give it just enough water to keep it moist and fertilize it lightly only once every 4 to 6 weeks. If the area doesn't have natural light, the tree will go dormant. Water a dormant tree lightly every 2 weeks—just enough so that the soil doesn't shrink away from the sides of the container—and don't fertilize the tree at all.

In the spring, after the last frost date has passed, start watering and fertilizing it again as before. Bring the tree outdoors for a few hours at a time, gradually increasing the time over a week or two, until it stays outside full-time.

Swinging Veggies

▶ Use that old metal swing set to make a one-of-a-kind vertical garden for various edibles. Plant tomatoes at the base of each leg, using the legs as sturdy supports. Run twine from the top crossbar and tie it to a stake stuck in the soil as a support for pole beans, peas, gourds, and more. You can plant a variety of lettuces and greens underneath the swing set, where they will thrive in the light, cooling shade created by the vines.

A Chair Centerpiece

▶ Quaint, bottomless wooden chairs are often displayed in flower gardens, but why not put one in the middle of your veggie patch to serve as a pretty and practical focal point?

Sink an expendable bushel basket or large pot into the seat and fill it with heat-loving pepper plants and onions, alongside petunias, or anything else you'd enjoy seeing on display. Culinary herbs, such as oregano, thyme, parsley, basil, and sage, are other options.

Perhaps you'd like to experiment with flowers known to attract insects that are beneficial to your vegetables. Plants in the aster or daisy family (*Asteraceae*), as well as those in the carrot family (*Umbelliferae*), attract lots of these good guys.

VEGGIE SUPPORTS

A New View

▶ If you have a couple of divided-light windows left over from a remodeling or repair project or find some on the curb, turn them into excellent storable supports for peas and other low-growing vines.

Remove any glass from the windows. Then attach the windows to each other to create a sort of A-frame by screwing large metal hinges into the edges. Position the frame in your garden and plant your peas at the base of it.

A bonus: Toss a piece of plastic over the A-frame and anchor the plastic with rocks. You'll have extra space to stash tomato and other frost-sensitive seedlings until planting time.

Whether you have some old windows on your hands from a remodeling project or you couldn't resist collecting them from the curb, they'll find new life as charming country-style plant supports in your vegetable garden.

Crib Notes

▶ When you're going through the old baby gear and pitching it, save the slats from the crib and playpen, as well as that accordion-style baby gate. They make ideal low supports for pod peas, snap peas, and snow peas.

Keep the slats upright and sturdily in place by pounding tall stakes in front of and behind each. Or connect the slats together, if possible, with hinges, so that you can place the support in a zigzag pattern in your vegetable garden.

VEGGIE LABELS

Let's See Some ID

▶ Hmmm . . . did I plant green beans here or carrots? Keep track of your produce by using empty cans of vegetables, such as corn, green beans, carrots, and tomatoes, as plant labels. Cut out the bottom of each can so that it doesn't collect water and wiggle it into the ground at the end of each row. You'll avoid any confusion as to which budding veggie is which.

So Plastic

▶ What were you thinking when you bought those plastic replicas of veggies to display in your home? They might work marvelously, however, as whimsical plant labels in the garden. Heat a Phillips screwdriver over a flame to punch a hole into each piece of fake produce. Insert a dowel or stick into the hole and mount the stick at the end of the appropriate row.

TOMATO TIPS

Seeing Red

▶ Several university studies prove that tomatoes ripen quicker when red plastic is placed around the roots as a heat-retaining mulch. Accomplish this by saving and storing red plastic shopping bags (they're all over the place during the holiday season). Cut them so they'll lie around the tomatoes in a single thickness, then make a number of slashes in them to allow water to pass through. When planting tomatoes in the spring, lay this mulch around your plants to give them a jump start.

Do Litter

◗ Growing tomato plants out of the bottom of a hanging container has become all the rage. It's also an efficient way to save space and keep the fruit clean. An ideal container is the plastic bucket cat litter comes in—the kind with a handle and an attached lid that flips open. Cut a small opening in the bottom of a clean bucket and slip a small tomato transplant through the hole from the inside. Fill the bucket with a loose, lightweight soil mix and water well. Close the lid and use the handle to hang the bucket. When the soil dries out, just pop the lid open to water the plant.

Grow your tomatoes upside down with the help of a cat litter or other durable plastic bucket. It's a major space-saver and keeps the fruit clean and healthy.

Cozy Tomatoes

◗ When the first frost is threatening in the fall, keep those last, precious vine-ripened tomatoes of the season safe with protectors made from 2-liter soda bottles. Just cut off the top of a clean bottle and slip it over a single tomato or a cluster of tomatoes for the night. Most of the time, the leaves and branches will hold it in place. If not, punch two holes near the rim and attach lengths of twine through the holes. Use the twine to tie the protectors in place.

If the following day is cool and overcast, there's no need to remove the protector. Otherwise, slip the soda bottle off so the fruit doesn't overheat.

Tomato Trellis from Trash

Everyone, it seems, has a favorite method for staking or caging tomatoes, but all involve growing them vertically. This year, if you have the space, try something different. Take advantage of tomatoes' natural tendency to sprawl and grow them horizontally. Growing tomatoes this way spreads them out into a single "layer" so harvesting them is a breeze.

Create a horizontal support to keep the foliage and fruit off the ground, where disease and pests could have a heyday. Make several stakes about 18 inches high from scrap lumber and pound them into the ground. Then string strong twine back and forth to create a net.

Or rummage around the house and garage for other suitable trellis materials: the slats of an old wooden crib or playpen, sections of old fencing, or pieces of lumber laid crisscross. Set them atop stakes or, better yet, use some of those gallon paint cans that have nothing but a bit of dried-up paint in them. They make amazingly sturdy legs.

Swab Away

▶ Your tomato harvest will be much heavier if you improve on Mother Nature and hand-pollinate your tomato plants. Wait until the flowers form and then use a cotton swab to gently touch the inside of each flower, gathering and distributing pollen on the tip of the swab much as a bee would do. Hand-pollinating is especially helpful during a spring when conditions are cold or rainy and the insects aren't as active as they would be in sunnier weather.

Green Tomatoes Longer

▶ When frost threatens and you need to harvest underripe or green tomatoes, put them in a box filled with foam packing peanuts. It's a compact way to store them, and the peanuts prevent bruising and allow air circulation so the tomatoes don't rot.

MELONS AND MORE

Melon Protectors

❯ Prevent your favorite melons, such as cantaloupes and honeydews, from rotting because of contact with the soil.

Make a little cradle for them by cutting plastic milk jugs in half lengthwise. Punch a few holes in the bottom of each half for drainage. As the melons develop, set each into a "cradle" to keep them high, dry, and oh-so-perfect. The plastic cradles also discourage nibbling by rodents.

If you don't want to go to the trouble of cutting up milk jugs, just grab some of those plastic container lids that are always losing their mates or the plastic lids of coffee cans or oatmeal canisters. They'll help keep the melons off the ground as well, although they won't do much to deter pesky nibblers.

Support Your Melons

❯ One of the best ways to grow melons is on a trellis or other upright support. Keeping those leaves high and dry prevents a plethora of diseases. The problem is that the melons grow heavy and tend to drag down or break off prematurely. To prevent this, pamper your melons with some old panty hose. Cut off the legs and use them to form slings around the melons, securing them to the trellis until they're fully ripe and ready to be harvested.

High and Dry

❯ Leftover lattice or trellis plus sturdy PVC or metal pipe equals horizontal support for melons and pumpkins.

Make legs for the support by starting with four T-shaped pipe fittings.

SAVE THE PLANET

Cute, Not Cluttered

When you're reusing things around the house, your veggie garden can get awfully cluttered and junky-looking—all those stakes and furniture parts and bits and pieces. Leftover house paint can come to the rescue. Paint all those odds and ends a single color, and suddenly they'll look decidedly more unified and intentional. The paint also will protect the items so they will last longer outdoors.

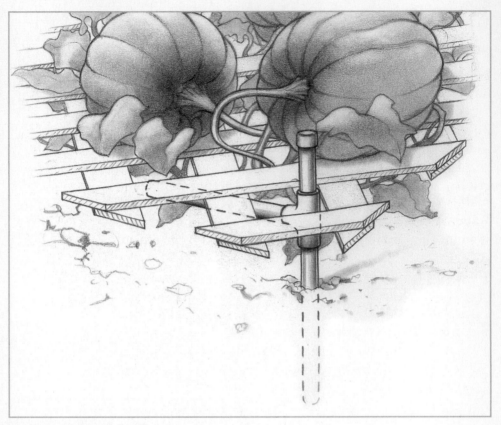

A scrap piece of lattice is ideal for keeping melons and other produce growing high and dry and ripening to perfection.

Cut the pipe into four 2-foot lengths, four 10-inch lengths, and four 4-inch lengths.

For each support leg, fit a 12-inch length and a 4-inch length into opposite ends of a T fitting. Set a 10-inch length into the remaining opening. Add a cap at the end of the 4-inch length to protect you from pokes and scrapes when you're working around the support.

Force the longest length of each pipe leg into the ground, positioned to support a corner of the trellis. Set the trellis over the pipe legs so that it rests horizontally on the 10-inch horizontal pipes, with the 4-inch pipes poking through.

Lift off the lattice to plant. As the melon or pumpkin vines grow, guide them up through the trellis. Growing in their perch above the soil, the fruit will be clean and safe from many diseases and pests.

Tomato Tower Twist

▶ Those wire tomato supports are practically useless for most varieties of tomatoes, which quickly outgrow the tiny supports. If you have some supports collecting dust in the garage, however, bring them out. They're just the right size for sweet and sugar snap peas.

SUPER SQUASH

Patch It Up

▶ Squash vine borers love to invade our favorite winter and summer squash. To stop an invasion, look no further than your first-aid kit.

When you spot any borers (the beetle-like insects burrow into the stems of squash, usually close to the roots), take a sharp paring knife and cut out the affected area. Pick out and smash as many of the borers as possible. Then wash the area with cotton swabs dipped in rubbing alcohol. Stuff a cotton ball or two into the "wound" to prevent the borers from reentering.

LETTUCES AND GREENS

Blanch with Panache

▶ You have probably seen the lovely— and expensive—blanching pots advertised in upscale garden magazines and catalogs. These pots are set over endive, rhubarb, sea kale, celery, and asparagus plants a few to several weeks before their harvest to prevent them from maturing green, a process known as blanching. Gourmets say this creates a more delicate flavor and texture.

But there's absolutely no need to rely on fancy blanching pots. Look

---

SAVE THE PLANET

Hampered Compost

That old wicker hamper makes an efficient compost bin for your vegetable garden. Just set it in the garden and toss weeds, over-the-hill produce, and other refuse into it. If the lid is moisture-resistant, you can keep the heap drier by closing the lid. If you want to keep the pile moister, keep the lid open. Depending on your area's climate, the hamper may last for several seasons.

around your home for easy substitutes. A cardboard milk carton works well for smaller vegetables. For larger vegetables, tip a large pot over the plant. (Anchor a plastic pot with a stone or brick.)

Lettuce Have Relief

▶ Lettuce needs shade on hot days, or it gets tough and bitter. To delay bolting, stick the handle of a croquet mallet into the ground at either end of the row and drape old sheer or lace curtains over the lettuce on very hot days.

Greens Longer

▶ In late spring and early summer, many types of lettuces and other greens "bolt," that is, they get tall and leggy and bitter because of the heat. You can delay this process with the help of a laundry basket.

When temperatures start to hit the 80s, tip a plastic laundry basket (or two or three) over the greens so the bottom shades and cools the plants underneath. Top with a brick or stone or two to prevent the basket from blowing away. You'll add as much as a week to your harvest time.

FRUIT TREES

Wrapped Up in the News

▶ The key to ripening pears from your fruit trees, especially those Kieffers that don't seem at all edible at first, might be lying right on your doorstep. Wrap pears individually in newspaper and store on basement shelves in cardboard boxes until the pears soften. This might take almost until Christmas for eating out of hand, but they will be well worth the wait.

Mulberries in Minutes

▶ If you are lucky enough (or unlucky enough, depending on your viewpoint) to have a mulberry tree on your property, you can harvest the fruit quickly with the help of a large sheet or plastic tarp. Just spread it on the ground and lightly shake a large branch over it. The overly ripe fruit will fall onto the sheet, and you can simply throw the berries onto your compost pile. Then replace the sheet and shake the same branch, this time much harder. Now the perfectly ripe berries will fall onto the sheet. A lot of insects will fall with the fruit, so wait about 5 minutes for them to disperse before you gather up the berries.

HARVEST HELPERS

Harvest in a Hurry

▶ One of the most convenient harvest baskets of all is right in front of your eyes—in or next to your kitchen sink. It's that plastic, metal, or wooden basket-type drainer that you use for drying dishes. When it's free of dishes, take it outside and load it up with produce. Just place the drainer in the sink and rinse off your vegetables and the drainer at the same time.

In a hurry? Grab that dish drainer on your way to the veggie garden for a fast, easy harvest basket.

Save That Bubble Wrap!

Bubble wrap is invaluable in harvesting any fruit that can split or bruise. Use it to line buckets or baskets. If you want to be extra careful, add a bit of bubble wrap between the layers of fruit as you fill a container.

For trees laden with small ripe fruit, such as cherries, try shaking some of the cherries down onto the bubble wrap. For bush fruits, lay a piece of bubble wrap on the ground near where you're harvesting and drop the berries directly onto the wrap. Then just gather up the wrap and take it indoors.

Best of all, bubble wrap comes clean with just a quick blast of water from the hose.

Beyond Eggs

One of the best all-around harvest baskets is a metal egg basket—the kind you might have picked up at an antiques store or flea market for other uses. It's not only decorative and looks pretty even when rusty, but it's also ideal for loading with fresh produce. Just wash your harvest outside under the hose before bringing it into the house.

Step Right Up

If your knees aren't what they used to be, borrow your kids' or grandkids' outgrown step stool—the kind they used to reach the sink and wash their hands. Leave it in the vegetable garden 24/7 so that whenever you go out for a little weeding or harvesting, you have an easy seat from which to work. This is especially useful if you have raised beds.

Fantastic Floss

When it comes time to braid onion or garlic, dental floss makes a light but tough string with which to braid and hang the produce. Floss is also ideal for stringing up apple slices to allow them to dry. Or thread some floss through a darning needle and run it through beans that you want to dry. They'll stay high and dry and take up less precious counter space.

Stash That Produce

If you have squash, melons, tomatoes, peppers, eggplants, potatoes, zucchini, apples, or other produce coming out of your ears with no place to store it until you can give it away or process it, dig out that ratty old duffel bag. Use it to store produce for a day or two until you need it. Line it with bubble wrap to cushion the harvest. It's also a convenient solution if you're going to a friend's house to share your garden bounty (or pick up some of hers) and need an easy way to lug all those tasty goodies.

Bagged Lettuce

❯ Those mesh bags that onions and potatoes come in are handy for harvesting and washing lettuce. Tuck the freshly picked lettuce into a bag right in the garden. Then bring the bag indoors and wash it by repeatedly dunking the bag into a large bowl (or your kitchen sink) filled with water.

If you're not in a hurry, just hang the bag on the knob of an upper cabinet and let it drip onto a cloth. If you are in a hurry, you can blot the lettuce dry in the kitchen, but even easier (and kind of fun) is taking the lettuce outside and swinging it gently around in circles for a few seconds. An instant salad spinner!

Bounteous Berries

❯ When harvesting blackberries or other thorny berries, wear a canvas apron with lots of pockets in front. Stash kitchen tongs and/or spring-type clothespins in one of the pockets. These are indispensable for grabbing a thorny branch to pull it out of the way so that you can get to other branches and berries.

Fork It Over

❯ If you're lucky enough to have elderberries growing on your property, you know they're delicious but labor-intensive to harvest. Make the job easier by cutting off the clusters and then using an ordinary table fork to pluck berries off each cluster (a

 Drying Racks

Onions, potatoes, garlic, winter squash, and pumpkins all need to be "cured" by drying them in a warm, dry, well-ventilated spot out of direct sunlight. They'll dry better if you put them on a rack of some sort. Here are some ideas to get you started.

1 Old screens, set on bricks or stones
2 Old or extra oven racks
3 Old outdoor grill racks
4 Old cookie or baking racks
5 Inverted wicker laundry baskets
6 Old fencing, propped up on bricks
7 Slatted wooden or metal mesh benches, chairs, or tables
8 Wire shelves

cluster can contain hundreds of individual berries). Alternatively, if you have some ½-inch hardware cloth lying around, position it over a bucket and rub the clusters over the wires for even faster separating.

Belt Bucket

❱ When picking berries or other small fruits, free up both hands with a belt bucket made of a clean plastic milk jug and an old belt (or even the belt you're wearing at the time). Cut off the top of a 1-gallon milk jug, above the handle. Holding the belt and the jug in your hand, loop the handle through the belt and buckle it on. As you pick, drop the berries (the ones you don't eat) into the bucket.

If the berries are especially fragile, such as raspberries, punch several holes in the bottom of the jug and store them right in it. That way, you won't have to risk damaging them by dumping them into a larger container. And with the holes, you can rinse the berries in the jug immediately before serving—even less bruising!

Long Tongs

❱ Reaching higher-up branches on many fruit trees can be difficult. Add another foot or two to your reach with a pair of barbecue, fireplace, or long kitchen tongs. They're surprisingly efficient for grabbing a branch and pulling it down toward you.

Barbecue or other tongs are a handy harvest helper when it's time to pick cherries, pears, and other high-up fruits. Use the tongs to pull each branch down toward you.

Bunches of Berries

❱ You can put together a terrific system for collecting, toting, and temporarily storing berries with the help of half-gallon milk cartons. Just cut off the bottom few inches of each carton. If you want to wash the berries in the carton, make a number of slashes in the bottom. These cartons fit neatly into those plastic flats that three- and four-packs of annuals come in for easy toting.

Bungee the Bounty

▶ Make a quick and handy harvesting bucket by wrapping a bungee cord around your waist and attaching each end to the handles of a strainer. Now your hands are free for picking, and the beans or peas go right into the strainer, ready to rinse.

Easy Digging

▶ A large spading fork makes harvesting root crops such as carrots and potatoes much easier. But if you don't have one, you don't need to go out and buy one just for harvesting. Grab that barbecue fork instead. Used in conjunction with your spade, it's a slick way to remove root crops from the soil.

Going to Pots

▶ If you have lots of tomatoes or if green beans just keep coming, the simplest, cheapest storage solution may be lurking in your garage: plant pots. Whether they're black plastic or beige foam types, large pots are super for collecting and temporarily storing produce. They even have drainage holes so you can rinse the produce right in the containers. For best results, wait to rinse until right before using.

Handy Harvest Haulers

▶ Those giveaway canvas tote bags or your kids' old book bags or backpacks can be the foundation of a convenient harvest kit. Stash one by the back door packed with your

Suited to a Tee

What could be nicer than dashing out the door right before dinner to grab some garden-fresh produce? Staying clean while you do it, that's what!

If you still have on your nice work clothes, going out to the garden and lugging in a melon or hauling mud-spattered tomatoes and lettuce can get a bit messy. Prevent this by keeping an extra-large T-shirt near the back door and slipping it on before you harvest. Hem the bottom into a pouch to make a convenient impromptu sling for bringing in more veggies than you anticipated.

If conditions are really muddy, slip plastic grocery bags over your shoes to protect them as well.

harvest supplies—a knife, scissors, plastic bags, and so on. The bag is also great for loading up with produce to bring indoors.

A Berry Welcome Mat

▶ An old section of carpet or an old scatter rug can come in handy when you go into the berry patch for some serious picking. Lay the carpet or rug down on top of the overgrown brambles and then stand on it to prevent stickers from clinging to your pants.

Catch All

▶ Have an old plastic basin lurking about? Store it outside by the garden hose to use as the perfect combination harvester/produce washer.

A basin is flat and shallow, making it ideal to spread out fragile produce—even fruit as easily bruised as strawberries and raspberries. It's also the ideal shape and size for filling with water from the hose outside and giving produce a preliminary rinse before bringing inside.

Store it where it's easy to access by driving two large nails into the siding above the hose. Or punch a hole in its side with a hot nail, heated over a candle. Thread a short length of twine through the hole and knot it to form a loop. Hang the basin from a nail or hook above your garden hose.

Scrub A Dub Dub

▶ If you decided that that plastic bath scrubber, the kind sold for use with moisturizing liquid body soaps, isn't for you, you can still use it outside on your veggies.

ONE MAN'S TRASH

Pallet Planters

Can we ever find enough uses for wooden pallets? They're widely used in transporting freight, but once they're damaged, they often end up in the landfill.

Check with your local supermarket or other retailers about saving damaged pallets for you. If you stack two of them, open sides facing up, they make an effective raised bed for shallow-rooted plants such as squash, cucumbers, melons, and other vining plants. Nail the two pallets together, position them in the garden, and fill with a blend of compost and topsoil.

It's great for cleaning mud and dirt off potatoes, carrots, and other root vegetables. And best of all, it hoses off nicely and dries quickly. Hang it from a nail or hook right above your outdoor faucet.

WEEDING HELPERS

Paper Pushing

▶ Newspaper, topped with grass clippings, is one of the best mulches around for the vegetable garden. Weeds find it nearly impenetrable, and it prevents disease-inducing mud and soil from making contact with produce.

However, it's not easy to fit pages of newspaper around tighter plantings, such as rows of beans or lettuce. Solve the problem by tearing newspaper into strips anywhere from 2 to 8 inches wide. Roll them up into neat bundles and keep them close at hand with the rest of your garden supplies in a carryall.

When you're out weeding in established, tightly planted rows or patches of veggies, you can just lay these strips where you need them. Top with grass clippings or, better yet, the weeds you just pulled up.

Rugged Rugs

▶ If you are ready to discard a rug—or see somebody else's going out on trash day—remember that rugs are extremely useful in the garden. Use heavy shears or a box cutter to slice the rug into strips approximately the same width as your garden rows. These strips are invaluable for blocking weeds and providing a mud-free path for walking or sitting while gardening. (If you use the strips as mulch, you can always top them with straw, pine needles, or wood chips for a more natural look.)

In the fall or spring, when you're getting ready to work the soil once again, just roll up the strips and put them aside. Then lay them down again come planting time. Your rug strips are likely to last for years.

Off the Hook

▌ There are too many telephone books in the world—especially after telephone book delivery days, when you see phone books poking out of everyone's trash or your office is getting ready to pitch the oldies. But you can use these books as mulch in your vegetable garden.

First, remove the covers. If the phone books are slender—just a half inch or so—lay them singly in a row. Fatter phone books can be ripped into sections about $\frac{1}{2}$ inch thick.

This mulch will last a surprisingly long time—a year or two. And as the books break down, they'll feed the soil nicely. When they become too decomposed to serve as mulch, just till them into the soil or toss the chunks onto the compost heap.

Noodling Around

▌ Don't have a hand cultivator—that funny forklike tool designed for loosening and breaking up the top layers of soil? You can always grab a pasta fork instead. Its clawlike construction makes it nearly as well-suited to the task.

Cultivating the soil allows water to penetrate more easily and prevents small weeds from taking hold.

PEST AND DISEASE CONTROL

Prevention Is the Best Cure

▌When you're pruning fruit trees or working in the garden in late summer with diseased plants, you can easily spread diseases from one plant to another.

One solution is to use those sanitizing wipes from your kitchen to wipe off your hands and tools in the garden as well. Or make your own

Sanitizing wipes can disinfect more than your hands. Take them out into the garden to prevent the spread of diseases when you're pruning trees or working with diseased vegetables.

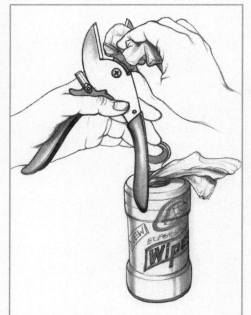

homemade version. Just mix together about a pint of water and a cup of rubbing alcohol. Add a tablespoon of liquid hand soap (preferably the moisturizing kind to keep your hands soft) and shake well.

Use the mixture to moisten a few rags or reusable paper towels. Tuck them into a plastic bread bag or a resealable plastic bag. Store them in your garden carryall to keep at your side while you're working in the garden.

It's Curtains for Pests

▶ Put those old lace or sheer curtains to use even if they are soiled, torn, or worn. Drape them over cabbage, broccoli, and carrot plants to keep out carrot rust flies and cabbage butterflies. If the curtains grow heavy after a rain, add stakes at the ends and middle of each row so the fabric falls like a tent over the vegetables and keeps out the insects.

Scarecrow on the Go

▶ A scarecrow is most effective if you move it around often. Make the moving process easier by building a scarecrow on wheels. Simply put a pail head and clothes on an old golf cart or upright vacuum cleaner. Now you can wheel this bird deterrent to different parts of the garden on a regular basis, and you don't need to pound a stake into the ground at every new location.

Bye-Bye, Worms

▶ Don't you hate it when little green worms hide in your lettuce, broccoli, and cabbage? Fortunately, the solution to getting rid of those harmless but icky worms is no farther away than your saltshaker. Place the freshly harvested crops in a basin or large bowl of cold water, then add a teaspoon or two of salt. In a few minutes, any stowaways will float to the surface.

Hang Those Baskets

▶ If you have any wire forms for moss hanging baskets lying about, consider putting them to new use protecting tender seedlings from crows, digging animals, and pets. Just invert

If they're not otherwise engaged, wire forms used for moss hanging baskets are excellent protection from dogs and rabbits for small tomato and other seedlings.

the baskets over tomato, pepper, and other plant seedlings. Anchor each basket with a stone on top, or make wire "staples" by cutting and bending lengths of coat hangers into elongated U shapes. Once the plant brushes the top of the basket, remove it.

Let 'Em Sprawl

▎Staking or caging tomatoes is the traditional way to keep them up off the soil and therefore more disease-free. But if you have neither the time nor the inclination to stake or cage, try letting your tomatoes sprawl. Keep them up off the ground with items you may have around your house or garage, such as screens set on top of bricks, wooden pallets, or milk crates.

CONTROLLING FRUIT PESTS

Scary CDs

▎Birds love to steal ripe cherries, but give this novel method of thwarting them a try. Fill the tree with old or freebie CDs. The reflective, moving CDs are believed to frighten off birds.

Spread the CDs throughout the tree, hanging some directly on branches and threading others on monofilament fishing line to make a garland. Knot the line around each CD to spread them out evenly and string this unusual garland on the branches.

Be sure to remove the CDs after harvesttime because supposedly, birds will eventually catch on that the CDs are harmless, rendering your clever trick ineffective over time.

Neater Netting

▶ When placing netting over blueberries, strawberries, and other fruits to protect them from birds, the netting is more effective if you can hold it up off the crop so that the smart critters can't just nibble right through it. Stakes work reasonably well, but they have an annoying tendency to poke through the netting. Prevent this with the help of aluminum soda cans. Just slip them over the stakes to round the ends and prevent poking. Plastic soda bottles also work nicely.

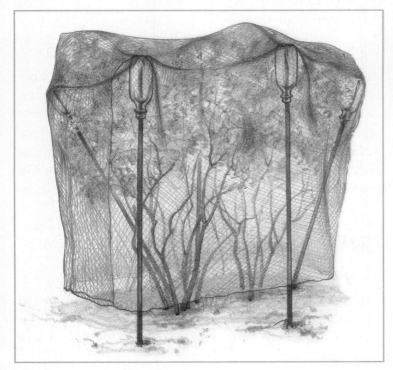

Prevent stakes from poking through protective netting by slipping soda cans or plastic bottles over the ends.

No Blueberries for the Birds

❯ If you've ever had a bride or a ballerina in the family, chances are you have some tulle around the house. This is an excellent free netting to use over blueberry bushes to prevent birds from snitching the fruit. Just wrap the bushes gently with the tulle. It should catch on the branches to hold it in place, although in some cases you may need some twine to hold it down.

MORE GROWING TIPS

Buckets of Potatoes

❯ You can grow potatoes even if all the gardening space you have is on your patio. Just punch drainage holes in the bottoms of 5-gallon buckets or oversize black plastic nursery pots. Plant your potatoes right in the buckets. When it's time to harvest, just dump the buckets.

Veggie Sunscreen

❯ Not only do people benefit from sunscreen, but spinach, lettuce, and peas do, too. After all, if they get too hot, greens such as lettuce and spinach tend to bolt—that is, send out long flowering stalks and go tough and bitter. Peas become tough with too much heat.

So when you finish a home window replacement project, save those old window screens and use them to block the light from late-spring crops. You may simply lean them against each other, forming A-frames. (Velcro is the simplest way to hold them together, but if you are planning on years of use, hinges are a better option.) Or you may prefer to form a screen roof over the rows by laying the screens horizontally on cinder blocks, hay bales, inverted pails, or whatever vertical supports you have on hand.

CHAPTER NINE

Low-Care Lawns

Nothing sets off a garden like a beautiful green lawn. And a beautiful lawn doesn't mean spending lots of money or using lots of chemicals. It just takes a little scrounging and a bit of know-how. Use newspaper as a mulch to establish ground cover on a slope; try vinegar to spot-treat weeds; use a coffee can as a low-tech chinch bug detector. You'll find your lawn never looked better.

An oatmeal box or similar container makes an innovative, free seed spreader. Just shake!

Help sod get established faster by holding it securely in place with sod staples you fashion from wire coat hangers.

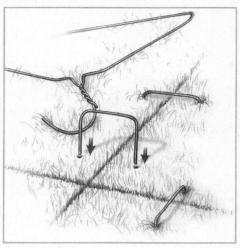

PLANTING LAWNS

Seed Shaker

▶ When you're planting or overseeding a lawn with grass seed, spread the seed more efficiently and evenly by creating a seed shaker, not unlike a giant saltshaker.

Start with any sealable plastic or cardboard container, such as a plastic milk jug or an oatmeal box. Use a sharp paring knife to whittle small holes in the bottom of the container. It's better initially to make too few rather than too many holes—you can always add more holes even after you've filled the container with seed. Once the container is filled, put the lid back on and gently shake the container over the lawn.

Even more convenient, but not quite as efficient: Pour the seed into a plastic or clay pot that has just a few holes in the bottom. If the seed comes out too fast, partially block the holes with duct tape.

Sod Staples

▶ Planting sod on a slope? You certainly don't want it to slip even a millimeter out of place. Having those ends butted up firmly against one another is critical to keeping the sod moist.

Try creating large soil staples from wire coat hangers. Snip the hook off each hanger and cut the resulting triangle in half. You'll have two roughly V-shaped pieces. Make a bend in each to make a squared-off staple. (The long sides don't need to be exactly the same length.)

Another idea: If the soil is moist, grab a few of those croquet hoops and push them in all the way.

Apply a Damp Cloth

▶ The key to getting sod off to a vigorous start is keeping it adequately moist. Watering once or twice a day is important, but you can prevent drying out by creating what is essentially a large sheet of moist mulch over the grass.

First, lay a light-colored sheet, cotton or sheer curtains, or a tablecloth (lace is especially good) over the grass. Hold the sheet in place with a series of small rocks along the edges or stakes driven through the corners. Wet the sheet thoroughly and keep it moist for 3 to 4 days. Since the cloth is light-colored, it will let in enough light, but it's also thick enough to prevent evaporation. A bonus: The fabric will prevent hungry birds from pecking out the seeds. Remove the fabric after 4 days maximum.

Sledding in Summer

▶ When planting a new lawn, the last thing you want to do is mess up your neatly tilled or raked soil with the gouging wheels of a wheelbarrow or yard cart. So when you need to haul a heavy bag of a soil amendment over this pristine soil,

Dust off your kid's plastic snow saucer and use it to drag soil amendments and other supplies when planting a lawn and working on freshly tilled soil. It doesn't make ruts the way a wheelbarrow would.

3 Ways to Level a Lawn for Planting

When preparing a large area to plant grass, you usually need to level the area first. If you have dumped a lot of topsoil or compost onto your lawn in an effort to fill low spots, you also need to level the area. Try these innovative devices for a more level lawn.

1 Make a drag made from a wooden pallet and rope. Tie the rope to the pallet and pull it across the lawn. (Knotting the rope and wearing sturdy gloves makes this task easier.) After the first drag, you'll get even better results if you weight the pallet with about 50 pounds, using rocks, buckets filled with soil, or, for some good clean family fun, a kid.

2 Pull a hose across the area.

3 Drag a board across the lawn.

plunk the bag on a child's plastic snow saucer. Tie a rope to the handle and pull the saucer over to where you need it with only minimal disturbance of the soil.

An Ash Can

▶ When you know you'll be planting a new lawn come spring, save your wood ashes in a large garbage can during the winter. Come planting time, spread the ashes over the area to be planted to improve fertility. This works best in areas where the soil is acidic, such as many regions of the Northwest and Northeast, because ashes can make the soil more alkaline. Avoid adding ashes in areas where the soil is already alkaline, including many parts of the West.

Cover Up

▶ Bring old bedsheets out to the yard on the day you seed your lawn. Cover flowerbeds, brick or flagstone paths and patios, and other areas where volunteer grass might be a problem. Then seed as usual. The sheets will prevent windblown grass seed from falling into the beds or cracks and sprout as weeds.

How Cool

▶ After seeding a lawn, you'll often have quite a bit of grass seed left over in a plastic bag. Keep the seed dry and protect it from extreme heat and cold (critical to maintaining the viability of the seed) by storing it in a small foam or plastic cooler. This also protects the half-full bag from ripping or spilling.

Plug Away

▶ When you plant or sod a new lawn, get out one of those large plastic flats that annuals come in. Add top-quality soil to the flat and sprinkle it with grass seed or set sod on top of it. Water well and keep the flat in a sunny but sheltered spot. Keep this reserve of grass on hand for patching the inevitable mistakes or problem areas in your new lawn as they crop up.

Flat-Out Brilliant

▶ When sprinkling grass seed by hand over a freshly tilled, raked, and smoothed lawn, you definitely do not want to compact the soil by stepping on it. To avoid this, flatten a number of cardboard boxes and use them as temporary stepping-stones (or a bridge, depending on your preference and whether you'll be wheeling things in) to get to all areas of the newly worked soil. Remove the "stones" as you go so you can seed the spots underneath.

LAWN WEED CONTROL

A Shady Proposition

▶ If a small area of your Kentucky bluegrass lawn has been invaded by crabgrass, use this handy tip to defeat the crabgrass once and for all. Cover the infected spot with several sheets of wet newspaper. Weight the paper with stones or bricks, then remove it after 10 days. The bluegrass will be yellowed from the lack of light but

---

ONE MAN'S TRASH

In Shreds

Straw is often used as a mulch over grass seed to keep it cool and moist until it can germinate. But it's not always easy to haul straw in, say, the back of a compact car. If you work in an office or volunteer in one, however, it's quite likely that you have easy access to boxful upon boxful of shredded paper, which works just as well.

Scatter the shredded paper lightly over newly planted grass seed. It works the same way as straw, although it tends to mat down more, so be sure not to use too much.

Once the grass is a half inch or so high, remove as much of the paper as you can by hand to let in more light. Some bits and pieces will probably remain, but this is okay because it continues to provide shade. When the grass is about an inch high, it should be able to withstand a gentle raking, which should remove any of the remaining paper shreds.

will recover quickly. Because crabgrass isn't shade-tolerant, it will have died.

Put a Dent in Dandelions

▶ Do you have trouble bending down to dig out dandelions? A surprisingly effective way to prevent their spread is to knock off the flower buds before they go to seed. This won't get rid of the plant, which is a perennial, but it will at least prevent it from spreading.

Look to your sports equipment for handy tools to rip off those flower heads. Select the weapon of your choice—a croquet mallet, a badminton racket, or a tennis racket—and get out there and swing, knocking the buds off the tall, easily snapped stems. In just a few minutes, you can prevent the formation of thousands of dandelion seeds.

A Little Dab Will Do Ya

▶ Spot-treat problem weeds with this nifty trick. On a sunny, dry day, dip a foam paintbrush into some vinegar. Dab it on the plantain, creeping Charlie, or other broad-leaved weeds plaguing your lawn.

For even easier application, duct-tape the paintbrush to a 2-foot branch or dowel. No bending over!

Make a couple of snips on the end of a curtain rod to create a handy dandelion digger.

Dig Those Dandelions

▶Create a nifty dandelion digger for your garden that really gets the job done. With their long taproots, these perennials will not die unless you remove at least the top 2 inches of roots from the ground. A flat metal curtain rod does the job effectively. Make a V-shaped notch at one end with tin snips, and you'll have a handy tool for popping the weeds out. This tool, like all dandelion tools, works far better if you use it when the soil is moist and soft.

AERATION

Sport a Healthy Lawn

▶ If you have heavy clay soil with little organic matter in it, you need to aerate your lawn periodically. To do so, just put on those old sports shoes that have spikes or cleats. Even if your knees prevent you from rounding the bases, you can simply wear these shoes when you mow the lawn to aerate the soil.

Note: Unnecessary aeration can actually cause compaction because it introduces too much air into the soil and speeds the decomposition of organic matter, the presence of which helps keep the soil loose.

Spot Aeration

▶ Ever notice how some parts of the lawn really get a lot of traffic and compaction? How about that spot right at the base of the deck stairs, that strip along the driveway that you always seem to back the car over, and that path the neighborhood kids make on the corner?

You can keep these areas in better shape by aerating them three or four times a year, using a large screwdriver or a small crowbar. Make large, deep (a couple of inches) holes

There's no need to rent heavy equipment to aerate small problem areas of your lawn, such as at the base of steps. A large screwdriver will do the trick.

about an inch apart in the problem areas using the screw-driver or crowbar and a mallet. These holes will help water, soil, and air reach grass roots so the grass is at its lushest, healthiest best.

MOWING BASICS

Clean Up Your Act

▶ Have you looked at the underside of your lawn mower lately? You may discover the reason for its sluggish action—a buildup of matted grass. To help you get into the habit of keeping those blades clean, keep an old dustpan and hand-held brush or broom next to where you park your mower. After you finish mowing and turn off the mower, use the brush to whisk away the grass clippings around the blades and over the rest of the mower. Catch the clippings in the dustpan and toss them onto your compost pile.

Alternatively, salvage that brass- or steel-bristled brush that's gotten too beat-up to clean the grill. It's often just right, even with badly bent bristles, to clean a mower blade.

Mow High

▶ It's best to mow most cool-season grasses 3½ to 4 inches high. That's because tall blades of grass shade the soil, keeping it moister and preventing weed seeds from germinating.

A healthy lawn is a high lawn. A down-sized ruler made from a Popsicle stick helps you double-check the height at which your mower is cutting.

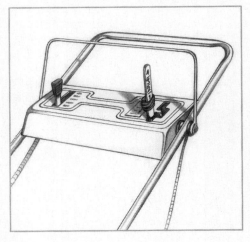

You can adjust your mower blade to a specific height, but sometimes it's still hard to tell whether you're mowing high enough. If you want a little reassurance, craft a mini-ruler from a Popsicle stick with 2-, 3-, and 4-inch marks. Secure it to one of the levers on the mower with a rubber band. Pull it off whenever you want to check exactly how high the mower is mowing and adjust it accordingly.

6 Items to Turn into Lawn Edging

Mowing is a pleasure when there's a good edging around the lawn. Flowers are less likely to flop into the path of the machine, and there is clear delineation of bed and lawn that makes it easy to figure out where to steer the mower. Also, a crisp, clean edge on a flower garden just *looks* nice.

Try these salvaged materials for edging.

1 Old aluminum gutters. Made from flexible aluminum, they are easy to straighten and flatten—just step on the curved seams. You can sink this former gutter 6 inches into the ground and shape it to match the contour of your lawn.

2 Strips of clear or dark plastic rug runner or carpet protector. Cut the plastic into strips 6 inches wide and use as an invisible barrier between lawn and bed. Top with a thin covering of soil or mulch to disguise them.

3 Scraps of 2-by-4s or similar lumber. Cut them approximately 6 inches long and use a hand trowel to set them into the soil, cut sides up and protruding just an inch or two above the soil. These resemble the pre-assembled wood edging available at garden centers.

4 Leftover 4- by 4-inch ceramic tiles. Dig a shallow trench about 1 inch deep and 5 inches wide. Fill it almost full with sand. Set the tiles into the sand and brush more sand over them. You can also set them flat along the edge of flowerbeds for a pretty mowing strip. (*Note:* Since interior ceramic tile doesn't hold up to severely cold weather, this works best in regions where temperatures seldom dip below 20°F or so.)

5 Leftover black rubber or plastic base trim. Used to finish off flooring in kitchens and bathrooms, this trim is wonderfully flexible. Dark-colored trim is the least conspicuous. Bury it so that just ½ inch or so is aboveground.

6 Old or leftover corrugated plastic roofing (the kind often used to cover patios). Cut into narrow strips about 4 to 6 inches wide. Insert into the soil by tapping with a mallet for a highly durable lawn edging.

Give 'Er a Squirt

▶ If you get into the habit of cleaning your lawn mower after each use, it will probably keep your repair bills down and extend the life of the mower. You can also enhance your mower's longevity with this quick step. After each cleaning, spray the undercarriage and blades with nonstick cooking spray. It both lubricates and prevents materials from sticking. Keep the can in the storage area near your mower for easy access.

Mow and Sow

▶ For most lawns, you can hardly seed enough. All season long, it seems as if there are bare patches to cope with and you never spot them until you're right on them. Solve this problem by keeping some grass seed with you at all times when you mow. It's easy. Simply duct-tape an airtight cylinder, such as an empty potato chip or tennis ball can, to the handle of your lawn mower and fill it with seed. When you spot a bare patch, repair it on the spot.

Early Riser

▶ The next time you absolutely need to mow early, well before a heavy dew might dry, try this trick—assuming you have a small lawn. Pull out all those old tablecloths, curtains, and sheets you keep in the garage for throwing over the annuals before a frost. Lay them over your lawn the night before you plan to mow. In the morning, just pick up the dew-laden cloths and mow to your heart's content. (The grass will be bent down a bit. If necessary, drag the garden hose crosswise across it to fluff it up.) After you have finished mowing, spread the cloths out on the grass to dry before packing them away.

A Clean Sweep

▶ When small bits of leaves or gravel get onto your lawn, it's tricky to get them out. Most rakes aren't up to the task because the tines are too far apart. As a solution, head into the house and reach into your broom closet. An old-fashioned whisk broom or any other fairly stiff broom works beautifully to sweep the debris into an easily removable pile. (Don't use a push broom. It's too dense, and you run the risk of brushing away chunks of grass as well.)

FERTILIZING TIPS

Flour Power

▶ Maybe you no longer bake your own bread. Or you don't want to throw out Aunt Florence's flour sifter. Either way, give that sifter a new job as a handheld spreader for fertilizer granules for a small lawn. Be sure to use a permanent marker to label it as a fertilizer spreader so that others in your household won't use it for food purposes.

Shake It

▶ You don't need a fancy spreader to apply lime or fertilizer to your lawn. Instead, just fill a sturdy brown paper bag with the amendment and poke the bottom with an ice pick several times. Walk back and forth across the lawn, dusting the grass as you go.

Dust Off Rust

▶ A lawn spreader used to apply moss control products or fertilizers usually throws small amounts of the products onto your sidewalk or patio. If a soil amendment contains iron, you wind up with rusty orange stains on the concrete. Next time, prevent rust spots by laying an old sheet or two on top of the concrete. After you're done, just shake the sheets out into the lawn and stow them away.

WATERING HOW-TO

How Dry Is It?

▶ Give an old, long screwdriver new life. When you're not sure whether your new lawn has been watered enough, push the screwdriver into the soil. If you find it hard to penetrate 6 inches or so, your lawn needs water. You can easily plunge a screwdriver into an adequately watered lawn.

LAWN PEST CONTROL

No Rinsing Necessary

▶ If you're noticing fine webs on your lawn laced with dew, you may have destructive sod webworms. To check for these, combine 2 tablespoons dishwashing liquid and 1 gallon water. Saturate infested areas of the lawn with this soapy mixture and watch for webworm larvae to float to

5 Ways to Reuse Water for Your Lawn

"Gray water" has long been the term for water used in the house and then recycled for landscaping purposes. There are elaborate gray water recycling systems, but you can recycle water for your lawn easily. (*Note:* Unless you're putting soapy water on your lawn constantly, such as every other week, it won't hurt the grass. In fact, it can suffocate certain harmful insects and actually help your turf.)

1 Bathe your dog and other pets on the lawn.

2 When you're cleaning the fish tank, dump it on the grass. It's chock-full of beneficial nitrogen.

3 Dump the kids' wading pool on the grass.

4 Wash the car on the lawn. Of course, you need to be careful of soil compaction, so you don't want to do this every week. But once a month or so, as long as the soil is dry, will be more helpful than harmful. Plus, the soil will absorb the soapy water, preventing it from getting into the gutter and polluting water supplies.

5 When emptying or cleaning out your water garden, use a hose to siphon the water to various parts of the lawn. Like the fish tank water, it's rich in nitrogen.

the surface. Applying BTK (*Bacillus thuringiensis* var. *kurstaki*) when pests are in their larval stage (about 2 weeks after moths appear) will help control also these nuisances.

It's a Chinch

▶ Chinch bugs are the bane of many a lawn, especially in dry conditions. To check whether these critters are taking over your backyard, do a little test in late winter as soon as the weather starts to warm up. (Chinch bugs can start to do damage as early as the end of March in some climates.)

Remove the top and bottom from an empty 2-pound coffee can. Sink it halfway into the soil and fill it with water. Any chinch bugs in the soil will float to the top.

Use a coffee can filled with water to check the chinch bug population in your lawn.

If you have a chinch bug problem, control it by keeping the soil very moist. In moist soil, a naturally occurring fungus keeps chinch bugs under control.

Get Rid of Moles

▶ They dig; they burrow; they make our lawns look like holy heck. Got moles? Try this home remedy. Stick empty, thin-necked soda or beer bottles upside down and at a slight angle in their holes. The sounds that result underground are said to drive the moles away.

ALTERNATIVES

Give It Up

▶ If you have some problem spots where turf just won't thrive no matter what you do, it may be time to give up on grass. After all, it does best as long as it has full sun (6 hours or more a day of direct, unfiltered light), ample moisture, doesn't have to compete with shallow tree roots, and doesn't have too much traffic or too much erosion.

The solution may well be a ground cover, but making the transition can be ugly and labor-intensive.

To ease the process, consult your daily newspaper. Just place a few layers of newspaper over the problem areas. Dampen them lightly and top them with mulch. Then water the mulch thoroughly. If you have Kentucky bluegrass or any other type of cool-season grass, the area will be ready to replant with a groundcover in 2 weeks. With bermudagrass and other, tougher warm-season grasses, it may take 8 weeks or longer.

When the site is ready, just use a knife to cut through the paper and plant each individual ground cover plant. The paper will eventually decompose.

CHAPTER TEN

Attracting Birds, Butterflies, and Other Beneficials

Birds and butterflies and beetles, oh my! Welcome these and many other small creatures into your garden. Leave them little treats made with scraps from your kitchen, including old cornmeal or bacon drippings. Or provide shelter with materials you might otherwise throw away. A plastic milk jug, for example, can make a quality bird feeder, or a teapot can become a toad house. Whatever you do to make these guests feel at home will be repaid in benefits to your plants.

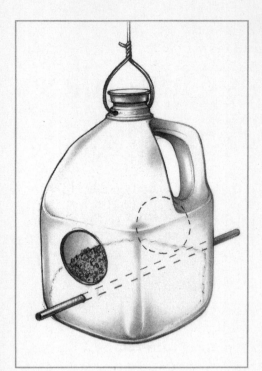

A plastic milk jug makes an excellent bird feeder.

CLEVER BIRD FEEDING

Out of Milk

▶ There's no need to spend money on a bird feeder from a store. You can make one for free with an empty plastic milk jug. Wash the container thoroughly with hot soapy water and rinse it well. Put the lid back on. Cut two holes 3 to 4 inches across on opposite sides of the container, being sure to make them high enough that you can put an inch or two of bird-seed in the bottom.

Using a large nail or a small Phillips screwdriver, punch a hole for a perch underneath each entrance hole and run a dowel or long, slender stick through the perch holes. Punch two more holes at the top of the jug in such a way that it will hang straight when a length of sturdy string or wire is run through the holes.

Fill the feeder with seed, hang it in a protected spot, and enjoy the show.

Thwart Squirrels

▶ Those pesky squirrels will empty a bird feeder in an afternoon if you let them. Prevent them from getting to your feeder by hanging it on a long wire suspended between two points, such as your house and a tree.

First, cut the length of wire you need and mount the feeder in the center. Then add a variety of objects that would cause a squirrel to lose its footing, such as old CDs, spools that once held thread, and empty plastic soda bottles with a hole punched in the bottom so you can thread the wire through them. The more objects, the more difficult it will be for that determined and acrobatic squirrel to get to the feeder.

A Bright Idea

▶ When your old lantern-type yard light goes on the fritz, consider turning it into a bird feeder. Remove the wiring and the outlet where the bulb screws in. Cut a piece of plywood to fit over the hole, or simply add a little duct tape to cover it up. Remove the glass from the sides of the lantern and add birdseed.

Greasy Good Eats

▶ Turn bacon grease into a tasty winter treat for birds. Start with an empty frozen juice can. Punch a hole in the can's metal bottom, then thread a strong piece of twine through the hole and knot it. Duct-tape it in place.

Keep the can in the freezer, and each time you cook bacon, pour the drippings into the can. (If you want, toss in a tablespoon or two of birdseed as you go.) When the can is full and frozen solid, peel off the cardboard and leave the metal bottom in place to support the frozen fat. Roll the fat in additional birdseed and hang it outside. This bacon log will stay fresh and firm as long as the temperature is at or below freezing.

3 Ways to Prevent Cats from Harming Backyard Birds

Create a safe haven for birds in your backyard by stopping cats from getting to your feathered friends' favorite spots.

1 Plant low, thorny bushes, such as barberries, raspberries, or roses, at the base of a favorite tree or feeder. Just make sure *you* can get in close enough to maintain the feeder!

2 Wrap chicken wire around the base of birdhouse supports or tree trunks where birds are nesting.

3 In out-of-the-way spots, leave a pile of bedsprings at the base of a feeder or another favorite tree.

Gobs of Cobs

❧ Use up that last bit of peanut butter or bacon grease by rolling a dried corncob in the almost empty container. Then cut a length of wire and wrap one end of it around the cob. Wrap the other end around a tree branch. The birds will perch on the corncob as they nibble this high-protein snack.

Hot Stuff

❧ Mix a bit of cayenne pepper with your birdseed. It won't bother the birds, but it will deter squirrels. For every quart or so of birdseed, add 1 to 2 tablespoons cayenne. Mix it thoroughly in a bowl, using two spoons to toss it if your skin is very sensitive. Either fill feeders immediately or store the seed in an airtight container until ready to use.

Walk the Plank

❧ Fancy bird feeders have their advantages, but if you don't want to spend a lot of money, you can craft a surprisingly effective one using nothing more than a leftover wooden plank. Just rest it across the corner of a deck or porch railing and scatter birdseed on it.

A simple plank bird feeder will attract a wide variety of birds.

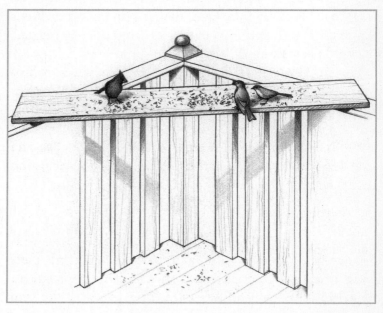

Cornmeal Special

▶ The next time you're smearing some peanut butter on a pinecone to put out for the birds, mix in one part cornmeal to four to six parts peanut butter. The cornmeal makes the peanut butter easier to work with and is nutritious for the birds besides.

Delectable Wreath

▶ Fret not when the wreath you acquired or made with a straw base fades and falls apart. Give the base new life as a bird feeder.

In a saucepan over low heat, melt two parts suet and one part peanut butter. Frost the straw wreath with this delectable mixture, then roll it in birdseed. Set it aside to dry. When it's dry, hang it outside for the birds.

---

5 Kitchen Leftovers for Birds

Have you been cleaning out the pantry and found some food that is a bit past its prime? It's very likely the birds might enjoy it.

1 Crumbs at the bottom of a dog food or dog biscuit bag, crushed

2 Uncooked oatmeal, corn-meal, or grits

3 Unsalted tortilla chips, crushed

4 Unsalted nuts, crushed

5 Unsweetened or lightly sweetened whole grain breakfast cereal crumbs

---

Whole Wheat Goodness

▶ Ever notice that whole wheat flour is the first flour to go bad? That's because the germ, the richest, most nutritious part of the wheat kernel, is in there—but that's also the part that's excellent for birds.

The next time you find weevils in your whole wheat flour, turn the remnants into a bird treat by mixing in peanut butter or bacon fat. Pack the mixture into baseball-size balls and freeze them. When you want to use one of the balls, cut out a section of a mesh onion or potato bag and wrap it around the ball. Tie the mesh closed with string and hang the ball outdoors for winter bird food.

Recycled Rinds

▶ Orange and grapefruit rinds make ideal mini–bird feed-ers. Just mix together one part birdseed and two parts peanut butter, then pack it into the rind of an orange or grapefruit half. Make a sling with string and hang the rind from a tree limb or on a hook where cats can't reach it—or the birds.

Fences Make Good Feeders

❭ Birds love to gather under bird feeders where birdseed has spilled. It is, unfortunately, a perfect place for cats and other hunters to pounce on unwary birds, especially if there are shrubs or rocks nearby.

The solution may lie in your garage. Look for anything see-through (so movement is detectable) to encircle the area. Even a low fence will slow down a pouncing predator. Reuse garden fencing intended for the tulip bed, tomato cages, plastic or wire milk crates, or closet accessories such as stackable shoe shelves, for example. Install the fence, creating an 8- to 15-foot circle of safety.

Whether your bird feeder is hanging or freestanding, a garbage can lid makes an effective baffle to keep out squirrels.

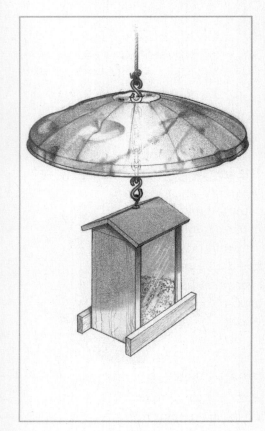

Baffle Squirrels

❭When that garbage can lid gets too battered to stay atop the garbage can, turn it into a squirrel baffle for bird feeders.

To install the baffle on a hanging feeder, you'll need a cup hook, two small S hooks, and an 8-inch length of chain.

First, screw the cup hook into the top of the bird feeder (as long as the feeder doesn't already have something similar). Slip one of the S hooks through the feeder hook and squeeze half the S hook shut with a pliers. Then slip the 8-inch chain through the other half of the S hook and close the hook around the chain with the pliers.

Next, slip the second S hook through the other end of the chain and close it around the chain. Then drill two holes in the center of the

Special Delivery

If you're upgrading your old large, metal mailbox, consider turning it into a birdhouse. The door makes cleaning out old nests a snap.

Using tin snips, cut a hole 2 to 3 inches tall and wide in the door, an inch or more from the bottom. Cover the sharp edges of the hole with duct tape or, if you've worked with it before and are confident of not getting a lot of cuts, strips of leftover copper flash-ing. (You can also buy sheets of lightweight copper at craft stores.)

Drill a hole right under the larger hole to insert a scrap of dowel, a length of chopstick, a twig, or a pencil stub to serve as a perch.

If you like, have fun painting the mailbox with leftover exterior house paint. Mount the mailbox on a freestanding post or a fence post and watch the birds play house.

---

garbage can lid, spaced close enough to slip the second S hook through. Slip one end of this other S hook through the holes in the garbage can lid and squeeze it shut.

Tie heavy twine or wire to the top of the S hook and hang the entire contraption from a tree or other support.

For a feeder mounted on a wooden pole, slit the garbage can lid from the edge to the center. Cut an opening in the center just large enough to fit around the feeder pole. Bend the lid gently around the pole, beneath the feeder, so it hugs the pole and stays in place. You may need to hammer on two wood cleats to hold it securely in place. If the lid is installed upside down, it serves a dual purpose by deterring squirrels and catching spilled seed, thus eliminating the mess that usually accumulates under feeders.

A Cheesy Idea

▶ Save that red plastic webbing that Gouda cheese comes in. It's the perfect size to encase a suet ball that you want to hang from a tree or hook. If necessary, secure one end with a twist tie. Slip in the ball and use another twist tie to close the top. Add string and hang.

5 Free Birdbaths

All a birdbath needs to do is hold a shallow expanse of water. A number of items you'll probably find around the house can do this quite well.

1 Set a flowerpot tray atop the flowerpot. If you use plastic, set a stone on top to keep the tray from blowing away.

2 Put a shallow bowl or dish on a stump, pedestal, or fence post and fill it with water. (In areas where temperatures hit freezing, avoid metal. A bird's delicate feet can freeze to it.)

3 Set a pretty pie plate on a vertical support.

4 Place a plastic garbage can lid, turned upside down, on the can or another support. Anchor it with a stone, if necessary.

5 Set out that crystal bowl that got chipped last Christmas. File off any sharp edges that might hurt tiny feet.

Double Duty

▶Those small woven berry baskets do excellent double duty helping our feathered friends.

In the winter, hang one of these baskets from the nearest tree limb and place a suet ball inside.

In the spring, wash the basket, then fill it with nesting material, such as dryer lint and bits of string and yarn.

Put Out the Welcome Mat

▶One of the problems with bird feeders is that so much of the seed ends up scattered on the ground. Stop this waste with a large plastic welcome mat.

Place the mat under your feeder. Not only will it prevent weeds from sprouting where the seeds fall, but it also will let you do a little recycling. Just brush up the seed and put it back in the feeder.

Cleaning Up

▶If you don't already buy dishwasher or laundry detergent in those medium-size buckets, you might want to start. Many are designed so that the lid can be snapped down securely all around the perimeter.

These are ideal containers in which to store birdseed. The secure lid thwarts raccoons and other animals that often raid birdseed. Just make sure you wash the container thoroughly before storing seed in it.

True Grit

❯ When you sweep the kitchen floor, dump the sand and dirt you gather onto the ground around your bird feeder, especially in the winter. Birds need grit to digest their food, and it may be hard for them to pick up sand and gritty soil when it is frozen.

BIRDBATHS

What a Drip

❯ Birds like birdbaths, but they'll *love* yours if you create a drip, which is a bird magnet.

Create that drip-drip-drip sound by poking a tiny hole with a pin in the bottom of a plastic milk jug or ice cream bucket. Fill the container with water, cover it to keep out debris that might stop up the hole, and hang it from a branch above the birdbath.

No branch? No problem. Make a tepee of three branches, curtain rods, broomsticks, or other similar objects and hang the container from that.

UNIQUE BIRDHOUSES

Teatime for Birds

❯ If you no longer want or need that teakettle, give it new life as a birdhouse. Use a power drill to punch a hole the size of a quarter into the side of the kettle for an entrance hole. For the perch, punch another hole with a nail right underneath the entrance.

Create the sound of dripping water—so enticing to birds—by hanging a milk jug filled with water over your birdbath.

3 Ways to Spruce Up Birdhouses for Spring

In late winter, before migrating birds return, it's important to clean and repair your birdhouses. There's no need to stock up on any special supplies. With a little ingenuity, you'll find everything you need right at home.

1 Wash out the houses. Remove old nesting materials and wash with a mixture of ¼ cup bleach and 1 gallon warm water. Rinse and let dry.

2 Do any necessary repair work. Hammer loose nails back into place. If the roof is leaking, plug the holes and cracks with nearly any type of leftover caulk. Or try dripping candle wax onto those spots.

3 Add a fresh coat of paint, if needed. Since you won't need much paint, use some of that leftover paint that's cluttering up the basement or garage.

Insert a long, slender bolt into the hole and secure it with two nuts, one on either side of the teakettle wall. Hang the house from a tree by the handle.

More Than Milk

▶ A simple milk carton can be the basis for an easy birdhouse that is fun to make with kids.

Just wash out an empty half-gallon milk carton. Staple the opening shut. Cut a round hole about the size of a quarter (or slightly larger) in one side of the carton about 3 inches from the bottom. Add a perch by punching a 2- to 3-inch pencil stub into the carton just below the hole so that at least an inch of the pencil protrudes.

Punch a hole through the top of the carton and string twine or wire through it. Create a waterproof roof by folding recycled aluminum foil into a rectangle large enough to fold over the top. Punch a hole through the center of the foil and thread the twine or wire through this hole. Fold the foil gently against the top of the carton to secure it.

Punch a hole or two in the bottom for drainage and hang the birdhouse in an appropriate spot.

Keep Out

▶ We all love purple martins for their mosquito-eating skills. But sometimes larger birds want to invade the purple martin houses we have so carefully erected. The solution lies in your handy dandy roll of duct tape. Cut each piece so that it curves a bit to reduce the size of each hole by about 25 percent.

FEATHERING THE NEST

Towels That Keep Going

▶ Toss that old cotton terry towel that's unraveling along the edges—but not in the trash. Pitch it across the crotch of a tree in the spring. Birds will love tugging at it to get fibers for building nests.

Neat Nests

▶ Dryer lint is much appreciated by nest-building birds. You can collect it efficiently with the help of a mesh produce bag—the kind onions and potatoes come in.

Keep the bag on a nail by your dryer. Each time you clean out the filter, put the lint in the bag. When it's reasonably full, secure the other end and pull a little lint out through the mesh to get things started. Hang it near your bird feeder in the spring. The birds will be grateful for the soft material to build their nests.

Tufts of Tinsel

▶ When the holidays are over and you're done with all that tinsel on the

Keep a mesh produce bag near the dryer. Fill it with lint after each dryer cycle, and you'll have terrific nesting material easily accessible to birds.

4 Items to Put Out for Nesting Birds

Hang an old wicker basket from a tree and fill it with the following items to encourage birds to use them in building theirnests.

1 Pieces of string and yarn no longer than 8 inches
2 Stuffing from damaged stuffed animals or pillows
3 Strips of soft cloth
4 Dental floss

tree, pull it off and save it for the birds. They love its glitter and gleam and are drawn to it for making nests.

In cold parts of the country, wait until very early spring when the snow starts to melt—prime nest-building time. Toss the tinsel over the crotch of a tree or stuff it into a net bag so birds can pull tufts of it out as needed.

Nesting Dispenser

▶ Birds love bits and pieces of string, lint, and other soft materials to use in making nests. And they like it even more if it's in a form that they can pull at with their beaks.

Make a nifty nesting material dispenser by filling two of those plastic mesh berry baskets with suitable nesting material. Place the tops of the baskets facing each other, then secure them together with twist ties. Use a pencil or crochet hook to pull out a few tufts of the material.

Hang the baskets by a wire or string from a tree. Birds will love landing on them and pulling out the material.

Attract Orioles

▶ Hang strands of red or orange ribbon or yarn on branches of shrubs or small trees near your bird feeder or birdbath. Baltimore orioles are attracted to the color and will carry the yarn away to use as nesting material. A bonus for bird-watchers: The bright color makes their nests easier to spot.

Grass That's Truly Greener

▶ Next Easter, instead of buying that nonbiodegradable green plastic grass, get excelsior (fine wood shavings) instead. It's widely available at craft stores in a multitude of colors. You can use and reuse it to your heart's content. When it starts looking a little weary, put it out for the birds to use as a nesting material.

Here Kitty, Kitty

▶ Even if you're trying to attract birds, having a cat can be a plus. Weirdly, all that soft, fluffy fur that ends up in the grooming brush is an ideal nesting material.

Keep a zippered mesh bag—the kind used for washing delicates—near your pet-grooming area. Slip it into a larger paper bag to keep the fur from flying. Each time you brush your pet, add the loose fur to the bag. When it's at least half full, hang it from a tree near the birds' favorite feeding area.

ATTRACTING HUMMINGBIRDS

Sugar: It's What's for Dinner

▶ Run out of hummingbird nectar for your feeder? Rather than interrupt the hummers' food supply (they may take their business elsewhere), whip up a quick batch of home-made syrup instead. Just bring to a boil 1 cup boiling water and ¼ cup granulated or brown sugar. Let cool and use.

---

3 Ways to Keep Ants off Your Hummingbird Feeder

Are those clever ants raiding your hummingbird feeder? Somehow, they're able to climb the tree, go along the branch, and continue down the hanger to the sugary nectar. Thwart their attempts with these methods.

1 Make a barrier of twisted and/or wadded-up masking or duct tape, sticky side out, and attach it to the hanger. The ants will get stuck to it, or avoid it.

2 Spray a mixture of 1 cup vinegar and 1 tablespoon ground cloves on the ant trail leading to the feeder.

3 Find a used spray paint cap that has two chambers. Punch or drill a hole in the center of the cap. Invert it, string the hummingbird feeder's wire through the hole, and hang it as usual. Then fill the outer chamber with vegetable oil or water. Ants won't cross this little moat.

OJ is Okay

▶ If you have a bit of orange juice at the bottom of the pitcher or there's a smidge left at the bottom of a glass, add it to your hummingbird feeder. It makes the nectar even more attractive to hummers. All it takes is a few drops per feeder, so be sparing.

BEAUTIFUL BUTTERFLIES

Belly Up to the Bar

▶ Butterflies flock to a source of water in the garden, especially if the water is shallow and fresh. To make a butterfly watering hole, turn an empty wine bottle (amber-colored bottles work especially well because the color attracts butterflies) upside down and push it, neck first, into an open, sunny edge of the garden. The indentation in the bottom of the bottle will collect water nicely. Consider lining up a series of bottles along the garden border to form a pretty edging.

3 Fast, Free Butterfly Baths

Butterflies love shallow water, especially if there's a spot to land where they can sun themselves. Try these ideas.

1 Recycle an old Frisbee. Add marbles to the bottom for weight and landing pads.

2 Sink a broken cup into the ground or into a large pot of plants on your deck or balcony. Cut up a sponge to fit into the cup or stuff in a well-rinsed net shower scrubber. Keep the cup filled with water.

3 Fill an old pizza or jelly roll pan with water to provide a shallow puddle on a sunny day. Line the pan with a cotton tea towel or paper towels.

Landing Pad

▶ Butterflies are drawn to water, but only if they can wade and flit in just the shallowest of shallows. (Ever notice gatherings of butterflies on the puddles along a creek or stream?) Encourage them to visit your birdbath by tucking in an object just below the water surface. Experiment with a flat stone, a brick, an inverted clay flowerpot, or perhaps even a small clay or stone statue or plaque.

For Butterflies Only

▶ Another way to attract butterflies is to make a small butterfly spa using a large plate, an old baking dish, or a shallow ceramic bowl. Sink the dish into the ground (preferably in a flowerbed, which is attractive as well as convenient—no mowing around it) and fill it with sand, which has absorbed or contains the salts and nutrients butterflies love. Or just toss a shovelful of dirt into the container. Wet the sand or dirt thoroughly and make sure it stays constantly damp.

Butterfly Buffet

▶ Just as you put out food for birds, try putting out food for butterflies. A platform feeder meant for birds works nicely. Or simply set a dish up off the ground (perhaps on a stump or an inverted flowerpot), where slugs and ground-dwelling insects won't bother it.

Put out an array of mashed bananas, watermelon, or apples. Change the fruit every day or two to keep the display presentable, although the butterflies won't mind (and

A Tea Party for Butterflies

One *child's* trash can provide the makings for an adorable butterfly feeding station.

When cleaning the attic and sorting through old toys, save that little table and tea set. Put the table in a sunny spot in the garden and set it not for teddy bears but for flutterers.

Fill some of the cups or bowls with sand mixed with a little soil for male butterfly "puddling'—their habit of sucking minerals out of the soil. Fill a saucer or two with water for drinking and some of the plates with mashed bananas and other over-the-hill fruit that butterflies love.

If you truly believe that old saying "the more, the merrier," fill a cup or two with birdseed as well.

Put out overripe fruit that you might otherwise toss in the compost to attract butterflies.

probably would prefer) rotting material. Swallowtails, painted ladies, and fritillaries are the most likely to visit a fruit station such as this.

It's Better with Butterflies

❱ Convert a hummingbird feeder into a butterfly feeder instead. First, tuck short strips of absorbent red fabric or red yarn into the holes to act as wicks. Then fill the feeder with red fruit punch, a butterfly favorite. Place the feeder near a window, porch, or garden bench where it will be easy for you to sit back and watch the butterflies come to feed.

Beckoning Bows

❱ Bulls aren't the only creatures that react to the color red. It turns out that butterflies are more drawn to reds and pinks than to yellows and whites. So if you want to beckon butterflies to your garden or yard, use some old red and pink bows from Christmas or birthday gifts or made from leftover fabric. Tie them around the stems of flowers and shrubs that butterflies love, or simply strew them over the branches.

OTHER BENEFICIALS

A Toad and Butterfly Resort

▶ Toads and butterflies love shallow water. Create a special bath for them right in your flowerbed, using a garbage bag as your liner.

Dig a hole about the depth and circumference of a bird-bath, roughly 2 to 3 feet across and about 6 inches deep. Smooth the garbage bag flat, like a pillowcase. Then lay it across the hole—no cutting required. Fill the hole with water to push the bag down into place. Fold and bury the ends of the bag so that as little as possible is showing.

Line the rim with stones, bricks, teacups, or whatever you have handy. Place lots of smooth stones, baseball-size or larger, in the water. Porous stones are best because they absorb water and leach salts that male butterflies love.

Create a shallow miniature wetland for toads and butterflies. The secret is a garbage bag liner.

Muffins No More

▶ If the number of years since you last baked muffins has entered the double digits, it's time to get rid of those muffin tins, be they full-size or mini.

Turn them into bird and butterfly watering holes by burying them in the garden just below the soil line in a sunny spot. The shallow water is ideal for sipping and splashing by feathered and fluttering friends alike. Accent with stones if desired.

A Home for Toads

▶Just how well toad houses work is subject to debate, but there's no debate over how cute they are. Make a toad house of your own by tipping a clay pot on its side near a water garden or other spot where toads are likely to hang out. For a whimsical touch, pull out a fat permanent marker and label it "Toad House" in fancy writing.

It's Tops

▶If the pedestal portion of your birdbath has gone missing or is damaged, put it to a new use—as a toad watering hole. Sink it into the ground in a flowerbed or other convenient spot and fill it with water. Add a few large, round stones the size of grapefruits to create convenient landing and frolicking pads for the creatures. If you want, add a few tough floating plants, such as water hyacinth or water lettuce. Toads like the cover, and the plants slow the growth of algae.

SAVE THE PLANET

Make Friends with Wasps

Predatory wasps, including paper wasps and mud daubers, are excellent hunters of caterpillars and other insects that like to munch on our favorite plants. One way to lure these helpful creatures into your garden is to play to their attraction to meat. Put that stinky kitchen sponge, the one you're ready to toss after scrubbing one too many skillets, in a lightweight plastic container and fill it halfway with water. Put it in a sunny spot that dogs and cats will have difficulty reaching.

Wasps also love overripe fruit such as cherries, melons, and peaches and will return to the same spot all summer to check for more. Put fruit out in a sunny spot where the wasps are likely to see it. Birds and butterflies, which also like overripe fruit, might stop by for a snack, as well.

A cracked or chipped teapot makes a charming, cooling haven for toads.

Teapot Toad House

▶ Turn that chipped or cracked teapot—or the one with the broken lid—into a one-of-a-kind toad house. Turn the pot upside down and sink it partially into the soil at an angle, so that half of the opening is underground and half is aboveground. Leave the spout outside the soil to increase air circulation and make the house more comfortable in hot weather. This teapot dwelling offers inviting shelter, safety, and a cooling-off spot for toads, those ever-so-helpful garden guests that devour many pests.

Lady Beetles Longer

▶ If you've invested in some lady beetles to control aphids in your garden, you want to do everything to make sure they stay in your backyard and not the neighbor's. First, ease the little creatures out of their container by taping a cotton ball to a Popsicle stick or chopstick and gently herding them out. Then encourage them to linger by offering them a mixture of one part sugar and four parts water. Spray it on the foliage right where the lady beetles are released. With a little luck, you'll convince them to stay.

Praying Mantis Protective Custody

▶Praying mantis eggs freeze in the winter, but you can help them survive and return them to your garden by storing them in your refrigerator until spring.

Start in the fall before the first frost by searching the garden for the foamy-looking egg cases. When you find them, snap or cut off the portion of branch or stem they're on.

Boost the population of helpful praying mantises in your garden by making a winter home for them in your fridge.

Tuck the branch into a jar. Add a damp paper towel in the bottom for humidity. Cover the top with foil and a rubber band. Keep the jar in your fridge, adding a little moisture to the jar every month or two.

After your region's last frost date, remove the foil and set the jar outdoors near a tree trunk. The warmer air will signal the eggs to hatch.

Pillow Power

▶ Those Japanese buckwheat pillows are delightful, but their stuffing does have a tendency to leak out. If you have a spill or decide to throw the thing out altogether, scatter the seeds in an open area of your garden—perhaps along the edge of the vegetable garden. The seeds will sprout into buckwheat plants, which are major magnets for tachinids. These flies control grasshoppers and caterpillars.

CHAPTER ELEVEN

Stretching the Season

Get more out of your garden longer. There's no need to be limited by frost dates or stretches of long, hot weather. Create protection from the elements or practice clever planting techniques, and you can add weeks, if not months, to your garden's growing season. Grab an umbrella for quick, effective frost protection for large containers. Use an old or damaged tent as temporary winter quarters for plants. Or make lightweight, storable cloches with nothing more than wire coat hangers and plastic grocery bags.

On chilly nights when frost threatens, a porch light may be all you need to keep your fuchsia or other tender hanging plant from getting nipped.

FROST PROTECTION

Leave That Porch Light On

▶Fuchsias are popular plants for hanging baskets, but they are extremely frost-sensitive. On nights when temperatures are predicted to go down to freezing or just a degree or two below, provide easy protection for fuchsias (and other tender hanging plants) by hanging them from your porch light, provided the light design allows for it and the basket isn't too large. If needed use wire to position the container so that the stems don't touch the light but are just an inch or two away from it. And, of course, leave the light on all night.

Wonderful Waxed Paper

▶ When a late frost is threatening and you don't want to bring in all those tender seedlings in flats by your back door, just whip out a box of waxed paper. It provides an instant, easy layer of protection between the plants and the elements.

Tape a sheet of paper to the sides of the container using duct tape. If mud and moisture make taping problematic, tear the sheet extra long and anchor each end with a stone or brick or simply tuck the paper under the container.

Read It and Reuse It

▶ Recycle your newspaper as an emergency row cover. It will last a night or two—just long enough to get your tender plants through an early light frost.

Staple or tape pages of the newspaper together top to bottom until you have a piece long enough to cover a row or two. Position the paper so the creases allow you to place them tent-style over the seedlings. Weight down the corners with rocks or soil. When it comes time to remove the row cover, tear the paper into strips and recycle it in your compost pile.

Forecast for Frosty

▌ The next time an umbrella starts to fall apart—the fabric breaks away a little from the frame; the wires get bent—don't throw it out. Save it to use as a quick and effective frost protector for plants a foot or two high or for large containers. When frost threatens, open the umbrella and insert the handle into the soil next to the plant.

Make a Frost Kit

▌ Don't you hate it when you're watching the evening news and you hear that the season's first frost is predicted for that night? That means frantically grabbing whatever you can to throw over your plants to ensure they make it through the night.

It's light, it's fast, and it's probably right by your door. Grab an umbrella to keep your favorite container frost-free near the end of the growing season.

Make fighting frost a little easier and more pleasant by creating a frost kit when you clean out your linen closet. Gather together old sheets, tablecloths, and lightweight blankets. Tuck them into an old pillowcase or laundry bag (the pillowcase or bag is perfect for slipping over a potted plant). Then tuck in some spring-type clothespins, which are good for clipping together several items to cover a long row or large tomato plant. They're also useful to shape, clip, and hold in place a single item around a large plant. Store your kit in your garage or toolshed, and you'll always be able to fight frost at a moment's notice.

PROTECTIVE STRUCTURES

Winter Picnicking

▌ That picnic table that collects snow all winter long can now have a new off-season use—as a winter plant shelter.

Push the table up against the side of a heated building. Slide borderline-hardy container plants underneath, as close to the building as possible. Then cover the table with waterproof material, such as oilcloth or plastic tablecloths, plastic shower curtains, or plastic drop cloths. Tuck the covering between the table and the building and under the legs. Also weight down the top, if necessary.

Window Well Nursery

▶ With the help of some bubble wrap, those window wells along the foundation of your house can be converted into excellent insulated greenhouses during the winter, protecting a variety of potted plants.

A window well and bubble wrap are the basis for a convenient, amazingly effective mini-greenhouse for overwintering container plants.

Put plants that are borderline hardy and need additional protection in the bottom of a window well. Water thoroughly and wrap each in a sheet of bubble wrap. Cover the tops with 6 to 10 inches of autumn leaves, straw, or even foam packing peanuts. Then lay a piece of plywood or any other rigid covering over the top of the window well.

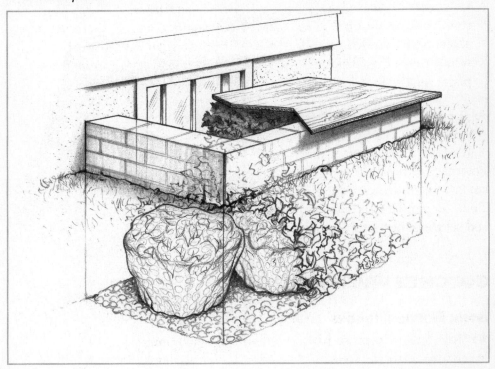

Have a Seat

Plastic yard or deck furniture is becoming one of our throw-away society's many problems in landfills. Nearly every spring and summer weekend, you will see white or green plastic chairs with one or two broken legs set out for trash pickup. Save them from the landfill and take them home. These imperfect chairs are great for making season-extending tunnels.

Lay the chairs down lengthwise every 6 feet or so and plant among the legs and open spaces. Then lay 5- to 6-foot-wide synthetic fabric row cover or clear plastic over the rows, making a tunnel. (The plastic chairs have rounded parts so they won't pierce the fabric, and the plastic will even warm the crops.)

Tuck the outer edges of the cover under the chair legs to anchor it, or use rocks.

Plant in the spring or fall with lettuce, spinach, broccoli, or other cool-season vegetables. The protective tunnel will allow you to plant 2 to 4 weeks earlier in the spring and 2 to 4 weeks later in the fall. Remove the tunnel after the last frost.

In early summer, change the covering to prevent cool-loving greens such as spinach and lettuce from getting overheated and bolting. Use a dark fabric, such as a dark-colored tablecloth, to provide shade. This can extend your harvest by a week or more into the summer.

In the spring, about 2 months before your region's last frost date, remove the plywood. About 6 weeks before the last frost date, remove the leaves, straw, or packing peanuts. Then, depending on the plants, remove the bubble wrap and set them out 4 to 5 weeks before the last frost date.

CLOCHES FROM SCRATCH

Soda Bottle Cloches

▶ Plastic milk jugs make nifty cloches for larger plants, but in tightly planted areas, you need something smaller.

From Books to Begonias

Small, upright mini-greenhouses the size and shape of a bookcase are all the rage these days. But why spend all that money when you might have the makings for something similar in your basement or attic? An old bookcase—wood, laminate, or metal—can easily be converted into a mini-greenhouse.

Set it outdoors in full sun. Place flats and pots directly on the shelves, or, to extend the life of the bookcase, set them in saucers made from found items such as plastic shoe boxes and margarine tubs.

Cover the bookcase by stapling, nailing, or duct-taping lightweight clear plastic over all the exposed sides, attaching the plastic just at the top. This will provide protection from cold but allow for easy access and adequate ventilation.

Depending on the size of the bookcase, you can use sheets of clear plastic cut from dry-cleaning bags, shower curtains, or drop cloths. If you don't have any of these handy, drop cloths and shower curtains are available for only a dollar or two each, and two of them certainly would cover even a large bookcase.

In the winter, store your bookcase in a protected area to extend its life.

Cloches made from 2-liter soda bottles are perfect. Cut off the bottom of each bottle and leave off the cap. Then nestle the bottles in over small plants; the openings at the top will serve as vents when daytime temperatures soar.

A bonus: The cloches make the plants almost impossible for rabbits to chomp. When you no longer need the warming effect of these cloches, trim off about 4 inches from the tapering tops and use the resulting cylinders around the plants to deter bunnies.

Molto Buono!

▶ Recycle those wonderfully sturdy, clear plastic glasses that Italian sodas are sold in at upscale coffee shops by using them in early spring to help harden off newly transplanted annuals. Immediately after planting, invert the glasses over the plants, nestling each glass into the soil to hold it in place. After a few nights, when the plants have had a chance to adjust, cut the bottoms off the glasses so the seedlings can harden off further. Allow the plants to grow right through the glasses, which will afford both rabbit and cutworm protection. When the plants begin to emerge a few inches above the glasses, cut the glasses away and remove them.

Quick Cloches

▶ When planting seedlings of tender vegetables and flowers in the spring, give them a few days of protection by inverting 1- to 3-gallon dark plastic pots over them. By day, the shade the pots provide will help the plants adjust to their new situations. At night, the heat they've absorbed from the sun will help warm the seedlings, speeding their overall development.

Be sure to leave the cloches on for no more than 2 to 3 days. Once the plants have overcome any transplant shock, they will need sunlight to thrive.

Not the Same Old Grind

▶ In early spring, gardeners have long placed coffee cans around their newly planted tender vegetable seedlings, such as tomatoes, peppers, and eggplants. The cans provide some insulation from cold spring temperatures and protection from rabbits, cutworms, and other pests.

You can take this idea one step further and top each can with a plastic produce bag used to collect fruits and veggies at the supermarket. Make a couple of slashes in the bag to allow for ventilation. The extra protection it provides will allow you to plant seedlings up to 2 weeks earlier than you otherwise would.

Take the old coffee can trick one step further and add a plastic produce bag. You'll be able to plant weeks earlier.

Zip Your Plants

▶ Those clear plastic zippered bags that blankets, pillows, and other bedding come in are handy early-season protection for large flats of seedlings or even entire small shrubs.

Slip a flat into a bag and zip it shut at night for maximum protection. (Slash the bag in a few places for ventilation.) In the morning, unzip the bag partway to allow for more ventilation. If the day is predicted to be really warm, unzip the bag completely and fold back the top to prevent seedlings from overheating.

Alternatively, slip a bag over a large pot, hanging basket, or small shrub. The zipper makes it easy to get a custom fit or to allow ventilation on a sunny day.

How Cool Is This?

▶If you have a foam cooler that has lost its lid or sprung a leak, you can turn it into an excellent winter protector for a rose or other small, borderline-hardy shrub.

Invert the cooler over the plant. Use a small knife to cut a series of holes in the top to allow for ventilation on sunny days. Anchor the cooler with rocks.

Remove the cooler a couple of months before your region's last frost date. Leaving it on any longer will invite overheating and disease problems from lack of sun and ventilation.

A Campy Idea

▶When your old pup tent gets an irreparable rip or you've just stopped using it, pitch it once again to protect marginally hardy container plants for the winter.

Call Around

Old storm or double-hung wood-frame windows and doors are ideal for building a cold frame or even an entire greenhouse. But they're hard to come by, especially in any quantity.

One of your best bets is to call around to remodeling contractors listed in the yellow pages. Contractors rip out old windows and doors all the time and seldom have any use for them, other than to toss them in the dumpster. As long as you're there to collect them, contractors are often happy to give them away. Use doors and windows with glass in them as the top of a coldframe, or the tops and upper half of greenhouse walls. Use solid doors for the sides of cold frames, or the bottom half of greenhouse walls.

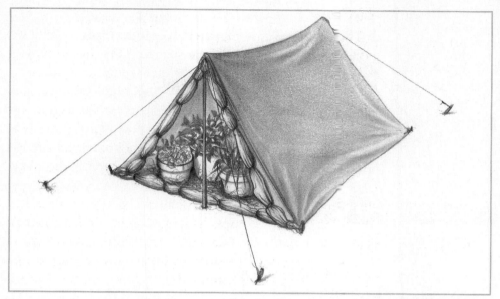

You can use it as is to provide protection for plants the same way it provided protection for you in the woods. Just add straw or autumn leaves around the pots and containers for additional insulation.

If you have just the metal tent frame, that's okay, too. Assemble the frame and position the plants underneath, filling in spaces around the pots with wadded-up newspaper for further insulation. Then drape a clear vinyl or plastic sheet over the frame. Anchor the sheet on the sides with stones or bricks.

If that old pup tent is a bit too battered or you're just not using it anymore, turn it into a large cold frame to over-winter borderline-hardy plants and to get other plants off to a faster start in the spring.

COOL COLD FRAMES

Coming Unhinged

▶ The next time you're remodeling, save the hinges from old doors and large cabinets. They come in handy when you're making a cold frame. Use them to attach the lid to the frame for easy lifting and lowering.

Disposable Blankets

▶ Save those thin, flexible plastic sheets that computers, televisions, and other electronics are packed in—the ones that look like white plastic blankets. They're ideal for throwing over your cold frame for extra protection in the winter.

Bubble Wrap Bonanza

▶ Use bubble wrap to insulate your cold frame on the coldest nights. If you have a large sheet of it, use it as is and anchor it on the sides of the cold frame with stones or bricks. If you have just bits and pieces of bubble wrap, cover an old window screen or window frame with the pieces and duct-tape or staple them in place. Then lay the screen or frame on top of the cold frame.

Cabinets Reborn

▶ If you're remodeling your kitchen or ripping out the vanity in the bathroom, turn a cabinet or two into a cold frame. Remove the doors and back of the cabinet, then set the boxlike frame into the soil. Position the frame so that it tilts an inch or two toward the south, allowing it to catch as much winter sun as possible. Then drape the frame with a sheet of clear plastic.

MORE COLD PROTECTION

Hoop It Up

▶ Row covers can be expensive. For quick, easy, and cheap frost protection, use old croquet hoops instead.

For row crops, space the croquet hoops about a foot apart along the rows. For larger plantings, place the hoops in a grid pattern.

In the spring, drape the hoops with plastic—anything from dry-cleaning bags to clear plastic shower curtains and drop cloths—to warm the soil and the plants. (Be sure to slash vents in the plastic to prevent overheating.) Remove the hoops and the plastic coverings after the soil has had a chance to warm up.

Come fall, place the hoops back in the garden and drape them with old sheets, lightweight curtains, tablecloths, worn towels, and other similar fabrics.

Hang-Ups

▶ Save the flimsy wire coat hangers you get from the dry cleaner for making cloches. Untwist the hangers and shape each into a U. Place a plastic grocery bag over each hoop, with the two ends of the hoop going through the handles of the bag. Push the ends into the soil over a tender plant. These guards are quick and easy to set in place, remove, and store.

Classy Cloches

▶ A clear glass or plastic dome rescued from a broken cake plate or a cheese server makes a classy—and free—cloche. Old glass light fixtures also make interesting minicloches.

Plastic grocery bags and wire coat hangers make perfect cloches to get tender plants going early in the spring.

They come in a variety of styles, but most are some variation of an inverted dome. Vintage light fixtures are downright pretty and can add a nice touch to the garden.

Since these items are not vented, they're best for use in very early spring before temperatures rise much. And always be sure to remove them on sunny days when temperatures inside the domes might cook your plants.

Parsley Power

▶ Parsley is technically a biennial, lasting 2 years. In areas where temperatures dip below freezing, however, it may die out the first year. With a little help, your parsley will stick around for 2 years even in those cold-winter regions.

In the fall, after the first light frost, mound a few large handfuls of leaves over the parsley. Then tip a bushel basket or 5-gallon bucket over the plant to make a cozy covering for the winter.

Twinkle, Twinkle

▶ Get those Christmas tree lights out early! In warm climates (Zone 9 and warmer) when a frost threatens,

Christmas tree lights might provide just enough heat to protect tropical plants from a winter frost in warm regions.

you can prevent damage to your cold-sensitive trees, such as citrus, gardenias, and camellias, by stringing them with Christmas tree lights and keeping the lights on throughout the night.

For even more heavy-duty frost protection, attach an electric work light—the kind with a metal reflector, a 150-watt bulb, and a pincher-clip base—to a lower branch of each tree, shining it upward. Toss a sheet or two over the tree to trap the warmth.

Note: Be sure to plug any fixtures into a GFIC (shock-resistant) outdoor outlet to prevent accidents. And be sure to remove the light in the morning so it doesn't collect rain or other moisture.

CHAPTER TWELVE

Pests and Diseases

They eat. They dig. They chew. They crowd out. Pests, diseases, and weeds are the bane of even the best-tended gardens. But you don't need to resort to harsh chemicals for control. Instead, rummage around in your kitchen cabinets. You might find the makings for a peanut bait to trap chipmunks, a cayenne pepper spray to apply to soil and plants to deter cats and some dogs, a rye flour dust to discourage cabbage butterflies, or a vinegar spray to zap weeds.

PEST SOLUTIONS

Damage Detective

▶ Don't know what's eating your veggies? In the late evening, bring an empty cardboard toilet paper roll or paper towel roll into the garden. Bait the inside of the roll with a dab of peanut butter and a drop of olive oil. Leave it lying on the soil and inspect it each morning as soon as possible after sunrise.

After a few nights, you should find inside the slugs, earwigs, potato bugs, or centipedes that have been nibbling your transplants. This will let you know what exactly is damaging your plants so that you can take appropriate action, such as applying an organic pesticide designed specifically for that pest.

 Ways to Get to the Root of Things

If you see young onion, carrot, or cabbage family seedlings wilt rather suddenly, uproot a few plants and check for grublike root maggots on deformed roots. If root maggots are the problem, you can take several steps to prevent them from hitting again next year.

1 Discourage adult forms of this pest, a type of fly that emerges from the soil in early spring, by leaving strips of leftover tar paper near each row of plants. The smell of the tar paper will discourage the flies.

2 Drape the seedlings with tulle or old sheer curtains cut into strips. Not allowing adult maggot flies to land on the seedlings will stop them from laying eggs.

3 In the spring, crush eggshells in a paper bag using a rolling pin. Use the shells to mulch around seedlings to further prevent adult maggot flies from reaching the plants and laying eggs.

4 Dust the ground around endangered seedlings with wood ashes, also to prevent adults from reaching the plants and laying eggs.

Erase Insect Problems

▶ When it comes time to empty your pencil sharpener, toss the shavings around plants that have been having insect problems. Work the shavings lightly into the soil at the base of the plants. The cedar scent will deter a variety of bugs.

Foil Destructive Insects

▶ Repel cutworms and squash vine borers from your vegetables by wrapping a strip of aluminum foil (new or washed and reused) around the base of tomatoes, squash, zucchini, peppers, eggplants, and other vegetables. Every week or two, check the aluminum foil. As the plants grow, you will need to loosen or reapply the foil. If you are concerned only with repelling cutworms, you can remove the foil completely once the stalk is ½ inch thick (too thick for the cutworms to damage).

Sprinkle shavings from your pencil sharpener around plants. Problem insects don't like the cedar scent.

Picky about Cutworms

▶ Here's a cutworm trick that takes seconds and you'll hardly be able to see. Tuck a couple of toothpicks into the soil beside each plant stem. Cutworms can't curl around the extra girth, and uncurled cutworms can't feed.

No More Ants in Your Plants

▶ Ants are usually harmless in the garden, but fire ants can be a pain, and a large anthill in the yard can take up valuable space. Ants are also guilty of tending aphids on beech trees, peonies, and roses. So if a resident anthill is making you antsy, here's a classic formula for getting rid of it without resorting to poisonous sprays.

Add several squirts of dishwashing liquid to a gallon of boiling water. Pour the mixture on the anthill while you poke it with a stick to stir up (and scald) the ants. Repeat three or four times over several days.

2 Methods of Whacking Whiteflies

Whiteflies are tiny flying insects that do most of their damage in greenhouses, on hanging baskets, or on indoor houseplants. You know you have them if you brush a plant lightly with your hand and a small cloud of tiny, grayish white insects rises into the air. Fortunately, whiteflies are easy to control with one of these solutions.

❙ Soap spray. Mix one part water, three parts rubbing alcohol, and a tiny squirt of dishwashing liquid in a spray bottle. Shake or brush infected plants with your hand so that a cloud of whiteflies appears. Spray directly into the swarm. In 5 minutes, repeat the process.

2 Fly buster. Put a piece of yellow tape on the end of a handheld vacuum cleaner or wear bright yellow gloves to attract the whiteflies. Brush the plant with one hand and then use the vacuum to trap the flies. (They are easiest to catch when days are cool and they're kind of slow.) Immediately after you suck them up, take out the vacuum cleaner bag and put it in the freezer overnight to kill the whiteflies inside. Repeat the process every day for a week.

Goodbye, Grasshoppers

▶ Grasshoppers and locusts can devour a vegetable garden and turn the leaves of your favorite ornamental plants into lacy skeletons. Fortunately, however, they like sugar even more than your prize plants.

Capitalize on this sweet tooth to create a trap for hungry hoppers. Mix together 1 gallon water, 1 cup molasses or honey, and a few squirts of dishwashing liquid. Pour the solution into small buckets or other waterproof containers. (*Note:* Avoid 5-gallon buckets, which are deep enough for toddlers to fall into and drown.) Set several buckets around the afflicted areas.

Grasshoppers, attracted by the sugar, will jump into the buckets, become coated with the soapy water, and drown. Keep an eye on the liquid. If too many beneficial insects, such as parasitic wasps, butterflies, or lady beetles, end up in the traps, remove them.

Fruit Fly Trap

❯ If you like to pile up your late-summer bounty on a screened back porch or in the garage or kitchen, you know how icky it is to have clouds of fruit flies feeding on your waiting-to-be-processed produce.

Trap fruit flies by the dozens or even hundreds with a simple trap. Just mix together 2 cups water, ¼ cup cider vinegar or leftover wine, and 1 teaspoon dishwashing liquid. Pour the mixture into a jar and set the open jar next to the produce.

The fruit flies will be attracted to the vinegar or wine smell and dip into the water, only to be coated with the soap and drown. Change the solution every couple of days or so to get rid of the dead insects and to keep the vinegar odor intense enough to attract more fruit flies.

Trip Up Thrips

❯ Thrips are tiny insects that travel in groups to feed on onions, carrots, cucumbers, and flowers, especially roses. They cause streaked foliage and deformed flower buds.

You can confuse and discourage them by reusing foil to mulch around their favorite plants. Lay pieces of foil around the base of each plant or curve a strip of foil around the plant to make a barrier 1 foot wide. Secure the foil with rocks along the edges. Apparently, this disorients thrips enough that they won't lay eggs.

Do this in early spring, as soon as daytime temperatures are reliably above freezing, before an infestation begins.

Roll Over Roly-Polies

❯ Whether you call them sow bugs, potato bugs, or roly-polies, these interesting little creatures (they roll into tiny gray balls if disturbed) are helpful to gardeners in modest numbers because they break down dead plant material. But in large numbers, they can cause considerable damage by feeding on flower petals and damp foliage.

Trap these segmented eating machines by playing on their love for moist, dark places. Lay a paper pet food bag with some crumbs inside in your garden. Moisten both the inside and outside of the bag with a spray of water.

Sow bugs will happily crawl into the dark dampness of the bag, attracted by the leftover pet food. Dispose of the bag and pests after a few days.

A Bug-Snaring Hose Guide

▶ Dahlias are earwig candy, and the larger flowers are easily toppled by the slightest brush of a hose. Fight earwigs and protect your dahlias at the same time with some easy, clever hose guard traps.

Insert a metal skewer or a large knitting needle through the drainage hole of a small clay pot turned upside down on the ground. Set several of these pots around your flowerbeds as hose guides.

Each morning fairly early, check inside the pots. They will lure both earwigs and slugs. If you're not squeamish, squish the pests you find. Otherwise, toss the pots into a bucket of soapy water for 10 minutes and then return them to your garden.

Turn small pots and knitting needles into combination hose guards and insect traps.

A Sticky Situation

▌ Take advantage of whiteflies' and aphids' lust for yellow by covering a yellow paper tag, gift bag, or other bright yellow object with a plastic sandwich bag. Smear the plastic bag with petroleum jelly and hang it on or right next to a problem plant. The insects will fly to the yellow and get stuck. Replace the plastic bag and reload it with petroleum jelly every few days.

Monitor the bag carefully. You want to be catching harmful insects, not beneficials, such as bees or butterflies. If you start capturing the latter, remove the trap.

Adios, Aphids

▌ Those tiny, soft-bodied aphids love roses and many other plants. Control them with this classic soap spray. It's an oldie but a goody.

Make a soapy water spray with 1 quart water and one good squirt of dishwashing liquid. Spray an afflicted plant thoroughly, being sure to get under the leaves and into the spots where the branches meet the stems, a favorite aphid hangout.

Great Garlic

▌ Cloves of garlic can help keep aphids away from your prized plants. In the spring, before aphids get seriously established, tuck peeled garlic cloves into the soil around plants where aphids are a problem. Replenish with fresh garlic every month or so.

All-Purpose Spray

▌ Chile peppers can keep a multitude of insects and four-legged pests—even most deer, rabbits, and squirrels—away from your plants. Once they taste or feel the heat, these pests are unlikely to return.

In a blender, combine 2 hot fresh chili peppers, 2 cups water, 1 tablespoon vegetable oil, and a few drops of dishwashing liquid. Transfer the mixture to a spray bottle and spritz it on leaves and flowers. The soap and oil will hold the mixture in place for several days. Reapply every 5 to 7 days, as needed.

Special Edition Bug Traps

▌ Bothered by millipedes, centipedes, slugs, sow bugs, earwigs, and other moisture-loving insects? Catch them with simple but effective traps made from newspaper.

Crumple and moisten several pages of newspaper, wadding each up into a ball about the size of a melon. The ball should be thoroughly damp but not sopping wet. Place these balls in areas where the pests are causing damage to your plants.

2 Ways to Eliminate Earwigs

Earwigs can be beneficial when they munch on decaying plant parts, creating compost. But in too-large numbers, they will nibble the edges of pansies and invade the petals of dahlias, phlox, and hydrangeas. Create traps to capture them dead or alive. If you opt for alive, dispose of them in your compost heap or in a garbage can with a tight-fitting lid so they'll go out with the trash.

▌ Bacon grease. Reuse bacon grease by smearing a circle of the chilled fat around the inside of a glass jar or tin can. Sink this container into the ground where earwigs are a problem and fill with soapy water to just below the grease line. Earwigs will be attracted to the grease and then fall into the water.

2 Fast-food wrappers. Collect the french fry bags from a fast-food meal, crumple them up, and lay them in the garden. Use rocks to keep them from blowing away. Earwigs will collect in the crumpled bags. To capture them, slip your hand inside a plastic produce bag. Use this as a large glove to grab the paper bags and quickly pull the produce bag around it before any earwigs escape.

Destructive insects like their morning paper, too. Crumple damp newspaper around the garden to trap and destroy slugs, earwigs, and other pests.

First thing in the morning—shortly after sunrise, if possible—pick up the traps, insects and all, and throw them into a plastic garbage bag. When all the papers are collected, use a twist tie to close the bag securely and dispose of it with the rest of your garbage.

With a Net, You Bet

▶ Prevent carrot rust flies and cabbage butterflies from damaging your vegetable garden by recycling old curtain sheers. In early spring and summer, when the pests are at the fly stage, drape crops that have been damaged in the past with the sheers. Anchor them with stones or bricks, then remove the sheers later in the summer.

Net Gain

▶ Panty hose make your legs look lovely, and now they can make your plants look pretty darn good, too.

Protect small plants from flying pests such as cabbage butterflies with a cage of sorts covered with panty hose. Bend a wire coat hanger into a U shape and press into the ground so it arches several inches above the plant. Stretch

6 Ways to Say So Long to Slugs

Slugs and snails are a huge problem in many gardens, especially those with tender-leaved plants that have lots of folds or large sheltering leaves low to the ground, such as lettuce, hostas, and tender seedlings. Luckily, there are many ways to stop these critters.

1 Ammonia and water. Mix equal parts nonsudsing ammonia and water in a spray bottle. Visit the garden on a rainy morning or cool evening and spray the slugs as they feed. This technique is most effective on baby slugs, which thrive in the crowns of hostas and daylilies. As an added bonus, the ammonia converts to nitrogen and acts as a foliar food for the plants. (*Note:* Some ferns and seedlings may suffer leaf burn from this spray. Test on a single leaf first.)

2 Vinegar and water. Mix two parts vinegar and one part water in a spray bottle. Spray the mixture directly on slugs you see or as you find them under boards or in the crevices of rock gardens. Be careful not to let the spray come in contact with plant foliage.

3 Wood ashes. A ring of wood ashes from your fireplace will discourage slugs from climbing up the stems of plants. Sprinkle the ashes in a band a few inches wide, but don't let them actually touch the stem of the plant. *Caution:* If your soil is alkaline, as it is in many parts of the West and Southwest, avoid putting ashes on your soil or in your compost heap. They can raise the pH even higher.

4 A window screen. Cut an old window screen into long strips at least 6 inches wide. Sink the strips 3 inches into the soil so that a fence surrounds your most vulnerable plants.

5 Clay pots. Lure slugs away from your plants to where you can find and destroy them. Set out small clay flowerpots turned upside down and propped up on one side with a flat rock. These traps are attractive enough to use in container plantings.

6 Damp cardboard, rolled-up newspaper, grapefruit rinds, or damp burlap. Position these materials around your garden to collect slugs. Gather the items each morning and destroy the slugs. Or move the slugs, "hotels" and all, to your compost pile.

old, light-colored, sheer panty hose (no black, brown, or blue) over the hoop and add some soil, stones, or plant staples to keep the hose in place.

Sunlight and rain will reach the plant, but flying enemies will be foiled by the barrier. You can keep the protection there all season, raising the hoop and the panty hose as the plant grows. If the plant is insect-pollinated, make sure to remove the covering when it blooms so the pollinators can do their job.

Beerfest

▌ Get rid of slugs with a dishful of beer. Just bury a shallow dish, such as a soup plate or cake pan, up to its rim in the garden in a problem area, such as around your hostas. Fill the dish with beer. Slugs will crawl in and drown.

Alternatively, use a mixture of 2 tablespoons baker's yeast, 1 teaspoon sugar, and 2 cups water. As with the beer, the yeasty fermentation will attract slugs.

Check the dishes daily and remove any dead slugs. After a rainfall, be sure to empty and refill the dish so the mixture is not diluted.

Espresso Exit

▌ Slugs and snails are not fans of Starbucks. The next time you have some leftover strong coffee, pour it into a spray bottle. At the first signs of the slimy pests, spray the coffee on the plant's leaves—top and bottom—as well as the stems. If you have the same luck as researchers in Alaska, the slugs will be gone in 3 to 4 days.

Baby Fresh

▌ Get rid of scale, mealybugs, and powdery mildew by wiping plant leaves—top and bottom—and stems with baby wipes or other cleansing wipes. The ones that contain alcohol work best. The alcohol removes the problem; the moisturizing emollients prevent it from recurring or suffocate any lingering pests.

Disposable facecloths can be used as well, but avoid those with any scrubbing particles.

Scale Down on Scale

▶ Scale appears as dark bumps on the stems and leaves of many citrus and fig trees, lilac bushes, and houseplants. For small-scale infestations (so to speak), use a cotton swab to dab rubbing alcohol on infested areas. For more extensive problems on larger plants, wad up a cotton rag, douse it liberally with alcohol, and rub it over the affected area. The alcohol dries up the scale.

One dose often does the trick, but if you're still seeing these critters, two or three applications 4 to 5 days apart might be needed.

Needs More Salt

▶ Control cabbage worms and butterflies with a mixture of 1 cup rye flour and 1 tablespoon salt. Sprinkle this mixture on the leaves of cabbage, broccoli, and cauliflower plants at planting time in early spring and then again 2 weeks later. It will not only discourage cabbage butterflies from laying eggs in the spring, but if the young, green larvae do hatch, they'll eat the flour, which they can't digest, and die.

Capture Codling Moths

▶ Although the larvae of codling moths burrow into apples, by midsummer they go into a caterpillar stage and climb down the trunk of the tree to overwinter in the soil. Get in their way in July by wrapping the trunk with one of the following barriers, placed 2 feet from the ground: burlap, flannel pajama pants, corrugated cardboard with the ribs toward the trunk, or an old sweater. Check daily for caterpillars hanging out in this barrier. Drop any insects you find into a bucket of soapy water to dispose of them.

Beer for Bugs

▶ These tiny black flea beetles hop around when disturbed and leave multiple tiny holes in the foliage of young tomatoes, eggplants, cole crops, spinach, beets, and radishes. Control them by filling a shallow bowl with beer and setting it near infested plants. The beetles will be attracted to the yeasty smell of the beer, dive in, and drown. And hey, you might snare some slugs, too.

Yuletide Cheer Year-Round

▶ Use those round red Christmas tree ornaments in the off-season to confound apple maggots. In early June, smear the ornaments with a thin coating of petroleum jelly and hang them from your apple trees. The maggots will go for the red, and the petroleum jelly will trap them hopelessly in the goo.

The Apple of Your Eye

▶ For flawless apples, the solution is in the bag. When the fruits are about the size of a marble, select those that are absolutely unblemished. Slip over each one a plastic sandwich bag and use a twist tie to close and secure the bag to the stem. But do so loosely—the apple needs some air circulation. Alternatively, tie a length of pantyhose over the developing apple. The bag (or hose) will protect the apple from burrowing larvae. Remove at harvesttime.

Bleach Your Borers

▶ When dividing German bearded irises, you might notice that some of the rhizomes are riddled with tiny tunnels. This is a sign that they've been infested with iris borers, a serious problem.

Discard the rhizomes that are badly damaged or rotting. Save the sound rhizomes and destroy any remaining borers by soaking the rhizomes in a mixture of 1 gallon water and ½ cup chlorine bleach for 1 hour. Then replant.

8 Ways to Collar Cutworms

One of the most effective ways to prevent cutworm damage is to create a collar around a plant. You can make this collar with a variety of materials.

1 Folded aluminum foil

2 Paper cups with the bottoms removed

3 Rings about 2 inches wide cut from plastic soda bottles

4 Milk cartons with the tops and bottoms removed

5 Square tissue boxes with the tops and bottoms removed

6 Frozen juice cans with both ends removed

7 Tin cans with both ends removed

8 Toilet paper rolls cut into three or four rings

PREVENTING DISEASE

See Spot Go

▶ You know all those black spots that show up in late summer on certain plants, especially roses? That's black spot, a fungal disease.

You can prevent it by spraying your plants with skim milk. (Do not use milk with any fat in it, as the fat will clog the pores in the leaves.) A month or so before your region's last frost date, use a clean spray bottle to mist the problem plants with milk, being sure to hit the stems and the undersides of the leaves. Do this in the morning so the leaves will dry quickly, further discouraging fungal growth.

Reapply every 5 to 7 days for the next 6 weeks. The milk will encourage an invisible milk fungus that is harmless to plants and keeps black spot at bay.

Rummage around your kitchen cupboards for the ingredients for an effective spray that prevents powdery mildew—baking soda, liquid soap, and water.

The Fungus Among Us

▶ Lilacs, bee balm, and roses are some of our favorite flowers, but they're very susceptible to powdery mildew, a disease that occurs in late summer and looks like a gray or whitish powder on top of the leaves. You can prevent powdery mildew with a potion of 2 tablespoons baking soda, 1 tablespoon liquid hand soap, and 2 quarts water. Spray the solution on the plants in early spring after they've started to leaf out but before temperatures regularly hit 80°F. Spray heavily enough to coat the leaves, top and bottom. Repeat once a week for 2 or 3 weeks. The spray affects the pH of the leaves at a critical time, preventing powdery mildew from taking hold.

Terrific Tomatoes

▶ It may sound simple, but one of the best ways to prevent all the many diseases tomatoes are prone to is to mulch like the dickens. Here's what many professional growers do.

In the spring, as soon as you've planted your tomatoes, lay several layers of newspaper around the plants. Moisten the paper well, then top with 2 to 3 inches of grass clippings (no more). This mulch will trap disease spores and other pathogens in the soil, preventing them from splashing onto the tomato foliage during watering or rain.

Collar Your Clematis

▶ Clematis are susceptible to a wilt disease that enters the plant from a broken stem. The point where the stem touches the soil is the most vulnerable part of the clematis vine. Protect your clematis from this malady with a metal collar made from a tuna can.

In early spring, remove the top and bottom of the can and wash it thoroughly. Slip the metal collar over the small clematis plant, pushing the can into the soil so that the vine emerges from the middle of the collar.

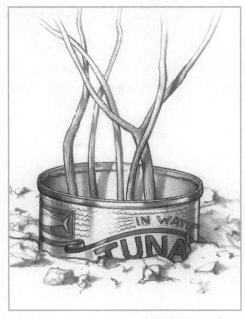

A tuna can makes a sturdy protector for a clematis's delicate crown, a key area for disease to enter.

WARDING OFF WILDLIFE

Cheerio, Chipmunks!

▶ If chipmunks have been terrorizing your bulb plantings and upheaving other plants in the garden, you can try to get rid of them by experimenting with a homemade trap.

You need a 5-gallon bucket with a snap-on lid. Remove the lid, cut a hole 3 to 4 inches across in the lid, and snap it back on.

Put a couple of cups of peanuts in the shell in the bucket. With a bit of luck—on your part, at least—the chipmunks will hop in to get to the peanuts and will then be trapped.

Check the bucket daily. When you catch a chipmunk, cover the hole with a plate, rock, or duct tape. Take the bucket several miles away, out to the country or to another area with plants and soil, and release the chipmunk.

It's a Wrap

▶ You don't need fancy tree wrap from the store to protect the bark of vulnerable trees from deer and rabbits. Brown paper bags work just fine. Cut them into thick strips and wrap the strips around the tree. Use bits of masking tape to hold the strips in place just long enough for you to wrap a web of string around it all to keep it in place until spring.

Chime In

▶ Keep rabbits and deer away from shrubs and trees by hanging lightweight chimes from the branches. For a festive touch, hang small bells recycled from Christmas decorations, too. The sound and motion of these items will frighten the animals away.

Get Grilled

A pinwheel or two, tucked into your strawberry patch, will deter hungry birds.

▶ In early spring, clean your barbecue, but don't fire it up. Instead, use those grill racks as protection from deer and rabbits. Surround a newly planted or emerging cluster of young, tender, tasty plants with a few bricks and top with a rack. It will discourage rabbits and deter deer.

Pinwheel Patrol

▶ If birds have a tendency to raid your strawberry patch, dig through your kids' or grandkids' old toys in search of a pinwheel or two (especially shiny ones). Tuck them into the strawberry patch when the fruit is starting to ripen. The movement and noise will deter birds and chipmunks. The pinwheels make fun, pretty garden ornaments, too.

By a Thread

▌ All those near-empty or odd-colored spools of thread in your sewing basket can be put to use thwarting birds in your berry patch. Just tap a few light stakes in place along the perimeter of the patch. String the thread back and forth among the stakes to make a web that will be difficult for birds to penetrate but will allow you to slip your hand through to harvest the fruit.

Use odds and ends of thread to make a barrier over your berries that birds will avoid.

The Cat's Meow

▌ Moles can cause quite a lot of havoc in your garden—and your lawn—with their constant digging. Fight back with the help of your cat. Save some of the cat litter you scoop from the litter box and sprinkle it into the moles' holes. They are not big fans of cats and may flee the scene in feline fright.

Keep Out Burrowers

▌ If moles, voles, or other burrowing animals are disturbing your perennial and bulb plantings, try planting them in a

Use those "shredded" plastic bags that grapes are sold in to prevent burrowing animals from nibbling your favorite perennials and bulbs.

"cage" that prevents those hungry rodents from getting at roots and bulbs.

Small plastic baskets—the kind sold for organizing various items in the home—work well as long as you cut drainage holes in the bottom. So do 1-gallon plastic ice cream containers with the bottoms cut out. Or, easiest of all, slip the bulbs or roots of perennials into one of those "shredded" plastic bags that grapes and other produce are sold in. (You know the type—they look as if they've been slashed all over with a knife.) Burrowing animals won't want to work through the plastic to do any serious damage.

Let Sleeping Dogs Lie

▶ Sometimes pet bedding gets so smelly or tattered that it has to be replaced. But don't toss it. If it smells too strong for you, it will be downright threatening to many animals that might be heading to your garden for lunch. Put the dog bed outside the garden, on the side nearest the field or woods where deer, raccoons, and rabbits come from. If they get a whiff of Fido, they may decide not to venture in.

To multiply the effect, take any old bath mats, floor mats, or fabric you may have and let the dog sleep on them for a few days, especially when she is wet. Those scented treasures make an excellent barrier, too, and periodic rain showers will refresh that strong odor on a regular basis.

Truly Furry Friends

▶ Even an indoor cat can help chase mice and squirrels away from a newly planted patch of spring-blooming bulbs. In the fall, just after you've planted the bulbs, and again in early spring, as they're emerging and growing, toss newly brushed cat fur onto the planting. Hold the loose clumps in place with a few sticks laid over them. One whiff and those rodents might head the other way.

NO MORE BUG BITES

Serve It Up to Skeeters

▶ Reduce the mosquito population in your yard and diminish the need for mosquito sprays chock-full of chemicals with this earth-friendly mosquito control.

Fill a white soup plate with water and a couple of drops of lemon-scented dishwashing liquid. Set the dish on your porch, patio, or other outdoor area. The combination of the white dish and the lemon soap will attract mosquitoes. You'll observe them drinking from it and then find them dead nearby, usually within 10 feet.

For even better control, set several of these dishes out around the garden, particularly in areas with a lot of mosquitoes, such as under shrubs. Change the soap solution every day or two.

Garden-Fresh Repellent

▶ Make a refreshing, chemical-free insect repellent using herbs from the garden.

In a 2-quart bowl, place ½ cup each fresh lavender, rose-scented geranium, mint, and thyme leaves.

Pour 1 cup vinegar into a 2-cup glass measure. Gently heat the vinegar in the microwave until it just begins to steam or boil. Pour the vinegar over the herbs.

Cover the bowl with a plate and let the herbs steep until the vinegar is cool. Strain the liquid through a fine-mesh sieve and funnel it into a spray bottle.

To use, spritz your skin with the herb vinegar before heading outdoors. Reapply liberally, every 2 hours or so. In fact, this spray is so nice that you can use it after gardening as a refreshing, cooling mist.

Store it in the refrigerator, where it will keep for up to 2 months.

Twinkling Bug Zappers

▶ Enjoy the lovely touch of candles in the evening garden and control mosquitoes at the same time. Fill small, pretty containers, such as margarita glasses or teacups, with water. Sprinkle in a pinch of BT (*Bacillus thuringiensis*) granules, more commonly used for disease control in the garden.

SAVE THE PLANET

Pickle Problem Plants

White vinegar makes an excellent earth-friendly herbicide. Just spray the vinegar, full strength, onto weeds, making sure they're well doused. This works best on a sunny day. (The acid stops the plants from absorbing moisture if it's warm and sunny.) The plants will turn black in a few hours.

The vinegar doesn't work well on deep-rooted plants, but it is excellent in eliminating those tiny reseeding plants that plague gravel and flagstone paths and patios. After a number of applications, fewer and fewer plants will grow in the areas you want to keep plant-free. Vinegar also performs well on moss growing on brick and stone paths and patios.

Use vinegar with caution, however. Test it first on a small area of pavement to make sure it doesn't discolor it or, in the case of limestone, dissolve it. Also, when vinegar is used repeatedly, it raises the acidity of the soil to the point that it can render a patch of ground temporarily sterile (an advantage in paths and patios where you don't want anything to grow). And finally, make sure none of it drifts over onto other, desirable plants. Use a piece of cardboard or a sheet of newspaper to protect nearby plants, if necessary.

Then top with a floating candle. Mosquitoes will be attracted to the standing water but will be killed by the BT.

Place these containers around the garden. They look pretty day or night.

EARTH-FRIENDLY WEED CONTROL

Cheers!

▶ All forms of alcohol, from rubbing alcohol to whiskey, will dehydrate and dry up small weeds. Combine equal parts alcohol and water in a spray bottle. Spray the mixture directly on weed foliage. If the weed isn't zapped the first time, a second dose should do it in.

Boiling Point

▶ Turn a teakettle of boiling water into an instant weed killer. Fill the largest pot you have, such as a stockpot, with water and bring it to a rolling boil. With pot holders, carefully take it out to a path, patio, or sidewalk that has small weeds sprouting. Pour the water onto the weeds to scald and kill them.

Boiling water kills problem plants. Just dump some on pesky weeds in your driveway or on paths and patios.

Weed Killers

▶ Got persistent problem weeds in a large area? Run to your closet or garage and look for ammunition to smother the life out of 'em.

Use sections of old carpeting, a bedspread, old clothes, a bath mat, a throw rug, or cardboard to cover the area. Spread a few inches of bark mulch over the smother cloth to hide it from view. In a few weeks, all but the most persistent weeds will have died, and you can replant. If the infestation is really bad, leave the material in place for a couple of months or more.

Plant Protector

▶ When applying even an organic herbicide, you need to be careful not to spray your garden plants. One of the easiest ways to prevent this is to keep a medium-size cardboard carton nearby. Just invert it over the plant you want to protect.

Or if you have a large, flat cardboard box—the kind a large picture or a mirror might be sold or shipped in—you can slit it at one end to create a two-paneled screen of sorts to position between you and the garden plant.

If you have just a small plant or two to protect, cut the bottom off a 2-liter soda bottle or plastic milk jug and slip it over the plant.

A cardboard box makes an easy, disposable guard to shield your garden plants when spraying an organic herbicide.

Getting Cagey

▶ That wire-type bird or hamster cage you have in the attic can be put to good use until you decide to get another pet someday. Lift the wire portion off the base and use it in the garden as a protective cage for young tomato, pepper, and lettuce plants to keep bunnies from munching.

Prevent blowing over by setting a stone atop, if the design permits.

PROTECTING FROM PETS

Doggy Don't

▶ If your raucous pup (or the neighbor's) has been frolicking in your planting beds, create a low, semivisible fence to keep her out.

Place small, low stakes around the perimeter of the planting area. (Paint them dark green if you'd like them to be nearly invisible.) Then string clear, strong monofilament fishing line from stake to stake, wrapping it around each stake to secure it. Or you can use a tack to hold into place as needed.

The height of the line depends on the size of the dog. Position the line so that it comes to the middle of the dog's chest. If you have multiple dogs of different sizes, add more than one line to the stakes.

Doggy Deterrent

▶ Those green plastic berry baskets make a nifty cover for a row of newly planted seeds. Just wire them together side by side. Place them over the seedbed, adding a chopstick every 2 feet or so to anchor them to the ground. The baskets will keep nosy dogs and other critters out, and the chopsticks will prevent the animals from disturbing the baskets or the wind from blowing them away.

When the berries are gone, those plastic baskets make an effective guard to put over newly planted seeds to prevent dogs, cats, and other critters from bothering them.

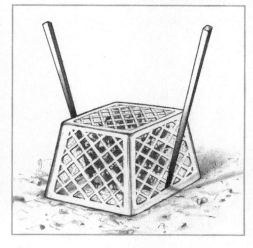

Mark Your Spot

▶ Think like a dog or cat and mark your territory—that is, your garden. Combine one part ammonia and two parts water in a spray bottle or squirt gun (a super-shooter type is particularly useful if you can't move as fast as your pet). When the pet digs or scratches, spray in his direction, being very careful not to hit the pet, especially in the face. In theory, the ammonia smell will tell the animal that you're marking your territory and he needs to back off.

A Pet-Free Zone

▶ If your dog or cat insists on lying atop your new plants, poke craft sticks, chopsticks, or bamboo skewers into the ground around the plants until they fill in. Space them so they protrude at least a couple of inches and are about ½ inch apart.

For larger dogs, you'll need to use larger stakes. Wooden paint stirrers work well.

Critter Control

If your garden shed is open-sided or has walls and windows but no door, you may be dealing with unwanted furry or feathered invaders. You could always add a door or window, but that takes time, money, and skill.

Instead, make a quick and easy door or window covering by recycling an old shower curtain or good-quality vinyl or plastic drop cloth. (Clear is especially good because it lets in more light.)

Reuse the tension rod used to hang the shower curtain, or simply nail the curtain in place from the inside.

The curtain is flexible enough that it's easy for you to get in and out of the shed, even when lugging filled buckets or pushing a wheelbarrow. Yet this flimsy barrier, amazingly, is enough to discourage bats, birds, skunks, raccoons, and other critters (as long as they're not too determined) from entering.

Go Nuts

▶ Keep cats out of the garden by sprinkling nutshell shards around the perimeter of a planting area. Cats won't walk across this uncomfortably poky barrier.

Save those nutshells! When used as a mulch around the perimeter of your flowerbeds, they'll keep kitty at bay.

You'll need a lot of cracked shells, so it's a smart idea to save them up over the winter. Store them in a large bag or box or two.

Come spring, spread the shells at least 10 inches into the planting area. (They'll blend in visually with wood chips and many other garden mulches.)

If nutshells are hard to come by, you can substitute a thick barrier of small, sharp-edged pinecones for the same cat-deterring results.

CHAPTER THIRTEEN

Indoor Gardening

Since ancient times, people have brought live plants into their homes to add beauty, color, and fragrance. But houseplants have some special needs. Gardeners need to be clever in finding ways to provide enough light, nutrients, and humidity for these beauties, as well as to fight pests and diseases. In this chapter, you'll learn how to fertilize plants with water from your aquarium, turn scrap containers into attractive pots, and protect plants from marauding pets with chili oil. If you follow our advice, you'll have lush, healthy houseplants that brighten your home all year long.

UPPING THE HUMIDITY

Cold Remedy for Plants

▶ That humidifier you run in your room when you have a cough or cold doesn't need to be tucked away in a closet when you're well. Instead, bring it out as the perfect Rx for humidity-deprived plants.

In the fall and winter, when your furnace is running and drying out the air, aim a cool-air humidifier directly at your plants. If you have a warm-air humidifier, point it away from the plants so you don't scorch them. Just an hour or two a day will make a significant difference.

Fish Tank Terrarium

▶ Are your humidity-loving orchids and Venus flytrap struggling? Solve the problem by turning an old fish tank into a terrarium for these and other humidity lovers, such as small ferns and woodland plants.

You can grow these plants in pots in the tank or, if you like, plant them directly in the tank. If you want to plant them in the tank, put a 1-inch layer of horticultural charcoal on the bottom. Top that with 3 to 4 inches of potting soil or bark potting medium, depending on the recommended medium for the plants.

After adding your plants, cover the tank with a sheet of glass, an old beveled mirror, plastic wrap, or even a dry-cleaning bag.

No Waste Here

▶ Provide more humidity for larger potted plants and create a handy cachepot as well by recycling a round plastic wastebasket.

Choose a plant whose container is 1 inch smaller in diameter than that of the wastebasket. Put a layer of gravel, marbles, or even crushed soda cans in the bottom of the wastebas-

An old wastebasket is an innovative cachepot for holding houseplants in plastic containers and providing additional humidity. Just put gravel and water in the bottom.

ket, just deep enough to position the plant so that it is almost even with the rim of the wastebasket. Add about 1 inch of water to the wastebasket and set the plant in place. The water will evaporate over time, providing humidity for the plant. Add more water occasionally.

POTS AND MORE

Count Your Containers

▶ Do you love houseplants but don't have much of a budget for fancy containers? If so, a can of faux granite spray paint—which costs just a few dollars—can turn an assortment of cheap plastic pots, tin cans, yogurt containers, gallon ice cream buckets, and other odds and ends into nice-looking earth-toned containers. You can even spray jar lids and mismatched ceramic saucers or plates to make matching saucers.

Rain or Shine

▶ If you have an old vase-type umbrella stand that hasn't held an umbrella for years, dust it off and put it to use as a pretty plant stand. Fill it almost to the top with crushed soda cans, squares of dry floral foam, or foam packing peanuts. Then set a large potted plant on top. (Be sure to put a saucer underneath to collect leaks.) Tuck this tall, elegant plant into a corner that needs a little interest or anywhere else in the house.

Tacky Idea

▶ We all like to perch small jars and pots on our windowsills, but sometimes the arrangement is a bit precar-

---

10 Creative Containers

Some of the prettiest plant containers are also the most clever. Slip an uninspired plastic pot into one of these concealing containers.

1 A teapot or teakettle
2 A soup tureen
3 A ceramic or metal cereal, serving, or soup bowl
4 A jewelry or decorative box
5 A wicker basket
6 A child's sand bucket
7 An iron or brass firewood holder
8 A ceramic or colored-glass flower vase
9 A copper pot or iron skillet
10 A purse

A Light Touch

You don't need to invest in a fancy grow light setup to provide a haven for houseplants. You can create an excellent houseplant garden in your basement (or any room of your home) using items found around the house.

Start with the lighting. Hanging lights, reading lights, and floor lamps can all provide additional light. For best results, you will want to equip these lights with special grow-light bulbs that provide both cool and warm light.

A shop light, if you have one, is ideal because you can equip it with a cool fluorescent and a warm fluorescent tube. This setup mimics sunlight the way a grow light does but costs considerably less. However, even plain incandescent bulbs will work. Plus, if you create this space in front of a window, you'll boost the amount and quality of light considerably.

An old table scrounged from the attic will keep things at convenient working height. Make trays for the plants by cutting out the bottoms of broken plastic laundry baskets. Put in a layer of gravel and a little water to raise the humidity.

Voilà! You'll have an ideal place to baby a variety of houseplants all year long.

ious. Hedge your bets by using a tiny wad of sticky tack—the stuff used to hang posters on walls. It's available wherever office supplies are sold. Make a ball or two about the size of a pea and tuck it in between the container (or saucer) and the sill. The pot or jar will be a little less likely to fall if jiggled a bit.

Protection from Pots

▶ Potted plants are beautiful on our furniture, but the water rings they leave can create a problem. You can do two things to minimize potential damage.

First, waterproof a clay saucer by giving it a coat of clear polyurethane spray. The saucer should be absolutely clean and absolutely dry before spraying. Spray and let dry for an hour or two. The polyurethane will prevent the clay from absorbing water.

Second, make a pot coaster of sorts from a flexible plastic lid—the type used on coffee and shortening cans. Cut it to fit just under the saucer of the plant. It will be nearly invisible but will provide a layer of protection.

And if your plant does dribble on your varnished wood furniture, wipe up the spill as quickly as possible. If it leaves a white spot behind, rub a little vegetable oil on the spot. It will be gone in a few hours.

CD Coasters

▌ Those free and no-longer-usable CDs can really accumulate. Put them to good use by tucking one under each potted plant in your house. It won't catch water, but it will create a barrier of air and plastic between the saucer and your furniture, preventing water rings.

HOUSEPLANT PLANTING AND PROPAGATION

Sweet Idea

▌ When rooting cuttings of ivies and other houseplants in water, add a pinch of sugar to the container. It's believed to nourish the cuttings and to encourage them to root faster.

A bit of sugar added to the water when rooting cuttings feeds the plants and induces better rooting.

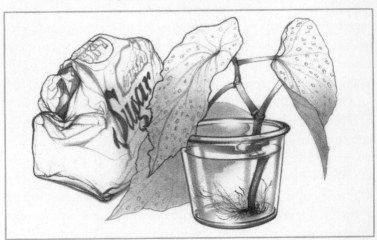

Put a Sock in It

❯ Where do all those stray socks go? No matter; you now have a good use for the odd mates left behind.

Tuck a folded sock into the bottom of your houseplant's pot. It will prevent soil from washing out of the pot, and if it's made from an absorbent material, such as cotton, it will hold moisture at a deeper level, encouraging roots to reach down deep and thus creating stronger plants.

Other excellent items to place over the drainage hole include a piece of folded newspaper, a coffee filter, or a recipe card.

FERTILIZING INDOOR PLANTS

Eggs and Tea

❯ The next time you make a batch of hard- or soft-boiled eggs, save the water. Allow it to cool and use it to water your African violets. The calcium leached from the shells during boiling will encourage more blooms.

And if you have any hot or iced tea left over, let it come to room temperature and use it to water African violets, too. The tea contains elements that will lightly fertilize the plants.

Put the Squeeze On

❯ Fish emulsion is an excellent organic fertilizer for plants, but depending on the formulation, it often needs to be pre-mixed. Make this planet-friendly fertilizer a bit more convenient to use with the help of a recycled flip-top squirt bottle, such as one that originally held dishwashing liquid, salad dressing, or ketchup. Premix the emulsion and pour it into the bottle. Keep it conveniently stored inside your watering can, and you'll never overlook fertilizing again.

Fast Fertilizer

❯ Those canisters that baby and other pop-up wipes come in make convenient containers to mix and administer water-soluble organic fertilizers for houseplants.

Mix each fertilizer according to the package directions in an amount that can be stored in one of these containers. Replace the lid, making sure the little pop-off tab is snapped on securely, and give it a hard shake or two to blend well. When it's time for fertilizing, just apply a dribble directly from the container.

Better yet, you can use a permanent marker on the side of the container to keep track of what you watered when, so you'll never under- or overfertilize again.

5 Steps to Fight Houseplant Problems

Is something bothering your houseplant, but you don't know what it is? A little spa treatment for your plant may provide the cure.

1 Rinse the plant thoroughly, again being sure to get under the leaves and along the stems.

2 Apply an insect-killing potion. Put aluminum foil around the base of the plant to protect the soil. Set the plant inside your shower or the kitchen sink. Fill a large spray bottle with a mixture of about 1 quart warm water, 2 tablespoons mild liquid hand soap (no moisturizers, please), 1 teaspoon Tabasco sauce, and ¼ cup vodka or gin. Spray the plant, still in the sink or tub, thoroughly, being sure to get under the leaves

and the spots where the stems meet the branches. Let sit for 15 minutes. Rinse off thoroughly.

3 Give the soil a long soak. Remove the foil and set the plant in a large bucket with several inches of tepid water. Water it from the top as well. Let sit for 1 hour.

4 Cut out diseased leaves and stems. Working carefully with scissors, trim out all yellowed or diseased plant material. In many cases, this will stop or dramatically slow the spread of a disease.

5 Move it. Give it more light. Or better yet, let it spend a couple of months on you porch or deck in a spot out of direct sun. Sometimes more light cures all.

WATERING

The Best Watering Can

▌ Why spend money on a watering can when all it will do is take up space? Instead, capitalize on what may be the best free watering cans there are—2-liter plastic soda bottles. They hold more water than a lot of overdesigned watering cans, and their narrow necks are ideal for reaching into foliage. Plus, they're free, so you can keep one on every level of the house and you won't have to run up and down the stairs to grab the watering can each time a plant is thirsty.

Fishing for Fertilizer

▌ If you're a conscientious pet owner and pump water from your aquarium every week as recommended, you also have a prime source of nitrogen-rich water for your houseplants. Either water your plants on the spot or pump the water into clean plastic milk jugs to save for your next plant-watering session. Make sure to use the water within a couple of weeks, however, or it will develop a foul odor.

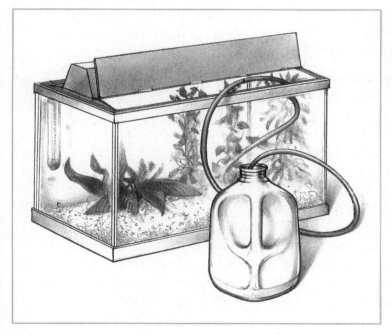

Don't throw out that aquarium water. It's an ideal source of nitrogen for your houseplants.

3 Ways to Keep Your Houseplants Watered

Going away for several days? There's no need to get someone to water your plants. Here are some easy ways to keep just about any houseplant hydrated for up to 10 days.

1 Fill a turkey baster with water, filling even the bulb. Hold your finger over the tip to prevent it from dribbling. Quickly insert it about 1 inch into the soil (deeper if it won't stand upright), creating a vacuum. It will slowly drip water for a day or two. This works best with medium-size pots.

2 Pour 2 to 3 inches of water into a mixing bowl and set a potted plant in the water. It will soak up water through the drainage hole(s) in the bottom. If you did this all the time, your plant would be overwatered, but for a week or so, it will be fine, especially if it's a type of plant that needs moist soil, such as a fern, arrowhead, or prayer plant.

3 Fill the bathtub with about 3 inches of water. (*Tip:* If your tub has a tendency to drain slowly even when closed, smear petroleum jelly thickly around the perfectly dry drain before filling. Top with a square of plastic wrap and press down firmly to seal.) Set larger houseplants in the tub.

Perfect Water

▶ If you have tap water that's high in minerals, your houseplants probably show it. They've developed crusty white mineral deposits on the surface of the soil and on the inner or outer rim of the pot.

If you use a dehumidifier, however, your problem is solved. The water pulled from the air is free of the minerals contained in tap water. When you empty the dehumidifier, pour some of the water into clean plastic milk jugs. (Use a funnel, of course.) Use this beautifully purified water to water your plants whenever they need it.

GOOD GROOMING

Give Them the Brush-Off

▶ African violets and other plants with fine hairs on their leaves collect dust, which can block much-needed sunlight. Remove the dust without damaging the leaves by using a paintbrush or soft toothbrush to gently whisk it away. And if you don't have one of those handy, a cotton swab, ever so slightly dampened, will work nicely.

Houseplant Hodgepodge

▶ If you have a wicker laundry basket or other large woven basket that is a bit tattered around the edges or has a broken handle, turn it into an indoor houseplant garden. Not only will you get rid of that hodgepodge look of little house-plants scattered all over, but you'll also have healthier house-plants, as they'll benefit from the additional humidity created by their being grouped together.

Line the basket with a black plastic garbage bag, tucking it into the weave or stapling it in place. To hold a collection

That battered laundry basket can find new life holding your smaller house-plants. The basket makes an attractive display container, and the plants' leaves hide the basket's flaws.

Houseplants flopping? Prop them back up almost invisibly with the help of chopsticks.

of smaller houseplants up to the rim of the basket, place some foam packing peanuts or crushed aluminum cans in the bottom. If possible, position the plants so that their large leaves and fronds drape over the broken part(s) of the basket. If there are unsightly gaps between the plants, just tuck in bits of dried floral Spanish moss.

Low Stakes

▶A wooden chopstick or two makes an instant stake for a floppy houseplant of small to medium height. Simply insert the chopstick alongside the plant. Tie with string or a dark green twist tie, if necessary. If several leaves need support, insert two chopsticks in the shape of an X as a framework to hold them up.

HOUSEPLANTS, PETS, AND CHILDREN

Keep Out Kitty

▶ If your cats have made your larger potted plants their favorite place to dig and make a mess, discourage them with small bamboo skewers—the kind used for small kebabs. Insert the skewers into the soil about every inch or so, with the pointed ends protruding ½ to 1 inch. (You can cut the skewers in half to make them go further, if you like.) Cats are smart enough not to try walking around on the sharp surface.

Hot Idea

▶ Occasionally, cats and dogs like to chew on houseplants. In some cases, this is a problem for the plants—the leaves get shredded and disfigured. In other cases, the pet might be ingesting enough of a toxic plant to become ill.

Discourage pets from chomping and batting houseplants with chili oil, used to add heat to Asian stir-frys. Wearing latex gloves (so your hands don't sting) or working carefully with a wadded-up tissue or cotton ball, rub a bit of the oil onto the affected leaves or the leaves most at risk for attack. The oil will do nothing more than make your dog or cat sneeze and drool a bit, and it will save the plant—and possibly your pet—from a much worse fate.

Plant Pen

▶ When small grandchildren or other pint-size visitors come to visit, your houseplants can take a beating. What could be more tempting for tiny hands than nice big leaves to shred into pieces or even chew on? And what could be more fun than digging in the soil or tipping the plant over to see all that soil spill out?

Dust off that old playpen and use it to keep harmful or fragile houseplants out of the way when children come to visit.

6 Mulches to Discourage Cats

One way to keep cats out of potted plants is to mulch them with something cats don't care to play with. Try one of the following:

1 Bottle caps
2 Wine corks
3 Dried beans
4 Buttons
5 Seashells
6 Marbles

Keep plants and children safe by placing plants out of harm's way. Dig that playpen out of the attic, and instead of putting the kids in the playpen—a less popular option these days than in years gone by—put the plants inside. As long as the leaves aren't poking through the slats, the plants and kids will be safe until your little visitors go home.

This is also a useful trick if you have a new puppy in your home. Use the playpen until the dog gets used to the surroundings and is less likely to explore by ripping things up.

Lemon Fresh

▶ Some gardeners say that their cats are less inclined to bother plants that have the scent of citrus. Try scattering orange or lemon peels on the soil of houseplants your cats have been bothering. Alternatively, soak a cotton ball in lemon oil (the kind you use to polish furniture) and leave a ball or two at the base of the plant to discourage those unwanted feline visits.

CHAPTER FOURTEEN

Flower Arranging, Water Gardens, and More

In this chapter, you'll find ways to save time and money—and have more fun—cutting and drying flowers, building a water garden, enjoying outdoor living, and doing much more. Use plastic wrap to hold flower stems in place almost invisibly, put a pancake flipper to use removing algae from your water garden, or dust off an old mirror in the attic and put it on your porch to provide more light for potted plants there.

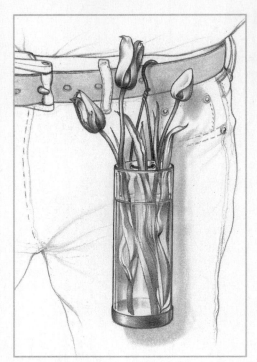

A powdered drink or tennis ball can makes a handy holster for collecting and conditioning cut flowers.

FLOWER ARRANGING

Flower Holster

▎As they're cut, flowers love to have their stems submerged in water for a few hours in order to become "conditioned"—that is, to absorb as much water as possible so that they can withstand the rigors of sitting in a vase for the next several days.

Condition on the spot by turning a canister that powdered lemonade or tennis balls came in into a holster of sorts. Poke two holes about an inch apart near the top of the canister. Thread a length of coat hanger wire through the holes and twist the ends together tightly with pliers. Shape the twisted wire into a hook that will fit over your belt or through a belt loop. Trim the wire as needed. Fill the canister with water and add flowers immediately as you cut them.

If you find the wire rubs at all against your waist, wrap it with duct tape.

Longer Lasting Spring Bouquets

▎Tulips and daffodils look so pretty in a vase together, but the daffodils give off a substance that shortens the life of tulips. Work around this problem by saving up tall olive jars. When making an arrangement, add water to a jar and slip it into a larger vase. Put daffodils (plus other flowers, if you want) in the olive jar. Then fill the rest of the vase up to the depth of the olive jar with water. Put tulips (and other flowers) in the vase.

If you're doing an arrangement of tulips and daffodils using floral foam, save the tiny slip-on tubes sold with single roses. Refill them and slip them onto the tulips before inserting them into the foam.

Looking through Rose-Colored Water

▶ If your favorite glass vase has become permanently cloudy or stained by hard-water mineral deposits, there's no need to throw it away. Instead, when arranging flowers, add a few drops of food coloring to the water. It will disguise the deposits and, if you choose well, look pretty with the flowers.

A bonus: White and pale-colored flowers may absorb some of the food coloring, adding a fun, ever-changing element to your arrangement.

Plastic Wrap to the Rescue

▶ If you have just a single flower to tuck into a narrow-necked vase, the flower may tilt and tip in a most annoying way. Solve the problem by stuffing a little clear plastic wrap into the narrowest portion of the vase near the rim. First, insert the stem. Then, using a pencil or chopstick, if necessary, tuck in a wad of plastic wrap. The stem will stay perfectly upright.

We'll Drink to That

▶ There's no need to get rid of chipped wineglasses, champagne flutes, or brandy snifters. They make elegant vases for all your favorite flowers. In fact, they're beautiful grouped in the center of a table, each at a different height and each with a different kind of flower.

A shot glass is just the right size vase for tiny flowers such as pansies and lilies of the valley.

Tiny Vases

▶ Pansies, violets, and lilies of the valley are diminutive flowers that need diminutive vases, but those are hard to find. Instead, dig through your cupboard for a shot glass or creamer. Both are just the right height and diameter.

Small flowers like these will look best if you use a rubber band to gather together a number of blooms into one tight bunch. Then cut the stems off evenly so they stand up nicely in the vase.

DRYING FLOWERS

Airtight Case

▶ Those circular tins English biscuits, shortbread, and other fancy cookies come in are wonderful for storing strawflowers and other fragile dried flowers. Layer them between crumpled sheets of waxed paper and snap on the lid. Use a strip of masking tape as a label on the outside of the tin.

3 Ways to Grow Air Plants

Those cute little "air plants" that grow in frost-free areas are actually tillandsias, members of the same family as the pineapple. In their native habitats, their curly little green or gray-green leaves absorb nutrients and moisture from fog, dew, and rain. Tillandsias have little in the way of roots and no need for soil, but they do need a place to hang. Here are some ideas for tillandsia displays.

1 Give a scrap of Peg-Board a coat of paint in a color that contrasts nicely with the air plants, such as a deep green or rich blue. Hang the air plants from the pegs sold to insert into the board. The pegs provide excellent circulation, a must for air plants.

2 Mount an old window screen vertically. Unbend the ends of small paper clips, then poke the paper clips through the back of the screen. Hook the tillandsias onto the clips.

3 Mount hardware cloth in a wooden frame or simply attach it to a wall. Make a slipknot using UV-stabilized monofilament line or heavy black button thread. Slip the knot loosely around a tillandsia, then tie it to the hardware cloth.

Use fabric softener as an inexpensive replacement for glycerin to preserve flowers better and longer.

How Dry I Am

▶ Fabric softener makes an effective and inexpensive substitute for glycerin when preserving some of your favorite flowers and foliage.

Fill a large plastic margarine tub or whipped topping container with fabric softener, snap on the lid, and use the tip of a sharp knife to cut a dozen or so quarter-inch Xs in the top.

Push as many stems of cut flowers or foliage as you can fit snugly through the Xs and into the fabric softener. Let the stems soak up the softener for several weeks until they are dried and well preserved. This technique works especially well for preserving baby's breath, statice, ferns, and magnolia leaves.

Efficient Drying

▶ Some of the best supplies for drying flowers are right in your home office, such as rubber bands and paper clips. Use rubber bands to gather together bunches of flowers to hang for drying. Unlike string, rubber bands will tighten as the flowers dry and continue to hold them fast.

Keep rummaging through that desk drawer for a handful of paper clips. Pull each apart into an elongated S shape. This is excellent for looping through a rubber band and over a nail. Or loop several onto a laundry drying rack, where the flowers will get plenty of air circulation.

WATER GARDENING

Pretty Pond Protection

The water dripping from that leaky or slightly sagging gutter can "feed" a pretty rain chain that leads to a water garden.

▶ In some areas, it's necessary to drape netting over small ponds to protect them from cats, raccoons, herons, and other fish-eating animals. However, most netting needs some support to keep it from sinking into the water. A cute and permanent way to add support is to use that old, defunct fishing rod. Fill a large nursery pot with gravel and insert the handle, at a pleasing angle, into the gravel, setting the pot in the bottom of a shallow pond. The tip of the rod will keep the netting out of the water and add a whimsical decorative element as well.

Great Gutter

▶ Have a gutter that overflows due to a problematic angle? Capitalize on the drip and drizzle by creating a water feature under the gutter.

Put a plastic-lined half barrel, an old black iron kettle, a rustic galvanized bucket, or any other rather large, waterproof container underneath. Fill with water.

Run an old chain from the point where the water drips to just below the surface of the water in the container, attaching it to the gutter with a bolted hook or a piece of wire. This rain chain will create a pleasing effect on drizzly days.

Add a few floating plants, and you'll have a one-of-a-kind water feature. Replenish the water during dry weather to keep the water fresh and the plants thriving.

Tabletop Treat

▶ Have a pretty soup tureen, large serving bowl, or deep copper or brass pan that does nothing but collect dust? Get it out, brush it off, and use it as the basis of a charming tabletop water garden.

Purchase a small electric pump-fountain, found at most garden centers for around $15. Position the pump-fountain in the bowl and fill in around it with whatever you have handy—pebbles, marbles, seashells, or smooth river rocks. Add water, plug in the pump-fountain, and enjoy.

Flipped Out over Algae

▶ One of the biggest problems in ponds is algae, which can easily get out of hand without diligent care. You don't need a fancy pond net to control algae in smaller ponds. Instead, use a large slotted spoon or pancake flipper from your kitchen. It will collect the algae nicely. If you need a little length on the tool to get to the center of the pond, duct-tape it to the end of a broom handle.

4 Uses for Christmas Trees after Christmas

After spending all that money on your holiday tree, it's silly to dump it in the landfill. There are plenty of ways to make that tree useful in the garden.

1 Cut off the branches and use them as a protective mulch over perennials and the bases of rose-bushes.

2 Cut off the branches and stick the cut ends into the soil in planters, pots, and window boxes. This greenery will last until spring.

3 If you have a pond or lake nearby, toss the tree into the water. It makes an ideal fish-breeding mini-habitat.

4 After the trunk has been denuded of branches, use it in spring as a rustic pole in the garden to support green beans, sweet peas, morning glories, and other vining plants.

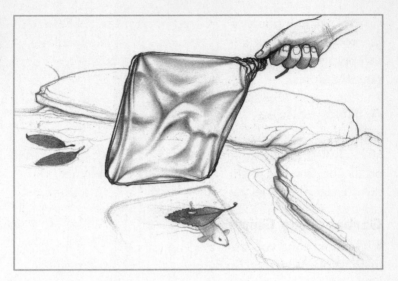

Turn a wire coat hanger and a length of panty hose into a pond net in minutes.

Neat Net

▶ To collect fish in your pond, you can fashion a freebie net with nothing more than a wire coat hanger, an old pair of panty hose, and a rubber band. Pull out the triangular part of the hanger to make a diamond shape. Cut off one of the legs of the hose and pull it over the diamond, fastening it

8 Creative Stake Toppers

How many times have you bent over in the garden and nearly poked out an eye on a plant stake? The sharp ends of stakes, whether they be wood, metal, or bamboo, pose a hazard when they're hidden among stems and foliage. Solve this problem by topping wooden or metal stakes with one of the following fun and funky toppers.

1 Old doorknobs
2 Salvaged drawer knobs
3 Curtain finials
4 Tennis balls
5 Table tennis balls
6 Wooden beads hot-glued into place
7 Wine corks nailed or hot-glued into place
8 Fishing bobbers

closed over the hook of the hanger with the rubber band. Try to keep the hose a little slack over the wire to allow for a cupping effect. You'll have a net as good as any you could buy in a store.

A Strained Idea

▶ The next time you need to collect a few fish in your pond, just grab a large kitchen strainer. It makes a fast, easy pond net. Just run it through the dishwasher when you're done to sterilize it so you can use it for cooking again.

Garbage Bag Gaiters

▶ The next time you need to get out in the pond for cleaning and planting, there's no need to get all muddy and wet. Grab two thick-ply garbage bags, cut the bottoms out of each, and slip one over each leg. Then use duct tape to secure them around your thighs or hips.

A sock filled with fiberfill or wadded-up panty hose makes an economical pond pump filter.

Sock It to It

▶ An old sock makes an economical filter for a pond pump. Stuff polyester fiberfill or wadded-up panty hose into the foot of a sock or even the foot of yet more panty hose. Slide the open end over the pump hose and secure it with a rubber band. Once a week, remove the filter and set it aside to dry, then clean and reuse it or replace it with a new one.

Panty Hose Planters

▶ Turn old panty hose into economical and practically invisible planters for your aquatic plants.

Cut off each leg 8 to 10 inches from the toe. Fill it about two-thirds full with a few rocks and clay-laden or aquatic potting soil. Tie the other end shut.

Cut a slit in the side of the hose and position a plant in the soil. If

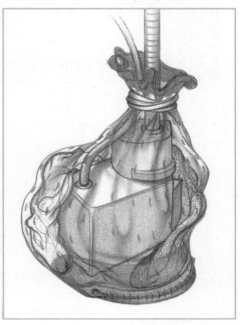

8 Great Materials for Tying Up Plants

Need something to tie plants to a trellis or stake? Before you run out to buy twine, consider using one of these found items instead.

1 Yarn
2 Ribbon
3 Several twist ties tied together
4 Rubber bands looped through one another to make a strand
5 Ropes from old double-hung windows
6 Old belts
7 Pull cords from blinds or draperies
8 Leaves of ornamental grasses or daylilies

necessary, secure the panty hose planter by bundling it with dark-colored twine (which won't show up well underwater). Then place the whole thing in your water garden.

Fish Hideaway

▶ In water gardens, fish do best if they have a place to lie low and hide from predators. A flat rock propped up on bricks or other stones works well, but if you don't have a perfectly shaped rock for this, an old pizza pan will do. Just lay two or three bricks at the bottom of the pond and place the pizza pan on top. To disguise the pan, top with a potted water plant.

Padded Carpet

▶ When laying a rubber liner to construct a water garden, lay down some carpet scraps first, putting the pile side up. The carpet prevents bits of glass or sharp rocks embedded in the soil from puncturing the liner. Also, it has more "give" than most soils do, so if something sharp pokes the liner from above, the liner is less likely to puncture or tear.

OUTDOOR LIVING

Screen the View

▶ Hide an unsightly compost pile or your messy workbench with old wooden doors. Vintage wooden doors with carvings, small windows, and other details are ideal, but even plain old hollow-core doors work well, too.

Hinge two or three doors together, folding-screen-style. Leave as they are or use leftover house paint to spruce them up. To further stabilize them, you may want to hold them in place with a few stakes, pounded into the ground in front of and behind each door. The stakes should be at least a couple of feet long and inserted so that 6 to 8 inches of each protrudes above the ground.

Reflected Glory

▶ Plants on a porch are wonderful, adding color and greenery up close where you can enjoy them. But too often, in the deeper recesses of a porch, there's not enough light for some of your favorite plants. You can increase the light for plants and add a nice touch to your porch by hanging a spare mirror behind the plants. It will reflect the available light back onto the plants, letting you grow a wider variety of plants in the limited light.

Resources

❱ If you contact associations or specialty nurseries by mail, please enclose a self-addressed, stamped envelope with your inquiry. Notes in italics indicate particular products, plants, or services offered.

ASSOCIATIONS AND ORGANIZATIONS

Backyard Wildlife Habitat Program
National Wildlife Federation
11100 Wildlife Center Drive
Reston, VA 20190
Phone: (703) 438-6100,
(800) 822-9919
E-mail: info@nwf.org
Web site: www.nwf.org/backyardwild
lifehabitat/

Biodynamic Farming and Gardening Association
25844 Butler Road
Junction City, OR 97448
Phone: (541) 998-0105,
(888) 516-7797
Fax: (541) 998-0106
E-mail: biodynamic@aol.com
Web site: www.biodynamics.com

National Gardening Association
1100 Dorset Street
South Burlington, VT 05403
Phone: (802) 863-5251
Web site: www.garden.org

North American Butterfly Association
4 Delaware Road
Morristown, NJ 07960
Phone: (973) 285-0907
E-mail: naba@naba.org
Web site: www.naba.org

Rodale Institute Experimental Farm
611 Siegfriedale Road
Kutztown, PA 19530
Phone: (610) 683-1400
Fax: (610) 683-8548
E-mail: info@rodaleinst.org
Web site: www.rodaleinstitute.org

BENEFICIAL INSECTS

Bountiful Gardens
18001 Shafer Ranch Road
Willits, CA 95490
Phone: (707) 459-6410
Fax: (707) 459-1925
E-mail: bountiful@sonic.net
Web site: www.bountifulgardens.org

Gardens Alive!
5100 Schenley Place
Lawrenceburg, IN 47025
Phone: (812) 537-8651
Fax: (812) 537-5108

E-mail: service@gardensalive.com
Web site: www.gardensalive.com

BULBS

Breck's

PO Box 65
Guilford, IN 47022
Phone: (513) 354-1512
Fax: (513) 354-1505
Web site: www.brecks.com

Brent and Becky's Bulbs

7900 Daffodil Lane
Gloucester, VA 23061
Phone: (804) 693-3966, (877) 661-2852
Fax: (804) 693-9436
Web site: brentandbeckysbulbs.com

Dutch Gardens

144 Intervale Road
Burlington, VT 05401
Phone: (800) 950-4470
Fax: (800) 551-6712
E-mail: info-dg@dutchgardens.com
Web site: www.dutchgardens.com

FLOWERS

Bluestone Perennials

7211 Middle Ridge Road
Madison, OH 44057
Phone: (800) 852-5243
Fax: (440) 428-7198
E-mail:
bluestone@bluestoneperennials.com
Web site: www.bluestoneperennials.com

W. Atlee Burpee & Co.

300 Park Avenue
Warminster, PA 18974
Phone: (800) 888-1447
Fax: (800) 487-5530
E-mail: custserv@burpee.com
Web site: www.burpee.com

Park Seed

1 Parkton Avenue
Greenwood, SC 29647
Phone: (800) 213-0076
Fax: (800) 275-9941
E-mail: info@parkscs.com
Web site: www.parkseed.com

Select Seeds Antique Flowers

180 Stickney Hill Road
Union, CT 06076
Phone: (800) 684-0395
Fax: (800) 653-3304
Web site: www.selectseeds.com

Thompson & Morgan Inc.

PO Box 1308
Jackson, NJ 08527
Phone: (800) 274-7333
Fax: (888) 466-4769
E-mail: tminc@thompson-morgan.com
Web site: www.thompson-morgan.com

Wayside Gardens

1 Garden Lane
Hodges, SC 29695
Phone: (800) 213-0379
Fax: (800) 457-9712
E-mail: info@waysidecs.com
Web site: www.waysidegardens.com

White Flower Farm

PO Box 50, Route 63
Litchfield, CT 06790
Phone: (860) 482-8915, (800) 503-9624
Fax: (860) 482-0532
E-mail: custserv@whiteflowerfarm.com
Web site: www.whiteflowerfarm.com

GARDEN SUPPLIES

Gardener's Supply Co.

128 Intervale Road
Burlington, VT 05401
Phone: (888) 876-5520

Fax: (800) 551-6712
E-mail: info@gardeners.com
Web site: www.gardeners.com

Gardens Alive!
5100 Schenley Place
Lawrenceburg, IN 47025
Phone: (812) 537-8651
Fax: (812) 537-5108
E-mail: service@gardensalive.com
Web site: www.gardensalive.com

Kinsman Garden Co.
PO Box 428
Pipersville, PA 18947
Phone: (800) 733-4146
Fax: (215) 766-5624
E-mail: kinsco@kinsmangarden.com
Web site: www.kinsmangarden.com

A. M. Leonard, Inc.
241 Fox Drive
Piqua, OH 45356
Phone: (800) 543-8955
Fax: (800) 433-0633
E-mail: info@amleo.com
Web site: www.amleo.com

The Natural Gardening Co.
PO Box 750776
Petaluma, CA 94975
Phone: (707) 766-9303
Fax: (707) 766-9747
E-mail: info@naturalgardening.com
Web site: www.naturalgardening.com

Worm's Way
7850 North State Road 37
Bloomington, IN 47404
Phone: (800) 274-9676
Fax: (800) 466-0795
E-mail: info@wormsway.com
Web site: www.wormsway.com

SOIL TESTING

Cook's Consulting
RD 2, Box 13
Lowville, NY 13367
Phone: (315) 376-3002
Web site: www.lcida.org/cooks.html
Organic recommendations; free soil-testing kit

Peaceful Valley Farm Supply
PO Box 2209
Grass Valley, CA 95945
Phone: (530) 272-4769
Fax: (530) 272-4794
E-mail: contact@groworganic.com
Web site: www.groworganic.com

Timberleaf Soil Testing Services
39648 Old Spring Road
Murrieta, CA 92563
Phone: (909) 677-7510
Basic and trace mineral soil tests; organic recommendations provided

TREES, SHRUBS, AND VINES

Carroll Gardens
444 East Main Street
Westminster, MD 21157
Phone: (410) 848-5422, (800) 638-6334
Fax: (410) 857-4112
E-mail: info@carrollgardens.com
Web site: www.carrollgardens.com

Forestfarm
990 Tetherow Road
Williams, OR 97544
Phone: (541) 846-7269
Fax: (541) 846-6963
E-mail: plants@forestfarm.com
Web site: www.forestfarm.com

Greer Gardens
1280 Goodpasture Island Road
Eugene, OR 97401

Phone: (541) 686-8266, (800) 548-0111
Fax: (541) 686-0910
E-mail: orders@greergardens.com
Web site: www.greergardens.com

Gurney's Seed and Nursery Co.
PO Box 4178
Greendale, IN 47025
Phone: (513) 354-1492
Fax: (513) 354-1493
E-mail: info@gurneys.com
Web site: www.gurneys.com

Pickering Nurseries Inc.
RR 1
3043 Country Road
Port Hope, ON L1A 3V5
Canada
Phone: (905) 753-2155, (866) 269-9282
E-mail: roses@pickeringnurseries.com
Web site: www.pickeringnurseries.com

VEGETABLES

W. Atlee Burpee & Co.
300 Park Avenue
Warminster, PA 18974
Phone: (800) 888-1447
Fax: (800) 487-5530
E-mail: custserv@burpee.com
Web site: www.burpee.com

The Cook's Garden
PO Box 1889
Southampton, PA 18966
Phone: (800) 457-9703
E-mail: cooksgarden@earthlink.net
Web site: www.cooksgarden.com

Irish Eyes—Garden City Seeds
PO Box 307
Thorp, WA 98946
Phone: (509) 964-7000
Fax: (800) 964-9210

E-mail: potatoes@irish-eyes.com
Web site: www.irish-eyes.com

Johnny's Selected Seeds
RR 1, Box 2580
Foss Hill Road
Albion, ME 04901
Phone: (207) 861-3900, (800) 879-2258
E-mail: johnnys@johnnyseeds.com
Web site: www.johnnyseeds.com

Park Seed
1 Parkton Avenue
Greenwood, SC 29647
Phone: (800) 213-0076
Fax: (800) 275-9941
E-mail: info@parkscs.com
Web site: www.parkseed.com

Ronniger's Potato Farm
Phone: (208) 267-7938
Fax: (208) 267-3265
E-mail: smallpotatoes@ronnigers.com
Web site: www.ronnigers.com

Seed Savers Exchange
3094 North Winn Road
Decorah, IA 52101
Phone: (563) 382-5990
Fax: (563) 382-5872
Web site: www.seedsavers.org

**Seed Savers Heirloom Seeds
and Gifts**
3076 North Winn Road
Decorah, IA 52101
Phone: (319) 382-5990
Fax: (319) 382-5872

Seeds of Change
PO Box 15700
Santa Fe, NM 87506
Phone: (888) 762-7333
Fax: (888) 329-4762
Web site: www.seedsofchange.com

Seeds of Diversity Canada
PO Box 36
Station Q
Toronto, ON M4T 2L7
Canada
Phone: (866) 509-7333
E-mail: mail@seeds.ca
Web site: www.seeds.ca

Tomato Growers Supply Co.
PO Box 60015
Fort Myers, FL 33906
Phone: (888) 478-7333
Fax: (888) 768-3476
Web site: www.tomatogrowers.com

WILDFLOWERS

Abundant Life Seeds
PO Box 157
Saginaw, OR 97472
Phone: (541) 767-9606
Fax: (866) 514-7333
E-mail: als@abundantlifeseeds.com
Web site: www.abundantlifeseeds.com

Wildseed Farms
PO Box 3000
425 Wildflower Hills
Fredericksburg, TX 78624
Phone: (800) 848-0078
Fax: (830) 990-8090
E-mail: orders1@wildseedfarms.com
Web site: www.wildseedfarms.com

RECOMMENDED READING

COMPOSTING AND SOIL

Gershuny, Grace. *Start with the Soil.* Emmaus, PA: Rodale, 1993.

Hynes, Erin. *Rodale's Successful Organic Gardening: Improving the Soil.* Emmaus, PA: Rodale, 1994.

Martin, Deborah, and Grace Gershuny, eds. *The Rodale Book of Composting.* Emmaus, PA: Rodale, 1992.

Martin, Deborah, and Karen Costello Soltys, eds. *Rodale Organic Gardening Basics: Soil.* Emmaus, PA: Rodale, 2000.

FRUITS AND BERRIES

McClure, Susan. *Rodale's Successful Organic Gardening: Fruits and Berries.* Emmaus, PA: Rodale, 1996.

Nick, Jean, and Fern Marshall Bradley. *Growing Fruits and Vegetables Organically.* Emmaus, PA: Rodale, 1994.

GENERAL GARDENING

Bradley, Fern Marshall, and Barbara Ellis, eds. *Rodale's All-New Encyclopedia of Organic Gardening.* Emmaus, PA: Rodale, 1992.

Bucks, Christine, ed. *Rodale Organic Gardening Basics: Vegetables.* Emmaus, PA: Rodale, 2000.

Coleman, Eliot. *The New Organic Grower.* White River Junction, VT: Chelsea Green Publishing, 1995.

Coleman, Eliot. *Four-Season Harvest: How to Harvest Fresh, Organic Vegetables from Your Home Garden All Year Long.* White River Junction, VT: Chelsea Green Publishing, 1992.

Logsdon, Gene. *The Contrary Farmer's Invitation to Gardening.* White River Junction, VT: Chelsea Green Publishing, 1997.

Stone, Pat. *Easy Gardening 101*. Pownal, VT: Storey Communications, 1998.

Swain, Roger. *The Practical Gardener*. Boston: Little, Brown and Company, 1989. Reprint, New York: Galahad Books, 1998.

HERBS

Herbs, Just for Fun: A Beginner's Guide to Starting an Herb Garden. Oak Grove, AR: Long Creek Herbs, 1996.

Smith, Miranda. *Your Backyard Herb Garden*. Emmaus, PA: Rodale, 1997.

Sombke, Laurence. *Beautiful Easy Herbs*. Emmaus, PA: Rodale, 1997.

LANDSCAPE AND FLOWER GARDENING

Bradley, Fern Marshall, ed. *Gardening with Perennials*. Emmaus, PA: Rodale, 1996.

Cox, Jeff. *Perennial All-Stars: The 150 Best Perennials for Great-Looking, Trouble-Free Gardens*. Emmaus, PA: Rodale, 1998.

DiSabato-Aust, Tracy. *The Well-Tended Perennial Garden: Planting and Pruning Techniques*. Portland, OR: Timber Press, 1998.

Phillips, Ellen, and C. Colston Burrell. *Rodale's Illustrated Encyclopedia of Perennials*. Emmaus, PA: Rodale, 2004 (revised edition).

PEST MANAGEMENT

Ellis, Barbara W., and Fern Marshall Bradley. *The Organic Gardener's Handbook of Natural Insect and Disease Control*. Emmaus, PA: Rodale, 1992.

Insect, Disease, and Weed I.D. Guide. Revised by Linda Gilkeson. Edited by Jill Jesiolowski Cebenko and Deborah L. Martin. Emmaus, PA: Rodale, 2001.

SEED STARTING

Bubel, Nancy. *The New Seed-Starter's Handbook*. Emmaus, PA: Rodale, 1988.

Ondra, Nancy, and Barbara Ellis. *Easy Plant Propagation* (Taylor's Weekend Gardening Guides). Boston: Houghton Mifflin, 1998.

Powell, Eileen. *From Seed to Bloom*. Pownal, VT: Storey Communications, 1995.

WEEDS

Hynes, Erin. *Rodale's Successful Organic Gardening: Controlling Weeds*. Emmaus, PA: Rodale, 1995.

Pleasant Barbara *The Gardener's Weed Book*. Pownal, VT: Storey Communications, 1996.

MAGAZINES AND NEWSLETTERS

The Avant Gardener, PO Box 489, New York, NY 10028.

Common Sense Pest Control Quarterly, Bio-Integral Resource Center (BIRC), PO Box 7414, Berkeley, CA 94707.

Country Living Gardener, PO Box 7335, Red Oak, IA 51591.

Organic Gardening, Rodale, 33 East Minor Street, Emmaus, PA 18098.

Index

▶ <u>Underscored</u> page references indicate boxed text. **Boldface** references indicate illustrations.

Seed packets, 50, 120–21, 126
Seed-planting tools
  cardboard tubes, 37
  chopsticks, 62
  gelatin mush, 38–39
  greeting cards, 37, **37**
  knitting needles, 36
  for lawn seed, 198, **198**,
    206
  pencil erasers, 36
  plastic flatware, 44
  plastic jugs, 52
  pool cues, 61
  PVC pipe, 173
  salt shakers, 37
  screwdrivers, 57
  seed stencils, 38
  seed tape, 38
  spice containers, 37
  sugar, 35–36
  toothbrushes, 43
Seed-saving
  information resources, 292
  in powdered milk, 39
  refrigerators and coolers,
    49, 200
  seed-collection kits, 50
  sharing seeds with others,
    35
  storage containers/
    organizers
    breath-mint containers,
      49
    clotheslines, 113
    hair clips, 72
    jars, 39, 49, 110
    planting pots, 113
    plastic cups, 111–12
    recipe boxes, 126
    Rolodex organizers, 50
    spice containers, 37
Shade
  for cool-season produce,
    177, 184, 196
  for hanging baskets, 155
  for new plantings, 137,
    137, 155
  plastic-chair tunnels, 235
  for seedlings, 45–46, **45**,
    62
  sunscald protection,
    45–46, **45**, 62, 140

Sharing books, 128
Sheets. *See* Blankets and
    sheets
Shelving
  bookcases, 97, 236
  as drying racks, 187
  kitchen or bathroom cabi-
    nets, 115, 240
  for plant displays, 101
  plastic-coated wire,
    109–10
Shoe racks, bags, and boxes,
    105, 116, 124
Shoes and boots, 82, 189,
    203
Shovels, children's, 58
Shower curtains
  as bird deterrents, 173–74
  as garden-shed windows,
    266
  soil solarization, 29–30,
    30
  as tarps, 63
  for winter protection,
    165–66
Shower wands, for outdoor
    watering, 65
Shrubs. *See* Trees and shrubs
Sinks, for potting benches,
    119
Skateboards, as trolleys, 61
Skewers, bamboo, 265, 278
Skis, as compost-mixing
    sticks, 18
Slopes, gardening techniques
    for, 8, 52, 198–99,
    198
Slug and snail control
  ammonia sprays, 252
  beer traps, 253
  clay-pot traps, 252
  coffee grounds and sprays,
    17, 253
  excluding from pots, 89
  newspaper traps, 250–51,
    251
  paper traps, 252
  peanut butter traps, 244
  planting-pot traps, 248,
    248
  screening plants, 252
  wood ashes, 252

Snow saucers, 63, 199–200,
    199
Soap pads, steel wool, 69
Soap sprays and soapy water
  ant control, 245
  aphid control, 249
  grasshopper control,
    246–47
  guidelines for using, 5, 10
  insecticidal soaps, 10
  mosquito control, 261
  powdery mildew control,
    256, **256**
  sod webworm control,
    208–9
  as wetting agents, 42
  whitefly control, 246
Socks
  for drainage holes, 273
  to protect skin and
    clothing, 65
  as twine, 57, 138
  as water-pump filters,
    289–90, **289**
Sod webworms, 208–9
Soil, information resources,
    296
Soil amendments. *See also*
    Compost materials
  applying, 52, 53, 207
  materials for, 21, 30–31,
    88
  moving, 61, 63, 110,
    199–200, **199**
  storing, 72, 73, 110, 115,
    115
Soil microbes, 8, 18–19, 29,
    30
Soil pH
  coffee grounds and, 17,
    145
  tea bags and, 28
  wood ashes and, 6, 19,
    200
Soil pollution, from soap
    sprays, 5
Soil solarization, 29–30, **30**
Soil testing, 29, 294–95
Soil thermometers, 34–35
Sow bugs (potato bugs or
    roly-polies), 247–48,
    250–51, **251**

USDA Plant Hardiness Zone Map

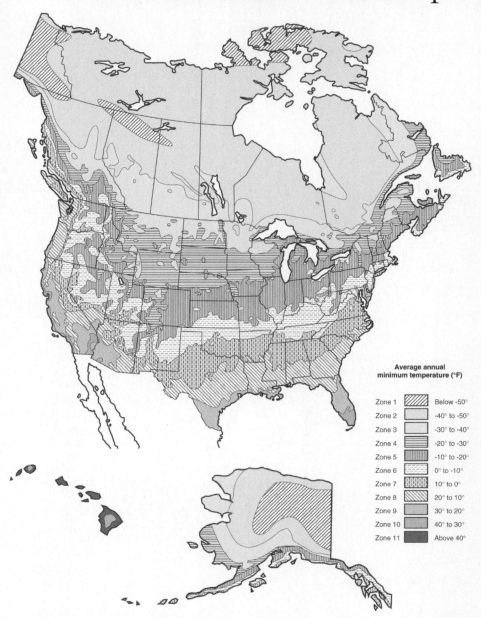

Average annual minimum temperature (°F)

Zone	Temperature
Zone 1	Below -50°
Zone 2	-40° to -50°
Zone 3	-30° to -40°
Zone 4	-20° to -30°
Zone 5	-10° to -20°
Zone 6	0° to -10°
Zone 7	10° to 0°
Zone 8	20° to 10°
Zone 9	30° to 20°
Zone 10	40° to 30°
Zone 11	Above 40°

This map was revised in 1990 and is recognized as the best indicator of minimum temperatures available. Look at the map to find your area, then match its pattern to the key above. When you've found your pattern, the key will tell you what hardiness zone you live in. Remember that the map is a general guide; your particular conditions may vary.